To John Gilmour

with all good wishes

during his post-surgical

recuperation

from

John Gyar.

March 1976

The Cambridge Mind

THE
CAMBRIDGE
MIND

Ninety Years of the *Cambridge Review*
1879–1969

edited by ERIC HOMBERGER,
WILLIAM JANEWAY *and* SIMON SCHAMA

JONATHAN CAPE
THIRTY BEDFORD SQUARE LONDON

Jonathan Cape Ltd, 30 Bedford Square, London, WC1

SBN 224 61914 4

The editors would like to thank the contributors
for permission to republish their articles
from the *Cambridge Review*

Printed and bound in Great Britain
by Butler & Tanner Ltd, Frome and London

Contents

INTRODUCTION   13

1 PROBLEMS OF WAR AND PEACE

Letter from India   WILLIAM CUNNINGHAM   1882   21

A Debate on Socialism at the Union   H. M. HYNDMAN and
J. ELLIS MCTAGGART   1889   25

Can England and Germany be reconciled after the War?
BERTRAND RUSSELL   1915   28

To the Front from the Backs   SIR ARTHUR QUILLER-COUCH
1915   31

Rex v. Bertrand Russell, June 5th, 1916   1940   35

A Letter from the Western Front   J.M.G.   1916   41

Keynes and the Slump
i Keynes on Money   MAURICE DOBB   1930   44

ii A Letter to the Editor   C. W. GUILLEBAUD, H. C. B.
MYNORS AND E. A. G. ROBINSON   1931   46

iii Lament for the Gold Standard   JACQUES RUEFF AND J. M.
KEYNES   1932   48

The Economic System in a Socialist State   JOAN ROBINSON
1937   50

Thoughts on War Thought   G. KITSON CLARK   1940   54

Letter to a Friend   GERALD BULLETT   1945   59

Egypt, Great Britain and the American People   D. W. BROGAN
1956   61

2 HISTORY AND HISTORIANS

Lord Acton: An Obituary   F. W. MAITLAND   1902   69

Acton on the French Revolution   J. H. CLAPHAM   1910   75

Maitland and his Work   G. R. ELTON   1965   77

Mr Belloc on Medieval History   G. G. COULTON 1920   79

The Dawn of Modern Politics   G. KITSON CLARK 1929   83

The Legacy of Napoleon   G. M. TREVELYAN 1945   86

Europe 1848–1918: The Balance of Power   DENNIS MACK
SMITH 1954   90

Classical Education   M. I. FINLEY 1956   94

The Originality of the Namier School   HERBERT BUTTER-
FIELD 1957   98

What Is History?   HERBERT BUTTERFIELD 1961   103

Tawney, Trevor-Roper and the Gentry   PETER LASLETT 1964   108

Christopher Hill and the 'Intellectual Origins of the English
Revolution'   QUENTIN SKINNER 1965   113

3 PHILOSOPHY AND THE SOCIAL SCIENCES

Sidgwick and the Old Ethics   G. E. MOORE 1902   123

Principia Ethica   AN UNSIGNED REVIEW 1903   124

On Logic, And How Not to Do It   LUDWIG WITTGENSTEIN
1913   127

Bergson on Metaphysics and Intuition   BERTRAND RUSSELL
1913   129

Whitehead on Nature   J. ELLIS MCTAGGART 1921   131

Oakeshott and the Modes of Experience   R. G. COLLINGWOOD
1934   132

Dialectical Materialism: An 'Official Philosophy'   MICHAEL
OAKESHOTT 1934   134

Collingwood's Philosophy of Art   MICHAEL OAKESHOTT
1938   139

Wisdom's Guide on How to Think   R. B. BRAITHWAITE
1935   142

'Paretology'   JOSEPH NEEDHAM 1936   145

Existentialism   JOHN WISDOM 1952   148

The Case of C. Wright Mills   E. R. LEACH 1959   151

Max Weber: A Colossus in Precis   W. G. RUNCIMAN 1961   153

Hannah Arendt on Revolution   JOHN DUNN 1964   158

On Reading Marcuse   RAYMOND WILLIAMS 1969   162

4 THE NATURAL SCIENCES

The Late Lord Kelvin J. J. THOMSON 1908   169
Thomson and the Cambridge School of Experimental Physics
  W. C. D. WHETHAM (LORD DAMPIER) 1903   172
Rutherford and Radioactivity F. W. ASTON 1913   175
Lord Rutherford: An Obituary J. J. THOMSON 1937   177
Mon Anxiété Devant Le Problème des Quanta LOUIS DE
  BROGLIE 1964   181
The Biology of Fate JOSEPH NEEDHAM 1930   188
The Brain and its Place in Nature FRED HOYLE 1951   193
The Structure of Large Molecules MAX PERUTZ 1955   196
The Two Towers JOHN ZIMAN 1961   200

5 ART AND ARTISTS

Art Under the Plutocracy WILLIAM MORRIS 1883   209
George Moore and Modern Art ROGER FRY 1893   211
Mr Murry and the Question of Style J. B. PRIESTLEY 1922   214
Forster and the Novel I. A. RICHARDS 1928   217
Wyndham Lewis and the Zeitgeist I. A. RICHARDS 1928   219
The Idealism of Julien Benda T. S. ELIOT 1928   223
Pascal: the Great Layman T. S. ELIOT 1941   232
T. S. Eliot: A Reply to the Condescending F. R. LEAVIS 1929   235
Cambridge Poetry F. R. LEAVIS 1929   241
On D. H. Lawrence F. R. LEAVIS 1930   246
An Early Romantic WILLIAM EMPSON 1929   252
Empson's Criticism F. R. LEAVIS 1931   256
The Poetry of William Empson I. A. RICHARDS 1936   260
Seurat ANTHONY BLUNT 1929   262
The Progress of Poetry: A Letter to a Contemporary JULIAN
  BELL 1930   266
Julian Bell: An Obituary F. L. LUCAS 1937   270
W. B. Yeats J. BRONOWSKI 1933   274
T. S. Eliot's 'Failures' in Criticism JOAN BENNETT 1933   278

H. G. Wells and Ourselves   C. P. SNOW   1934   280

The Energy of Dylan Thomas   THOM GUNN   1952   285

The Death of a Stranger   THOM GUNN   1953   288

Le Modulor   NIKOLAUS PEVSNER   1954   289

In Defense of Yvor Winters   TONY TANNER   1960   291

Poems from the 'Cambridge Manuscript'   SYLVIA PLATH
  1969   296

Sylvia Plath: The Cambridge Collection   A. ALVAREZ   1969   299

In Extremis   GEORGE STEINER   1969   303

BIOGRAPHICAL NOTES   308

List of Illustrations

The illustrations appear between pages 152 and 153

J. M. KEYNES
(*Radio Times Hulton Picture Library*)

G. E. MOORE
(*Chatto and Windus*)

J. B. PRIESTLEY
(*Radio Times Hulton Picture Library*)

HERBERT BUTTERFIELD
(*Ramsey and Muspratt, Cambridge*)

G. KITSON CLARK
(*Courtesy of Dr Kitson Clark*)

G. M. TREVELYAN
(*Bassano and Van Dyk*)

J. J. THOMSON
(*Mansell Collection*)

JOSEPH NEEDHAM
(*Ramsey and Muspratt, Cambridge*)

MAX PERUTZ
(*Courtesy of Dr Perutz*)

WILLIAM MORRIS
(*Mansell Collection*)

ROGER FRY
(*Ramsey and Muspratt, Cambridge*)

T. S. ELIOT
(*Radio Times Hulton Picture Library*)

F. R. LEAVIS
(*Chatto and Windus*)

WILLIAM EMPSON
(*Chatto and Windus*)

JULIAN BELL
(*Ramsey and Muspratt, Cambridge*)

SYLVIA PLATH
(*Faber and Faber*)

THOM GUNN
(*Faber and Faber*)

BERTRAND RUSSELL
(*The Observer*)

TO BERTRAND RUSSELL

Introduction

This is an anthology of the *Cambridge Review*, celebrating its ninetieth birthday as a magazine of 'University life and thought'. It is not wholly representative of Cambridge University, nor, precisely, of the *Cambridge Review* as it has changed throughout its exceptionally long life. Those many aspects of the 'Cambridge mind' not represented here such as the anthropology of Frazer and Harrison, the work of Adrian in medicine and Adcock and Shepherd in classics, did not appear in the *Review* for any number of reasons; but the areas of 'life and thought' which *are* included speak eloquently for what has arguably been the most brilliant period of intellectual distinction in the history of Cambridge University. *The Cambridge Mind* is an occasion to look back on a remarkable golden age.

The *Cambridge Review* was founded when the University itself was undergoing dramatic change. New statutes permitting college fellows to marry had been passed in 1868. Improved arrangements for teaching coupled with new curricula and examinations, mirrored the rediscovered sense of academic purpose which the Victorian fathers of Cambridge—men like Henry Sidgwick and Sir John Seeley—had done much to promote. In a smaller way, the founding of the *Cambridge Review* contributed to this formative time of the University. Modestly, it was an act of self-definition. The men who met in J. G. Frazer's rooms in Trinity, in 1869, would not have described it so portentously, but the *Review* was soon to prove itself an image and a record of the life of the University. For the first twenty years of its career it did not, save in an oblique manner, reflect so much of the 'thought' of the community. But it did carry University news, college reports, summaries of debates at the Union, sports columns, book reviews, obituaries and a weekly supplement containing the University sermon and essays on topical intellectual issues.

The University, as reflected in the early years of the *Review*, was a smaller and a 'sweeter' place than today. An earlier anthology of the *Review* was published in 1898 as *The Book of the Cambridge Review*.

13

Filled with gentlemanly essays, light verse, and much sentimental writing about Cambridge itself, it is an image of distance and irrelevance. A characteristic issue of the time, for example that of October 21st, 1885, is less foreign. It begins with brief notes of University news; Edmund Gosse was going to be the Clark lecturer later in the term. The recently completed Drawing and Smoking Rooms of the Union were now open. A public meeting was to be held on the departure of the missionaries to China. Oscar Browning wrote a long obituary of Richard Monkton Milnes, Lord Houghton, whose Cambridge was Hallam's and Tennyson's. There are several pages of sporting news ('No very startling excellence has as yet displayed itself among the recruits to the Boat Club' reads a report about St John's College), and then follow details of clubs, church services and extended reports of the debates of the Union. A long essay by Karl Pearson discusses 'The Coming Factor in European Progress' (i.e. socialism):

> ... the real Socialists in England ... are, as a rule educated, or better, thinking men and women, who are oppressed by the misery of their fellows, and who are convinced that this misery can only be remedied by very wide-reaching measures of social reconstruction.

Later in the same academic year appeared long reviews of Howell's *The Rise of Silas Lapham*, Jowett's *Politics of Aristotle*, and *Salammbô*. On May 19th, 1886, a motion at the Union 'that in the opinion of this House undergraduates should have a share in the management of University affairs' was defeated by 35 to 14 votes. The image in its smallness and self-consciousness is not unrecognizable and its place in the history of the University worth acknowledging. The letter from 'Q' (Sir Arthur Quiller-Couch) to a soldier fighting on the Western Front in 1916 may perhaps serve as a suitable epitaph.

But the character of Victorian Cambridge—its concern for the refinement of sensibility and the dissemination of classical values—was in decline long before the First World War delivered the coup de grâce. The work of men like Frederick Maitland and J. J. Thomson heralded a new and demanding commitment to the highest standards of research and inquiry. And as the University changed again, the *Review* changed with it. Belletristic essays and donnish poetry vanished, leaving the *Review* filled with reviews and discussions, articles and bulletins.

While ninety years of any magazine can hardly avoid barren stretches, there have been moments when some of the most valuable and important achievements of Cambridge scholarship have found recognition in its pages. In 1903 there is a (sadly) anonymous review of *Principia Ethica*; in 1913 F. W. Aston reviews Rutherford's book on *Radioactive Substances* and in the Easter term of 1928 the verse of Empson and Eberhart appears besides the criticism of Leavis, I. A. Richards and Eliot. These are the moments which redeem the efforts of successive generations of editors who have worked devotedly on a small weekly magazine which has never been able to pay its contributors, and which, for most of its life, has had a small readership. It is to acknowledge these moments that we have compiled *The Cambridge Mind*.

The organization of *The Cambridge Mind* has been designed to group loosely some of the major preoccupations of the *Review*. The first section looks outward to the world beyond the University. Beginning with the problems of the *Pax Britannica* and concluding with the problems of the *Pax Americana*, it traces the response of the community to war, depression and precarious peace. The second indicates something of the change that has taken place in historical scholarship since Acton's long shadow first cast its influence over successive generations of Cambridge historians. Significantly, it is Maitland, whose stature perhaps rose above Acton but whose Chair he felt unable to fill, who provides a moving tribute. Kitson Clark and Butterfield represent the rise of a new generation to professional maturity and are followed by the critical insights of reviewers levelling their sights at generalizations committed in the name of Oxford history.

The third section is dominated by the beginnings of analytical philosophy and by the attack on idealism instigated by G. E. Moore and his disciples. Wittgenstein, newly arrived in Cambridge, demolishes a book about logic in what is possibly his first publication in English. The 'thirties brought the debate on Marxism into prominence at Cambridge and provoked Oakeshott's dismissal of dialectical materialism. It also brought greater attention to the social sciences and the remainder of this section is given over to reviews and essays about Pareto, Weber, C. Wright Mills, Hannah Arendt, and a personal comment on Marcuse by Raymond Williams.

The fourth section is the one most permanently identified with Cambridge and yet perhaps the least expected in an anthology of this sort. The Nobel Prize winners—Thomson, Aston, de Broglie, Perutz—speak for themselves and impart some of the exhilaration involved in advancing the understanding, first of atomic physics and the discipline of quantum mechanics, and then of molecular biology.

The fifth section is that of literature and art, most neatly joined together in Roger Fry's essay, written in his early twenties, on the criticism of George Moore. The predominant weight of Richards, Leavis and Empson (as well as the happy discovery of Eliot's long, important essay on Benda and a shorter piece on Pascal) hardly needs comment. These are the voices of Cambridge English whose work still dominates what is being done here long after the departure of the great patriarchs. After the late 'twenties it was only Leavis who stayed in Cambridge, but the deservedly great influence of his work should not be separated from that of Richards who was in China and eventually Harvard, and Empson, who also taught in China before returning to England, the B.B.C. and the University of Sheffield. It is the combined influence of these three which so dramatically raised the ante, so to speak, of modern literary criticism.

There has been no attempt to impose a unity on what must inevitably be sometimes related, but just as often disparate, contributions. There is nothing so suspiciously Continental as a 'school' of Cambridge thought and we have extended benefit of naturalization to distinguished immigrants from Oxford or even further afield. If our title is mildly tendentious, it is because it seems to us that nearly all of the contributions in this anthology do exhibit common qualities which might be collectively identified with *The Cambridge Mind*: a rigour of logical analysis; an uncompromising exercise of sceptical inquiry; a commitment to verification rather than imaginative construction. The same severity of standard is applied to the function of language in poetry as it is to the explanation of genetic information or to the study of seventeenth-century society. G. E. Moore liked to believe that he was doing no more than relying on 'common sense'. That quality, along with the others we have tried to characterize, can hardly be considered exclusive to Cambridge. But faithfulness to its canons has led Cambridge scholars to be perhaps especially guarded when faced with metaphysical systems and universal propositions. If, as the devastating target-practice of Coulton, for example, suggests, the technique of exposing the grandiose has been refined into an art at

Cambridge, it is just because pretentious dogma so often conceals the commonplace or the false.

One of the consequences of this professional discipline has been the recognition of greater intellectual complexity than the Victorian scholars could have anticipated. The lettered gentleman has become something of a graceful anachronism and with him has departed some of the intellectual versatility of an earlier Cambridge. When shall we have another vicar of Great St Mary's, the University Church, who, like William Cunningham, will also be an accomplished economic historian? Rutherford and Leavis have made the world a more intelligible and more truthful, but also a more complicated and uncomfortable place to live in. In the smaller world of the academic community this has entailed a proportionately larger loss. Yet within Cambridge it remains possible through the intimacy of collegiate fellowship to talk over High Tables and across disciplines. The *Review* continues to assist this function. As the article by Professor Ziman, himself a past editor, makes plain, it is still feasible to reach common denominators of discussion without sacrificing standards. So the *Review*, in one of its roles, remains a kind of scholarly parlour, where the human, as well as the professional life of its readers is chronicled: their arrivals and departures noted, their new work noticed and their deaths mourned.

But this record of the intellectual life of a community has, we think, much more than diaristic interest. In the first half of this century, Cambridge experienced a time of advance and achievement such as few other universities can look back on, and in this anthology we wanted to reflect this work and this period as directly as possible.

ERIC HOMBERGER
WILLIAM JANEWAY
SIMON SCHAMA

The contributions to this anthology are republished verbatim, and without revision, in the form in which they originally appeared in the *Cambridge Review*. They do not necessarily represent the current views of the authors on their respective subjects.

I

Problems of
War and Peace

Letter from India

WILLIAM CUNNINGHAM

. . . Archæologists are fond of raving about the wanton van-
dalism that marked our proceedings in Delhi after 1857; they do not
seem to be reconciled by the reflexion that it is quite in accordance with
the eternal fitness of things. The structures a people rears shew what is
in them, and so do those they preserve.We are tolerant of the 'super-
stitions' of natives, and we spare the temples and mosques—though
we walk about the Jumna Musjid with dusty boots, and parade our
want of sympathy with the feelings of our fellow subjects. Our Philistine contempt for the luxurious splendour which Eastern peoples
admire, found vent in the destruction of palaces which we cannot and
they may not use; while barracks and railways give a very fair measure
of what we shew ourselves capable of creating.

Of course I don't mean to scoff at barracks and railways; they are the
means for enabling us to command the country and suppress disorder,
or, if necessary, resist attacks; without them we could never maintain
the peace of the country, and so far as India is concerned I am fast
becoming a peace-at-any-price man, even the price of a large standing
army, of expensive barracks with all their adjuncts, of hospitals and
sanitation. The quiet of the country is due to the reputation our soldiers
enjoy, and the prestige of our crown, and I believe we benefit the
country more by keeping the troops in full efficiency, and holding our
own in the frontiers than by anything else we attempt—for by so doing
we secure peace and order; and these are the only conditions under
which a healthy social life can be developed.

I have often heard at home that the security of our position here
was due to the benefits bestowed on the natives—that their experience
of the justice of our administration, and blessings of our rule was sure
to knit the hearts of the people to us. But for this to come about, it is
not only necessary that we should *be* just and benevolent but that our
justice and benevolence should *make themselves felt* by the ordinary
people; they do appreciate the blessings of the peace which our military
strength maintains: but our ideas of social order are so opposed to

theirs that every 'improvement' we make wears a different aspect to them.

We treat British India as one whole, with communications between all its parts with similar administration and laws everywhere; and native states stand well in our graces according as they copy our English models. But the natives are used to have their affairs settled by traditional customs, which differ for each locality; the more our uniform system advances the more do we sweep away the old customs, and settle the disputes on principles that do not accord with native ideas of justice; there has been a great row lately in the north west of this province, because a certain village refused on the occasion of a marriage to pay fines which the local rajah had always collected. The judicial department decided that these fines had no legal authority, and shortly after the whole village was burned down. This was thought to be an act of vengeance on the part of the rajah, who failed to see the justice of the decision, and no wonder; and it doubtless was so, because he was many miles away at the time it happened, and if the native who is interested in the perpetration of mischief is well out of the way, his obvious *alibi* is almost conclusive as to his guilt.

There is the same confusion about the benefits we suppose we have conferred by giving greater facilities for trade between various parts of the country. Each village was self-sufficing when the simple neces-saries of life were manufactured by the village carpenter, potter, and weaver, who were supported by common contributions from village resources. Manchester mills are now underselling the local weavers— for men's attire at any rate, they cannot dye the women's *saris* as yet— the Indian mills supply yarn to the village weavers, so that domestic spinning is dying out. The more prosperous men are withdrawing from the common responsibilities of village life, the authority of the *patil* is disappearing, and the village artisans are no longer supported. This may suit the more prosperous man who gets his goods cheaper, but the village, as a village is less independent, and less able to weather bad times. Trade is the great solvent which breaks up social organisa-tion, and what is obvious about the progress we are bringing on, is the disruption of a cherished system, not the benefits which may accrue when society is transformed.

But even so far as individuals are concerned, our ideas of getting on in the world are so different from theirs that they cannot appreciate the benefits of many changes on which we congratulate ourselves. We think a man is doing well in the world if he rises out of the sphere of life where he was born and bred, if having been an office boy he becomes the First Lord of the Admiralty. They on the other hand, think a man is doing well in the world, if he holds a good position in that sphere of life in which he has been born and bred: his ambition is to stand well with his own class, not to escape from it. We set ourselves against the 'idle extravagance' the Hindu shews in occasionally feasting the members of his caste; and congratulate ourselves when one of their scavengers is raised by a charity education into a position in which he can instruct gentlemen's sons. No wonder if one Aryan brother feels that the long predicted and much dreaded 'iron age' has come at length, and feels but little gratitude for the blessings of British rule; while we, too, are quite out of sympathy with the native social system and its vigour is being everywhere sapped. This struck me particularly at Ahundabad, because the old organisation in that town was so highly developed that it has not melted away so rapidly as seems to have been the case elsewhere. There each craft has a regular guild, which meets in its own lodge for the settlement of the hours of labour, the rates of wages, and the prices of wares. In those cases where all the craft are of the same caste they have common feasts twice or thrice a year, and when they are of the same religion they assemble for common worship in the temple at the lodge. If you are dissatisfied with a workman you cannot send him away and get another unless you apply through the *panchayat* of the craft, and prove the justice of your complaint, when he is heavily fined. There are about fifty of them altogether, and disputes between one guild and another are settled by the chief guild, that of the bankers. Not very long ago the potters tried to raise the price of goods, but the bankers regarded their claim as unfair; and they were 'boycotted' till they had to give in and return to the old rates. But even in Ahundabad the whole is breaking down; the lodges look dilapidated; the hours of labour are no longer regulated, and little children of ten or twelve are kept in garrets helping at the looms for twelve hours a day, and every day, at something less than two shillings a month. Any one can see how the old protection for the weak and poor has been destroyed, and it may be doubted if we should ever be able to provide a satisfactory substitute, even if we pass a factory act and engage an army of highly-paid inspectors. But that is no reason why we should not congratulate ourselves on removing obstacles from the free flow of labour into any employment that may open, and wonder that the ignorant natives are not more thankful to us.

It is when one realises the entire incompatibility of eastern and western civilisation that one realises the extent of the task on which we have entered in setting ourselves to substitute the one for the other; we cannot appear as benefactors to the people of India, because we are stark men, and the more we speak of law, the more we do unlaw; every step of progress means the impoverishment of some class, and we really are nihilists, overthrowing the institutions of society, and helpless to develop anything in their stead—for the establishment of foreign administration highly paid at their expense can hardly be regarded as the foundation of a true policy among them.

The real reason why we are so helpless to create, is because we do not know our minds, and are always at cross purposes—a house divided against itself. People like my friends here who feel strongly the need of keeping up our prestige as the source of our power for good, are apt to look with jealousy on any schemes for raising the natives to a European level: few things are less popular in military society than attempts at the higher education of the native. On the other hand, most civilians seem to me to talk airily about educating the people in self-government, and the Universities turn out an annual crop of 'enlightened' young natives, who are alive to the English ideas of getting on in the world, and value themselves on their subjective acquirements or the accidents of their wealth, not on their status in an objective society. No wonder if they are self-conceited and wear patent-leather boots. Our government is apt to vacillate between these two lines, and has never ventured to embark earnestly in a course of experiments in the native capacity for self-government.

So far as I can hear, the only serious attempt that has been made has been in the introduction of municipal institutions. There used to be elements of municipal self-government at Ahundabad, where, as the *Nagar Seth* told me, the bankers guild assessed the others with their share of the revenue contributions, and each guild arranged for collecting their payments from its members. But we have town councils of a brand new Brummagen pattern, consisting of European and native members who are nominated by the civil authorities. There is no pretence at self-government here, and when the Poona people asked for the right to elect one or two of the members of their council, even the ordinary civilian was surprised at their audacity, for he feared they would put in a lot of crotchety fellows who liked to hear themselves speak. So they might, but can they be educated to govern themselves, unless we run some such risk? If, as seems likely enough, the risk is too great to run, let us at least not deceive ourselves with the shams we have set on foot. . .

March 8th, 1882

A Debate on Socialism at the Union

H. M. HYNDMAN AND J. ELLIS MCTAGGART

The series of successful meetings held at the Union this term culminated in the enormous throng which assembled to hear Mr. Hyndman on Tuesday. Owing to the retiring speeches and other formalities incident on the elections held in the afternoon the House met at 7.30: at 7.35 it was almost impossible to force an entrance into the Hall. But as a debate the meeting was not so successful: indeed it resolved itself into something like a game of Aunt Sally, Mr. Hyndman personating the lady in question while the other orators did the duty of marksmen at his devoted head. After all the interest that has been shown in Socialism of late in the University, including especially the successful series of lectures delivered by members of the Fabian Society in King's a year ago, this result may excite some astonishment: it may be to a great extent explained by the fact that Mr. Hyndman from the beginning tied his supporters down to his programme of social democracy: to vote for him was to pledge oneself to support that programme and did not mean merely that one sympathised with the aims of socialism and with a socialistic tendency in legislation. Four or five years ago Mr. Hyndman had 53 supporters, this year he has 27: the decrease is due to an increased interest in socialism; in the interval we have learnt more about the subject and those who sympathise with the misery of the masses have come to see that no panacea is to be expected from a cut and dried system of state organisation.

Mr. HYNDMAN's speech was admirably moderate: once or twice indeed we caught a ring of anger but the impulse to blaze out was quickly suppressed and the speaker was listened to with attention and respect from beginning to end. After explaining that to support the motion meant giving in one's allegiance to undiluted state socialism, the speaker began to prove the existence of the class war which he wishes to abolish. He referred us to the blue books and reports to show the appalling condition of the workers of the country and to support his statement that the victims of the war were the weakest and most defenceless, *i.e.* the women and children. He went on to show that this war raged in all countries whatever their form of government might be, whether republican as in France or America, or despotic as in Germany. Party politics then are no cure for this evil state of things, where men starve because corn is too plentiful and go unclad because too many clothes are manufactured: having shown the evils of the present wage slavery which sends one out of every five labourers to die in the workhouse, the lunatic asylum, or the hospital, and which keeps the rest in a continual state of uncertainty as to the means of subsistence, Mr. Hyndman went on to show that the Capitalist system which had produced this state of things was not eternal, it was only 200 years old, and was already beginning to change; this change was accelerated by socialism which meant the substitution of co-operation for competition. He then answered some of the objections generally raised against Socialism; in the first place it will not ruin the State by destroying individual energy, on the contrary it will develop a vast amount of energy at present latent in the masses who are kept down in such a position that they have no chance to help the commonweal. Then Socialism is not opposed to the law of the survival of the fittest, rather the present commercial system is opposed to that law, for it furthers the survival of those who are unfittest from the point of view of the State's good. Co-operation is limiting competition in the case of capital as we can see from the great rings and trusts; it should do so in the case of labour also. Then as to the Malthusian fallacy, in the first place our power over nature increases out of proportion to the increase of the population, and secondly it is poor countries that breed the fastest, and thirdly to limit population does not remedy present evils, as we can see in the case of France whose population is stationary and who yet suffer from the same evils and trade crises as England. Then as to the alleged unpractical nature of socialists, this charge is disproved by the fact that Radicals and Tories are both competing with one another in stealing planks from the Socialist platform. And as to the evils of revolution, the present state of irrational anarchy where we have individual appropriation of social production is worse than any revolution. Mr. Hyndman then began to approach his own programme. He showed how railways were organised by shareholders who got the wealth without doing any of the labour and maintained that the State could do this for the public benefit as well as the shareholders did it for their own. Our present system of doing everything by great companies, which meant the anonymous robbing of our fellows, could be supplanted by a system of State Organisation. The evils of the present system are shown in the adulteration of all goods produced in the corruption of our great cities, and in the employment of women's labour to compete with men's, as seen in the Silvertown strikes, which showed that women earned 9/5 weekly for doing ten and a half hours work a day. This system must be ended somehow; it is doomed to be replaced by a new growth just as Feudalism was replaced by Capitalism. This new growth involves no autocratic state government; it will come by gradual growth of co-operation, this is what the socialistic party, the only party which has true principles supports; let us all study together to further the movement.

The speech was clear and excellently delivered, but it was eclipsed, as all the other speeches of the evening (though many were much above the average), were eclipsed, by the reply of the opposer; in a rather low but distinct voice, Mr. McTAGGART began his work of destructive criticism. He asked why the opener had dwelt so much on the present distress which was admitted by all, and so little on the proposed remedy. Individualists do not deny the existence of misery, and would do anything to cure it; but the opener's proposals would retard rather than further progress in this direction. Competition is a clear gain if the parties compete on equal terms; it is only the inequality which does the harm; the present system tends to the abolition of this inequality and consequently to the spread of happiness; this statement was supported by statistics from Mr. Giffen's book, showing that the workers had gained an increase of 10 per cent. in 40 years; and this improvement, quick though it is, is likely to continue, since Trades Unions are spreading, more capital is being saved, and consequently the rate of interest is continually falling, and the more workmen combine the more they will gain; it would be unfair to quote old economists to show this is not the present individualistic position. As to Marx's theory of wages sinking to the point of bare subsistence, if it means anything it is contradicted by facts; the dock labourers have an increase of wages and yet the prices of necessaries have not risen in proportion. Mr. McTaggart then asked for more details as to the new state of things advocated by the Opener, and insisted that the details were the principle of practical Socialism, since all would admit that a Socialist ideal would be pleasant, and the only dispute was whether it could be realised. How, for instance, could business be managed? Could a central government, which muddles even the little it has to do at present, control such vast affairs? Or would it be done by small municipal organisations? But this would combine the evils of both systems, for there would still be competition between the municipalities. And could an emotional democracy attain the hardness of head required in a man of business? Mr. Hyndman's plan is too vague; he is accelerating a revolution before he has planned the details of his new order; and in common with the other Socialists will not apply himself to this task until the catastrophe has come. Mr. McTaggart spoke with admirable precision and each of his incisive sentences hit the mark; indeed we cannot remember any speech at the Union which combined solidity of argument and terseness of style in so high a degree of excellence.

November 28th, 1889

Can England and Germany be reconciled after the War?

BERTRAND RUSSELL

The present war, though it began as a Balkan conflict, has gradually altered its character, and has become a contest between Germany and England for world-dominion. Ever since 1900, it has been evident that the Anglo-German struggle would be the chief issue in a European war whenever it might occur. The Germans have aimed at postponing the struggle until their navy was formidable to us, the English have aimed at securing the support of powerful Continental armies whenever the struggle should come. All European diplomacy since the time of the Boer War has been dominated by these two endeavours.

It does not seem probable that the rivalry of Germany and England will be brought to a definite decision by the present war. Unless the Germans could sink our fleet or starve us out by means of submarines, neither of which is at all likely, they could not decide the conflict in their favour. Unless we can force upon them, as part of the terms of peace, an agreement to be content with a small navy, we cannot decide the issue finally in our favour; and there are great difficulties about such an agreement. To begin with, the Germans would feel it an intolerable humiliation, and would fight to the last gasp to avoid it. Meanwhile France and Russia would be unwilling to prolong the war for an object contrary to their interests—since Germany without a navy would have more money to spend on the Army, and would no longer compel England to support France and Russia in their colonial or Balkan disputes. Even supposing such an agreement could be forced on Germany, an army of spies would be necessary to see that it was carried out; there would be constant suspicion that Germany was building surreptitiously, and armament firms would see to it that spies presented reports in that sense. The relations of England and Germany would grow more and more embittered, and in the end there would be another war because we should assert and the Germans would deny that they were building beyond what had been stipulated. In such a war, we could not rely upon the sympathy of other countries, since we should appear in the light of bullying tyrants.

If a stable peace is to result, some other way must be found, since an agreement limiting German ship-building is merely specious.

Our case against the Germans is that they have deliberately challenged our naval supremacy, without which we cannot insure our food supply, or be secure against invasion. This case is unanswerable so far that we cannot permit any other nation to acquire the command of the sea.

The German case against us is less understood in this country, because most people have not the imagination to see either Germany or England with German eyes. Germany has been rapidly becoming an industrial country, dependent, like England, upon importing food and exporting manufactures. So long as we retain a supremacy, exercising the right of capture, Germany thus becomes more and more at our mercy. If the present war had been postponed another ten years, Germany's dependence upon foreign food would have compelled surrender. Yet Germany does not wish to forego the advantages of becoming an industrial nation, and we have no right to demand any such sacrifice. And similar considerations apply to the question of colonies. Germany, with its high birth-rate and growing population, naturally wants a place in the sun; but whether in Asia Minor or in Africa, we have done our utmost to interpose a veto, and by the help of our navy we have been largely successful. And in the present war we are absorbing a large proportion of the colonies which we had graciously permitted Germany to possess.

What issue is possible from this situation? Nothing but absolute and irretrievable disaster would compel us to submit to a German naval supremacy. Yet our naval supremacy will more and more, as the German economic development proceeds, threaten Germany with starvation in the event of war. We may protest that we are lovers of peace, and that so long as Germany refrains from aggression we shall not use our sea-power to injure German trade. But we shall never succeed in making the Germans believe this, any more than we should believe corresponding professions on their part. To know what Germans think of us, we have only to ask ourselves what we think of them: all the melodramatic wickedness which we attribute to them, they, with equal sincerity, attribute to us.

We cannot, therefore, expect either side to submit to the naval supremacy of the other. Unless a really drastic change of system is adopted, we must expect the rivalry to continue after the war, poisoning the politics of Europe, filling the world with the dread of disaster, causing all the potential benefits of science to be swallowed up in the mad race of armaments.

The only way I can see (though doubtless other ways may be possible) is that all the nations of the world should abandon their separate navies, and that instead one single international navy should interpose an impartial veto on all invasions that had to cross the sea. In this way, England and the whole British Empire would be secured against the German menace, while German commerce would be secure against the paralysis which our navy is now able to inflict. All the defensive purposes of a navy would be fully served. If either our navy or theirs were designed to prevent injury rather than to inflict it, such a proposal would be welcomed with acclamation.

There are several objections to such a plan. First, it would not minister to national pride: we could no longer say 'Britannia rules the waves,' and Germans could no longer hope to cause proud Albion's downfall. Secondly, it would offend the professional pride of the navy, and by sympathy also that of the army. Thirdly—and this is by far the most serious objection—it would diminish the profits of armament firms, and thereby impoverish many of the leading statesmen and ecclesiastics of all civilised countries. I do not know of any other objection, except that it would lessen the likelihood of war, and so remove one of the chief supports of social injustice.

In England's attitude, as in Germany's, there is something arrogant, a claim to dominion beyond what international justice would warrant. On both sides, this claim is reinforced by the danger of allowing the opposing claim to triumph. An international navy would do away with the need of triumph, and would secure mutual safety without injustice. It would render possible a genuine friendship between two great nations, extraordinarily similar even in the manner of their hatred of each other, and both of immense importance to the civilization of the world. It is to be feared that men's imaginations are not yet ripe for such a change. But perhaps, in the period of weariness and sanity which is likely to follow the conclusion of peace, it may be possible to get a hearing for drastic proposals, and to make evident the utter madness and futility of reciprocal slaughter. Behind the rulers, in whom pride has destroyed humanity, stand the patient populations, who suffer and die. To them the folly of war and the failure of governments are becoming evident as never before. To their humanity and collective wisdom we must appeal if civilization is not to perish utterly in suicidal delirium.

February 10th, 1915

To the Front from the Backs

SIR ARTHUR QUILLER-COUCH

My Dear Dick— ... I must now try to answer your questions about 'the old place,' as you call it with true Cambridge affection and true Cambridge accuracy. 'What is it like in these days?' Well, I will start by annoying you. It is still very much like Oxford, and like no other place in the world.

At the same time it is curiously unlike Cambridge, even unlike the Cambridge of last term. We came up in October to find the streets desolate indeed. The good soldiers who had swarmed in upon town and college in August—a Commander of Cavalry occupied my rooms; too busy, I hope, to curse the dull contents of my shelves—had all departed for France. Nay, already many of them slept in French earth. They had left a historical piece of plate to the high table; and some photographic groups in Stearn's window. A Head of a House halted me before one of these groups and ticked off the cheerful resolute faces of those fallen, by the Marne or the Aisne, since he had entertained them a few weeks ago. In one row of a dozen West Yorks. he could find two survivors only.

These had come and gone like a summer cloud: and October in Cambridge might have passed for the Long Vacation turned chilly. In the courts and around the Backs the gardeners were sweeping up the leaves, as ever; but no men passed on their way to lecture 'with the wind in their gowns.' The University, one heard, was 'functioning' still: the bell of Great St. Mary's still, on degree days, suggested the hand of the ancient Mother smitten upon her Chest mourning for her fee-paying children, because they were not. In College one seldom met, never heard, an undergraduate. A few would gather to Hall, the most of them in their O.T.C. uniforms after a strenuous afternoon out by Madingley. The scholar read grace with an unwonted reverence. '*Sic Deus in nobis et nos maneamus in Illo*'—and we took our seats to a meal decently frugal. As I looked down the hall, this one undergraduates' table reminded me of a road in the West Country I had followed a few days before, with the telegraph running beside it and on the wires the swallows gathering, discussing flight: the fire burning variously in each separate heart, but with the same call, to cross the Channel ... We in Combination Room talked of our depleted numbers as a matter for pride (very creditably too—if you understand College finance). One, who had been lecturing at the Examination Schools, likened the theatre there to the Pool of Bethesda.

I have to talk of it lightly, my dear Dick, because your letters, so constantly and undefeatedly cheerful, impose this tone. You must not suppose, however, that we do not think—and think all the while—of what the young are doing and suffering for us ... Well, thus it was in the Michaelmas Term; a suspended Cambridge; for which we were, on the whole, pretty well prepared. The Belgian refugees from their Universities had found harbour with us. On the King's and Clare Cricket Ground lines of hospital sheds were growing up almost as silently as the Temple of Solomon in Bishop Heber's Newdigate; and the almost incomparable turf was selling (I am told) to some fortunate purchaser for incredible sums.

A notice-board at the entrance of Burrell's Walk advertised the 1st Eastern General Hospital, and on any afternoon you might see the Red Cross motor ambulances bringing in the wounded. A whole block of King's had been handed over to house the nurses. But here, as at the Research Hospital, the work had been so quietly and thoroughly organised that you had to go out of your way to find anything strange. For the rest, Cambridge life had merely been arrested. Youth had, for once, refused to revisit her with autumn, and was busy elsewhere. We, whom age or infirmity obliged to abide, laid our account with the War and settled down to the dull streets, the short unbrightened days, evenings without talk, the long nights on depopulated staircases, our own heavy thoughts. You will think it queer, but the feeling of the change first broke on me one day when, stepping incautiously off the pavement into the road-way on this side of Magdalene Bridge, I recollected myself, cast the old horrified glance behind, and found not a single motor-cycle, not even a bicycle, in sight.

We returned in January to a vastly different Cambridge. She had become a garrison town...

At this point I was proposing a start a description of it all: of the lines of artillery horses beside the Trumpington Road, Adams Road, Jesus ditch; of the mud (but that is indescribable) in which the poor brutes stand fetlock deep, each mournfully chewing his neighbour's head-rope. (You reported that head-ropes wore out at a terrible rate in your Brigade; and now I understand, as you will understand, why the price of bitter aloes has become prohibitive in Cambridge—not that I want to purchase any); of the mud on Midsummer Common, and the worse mud on the road to the Rifle Butts, where the M.A. warriors of the C.U.O.T.C. drill and improve their waists, though they may never serve their country; of Whewell's Buildings occupied by the Monmouths, who take it for an Elementary School, and Archdeacon C—— for its Chairman of Managers, faithful to his post; of— most wonderful spectacle of all—the crowds of Tommies navigating the Backs in Canadian canoes and other bounding shallops. The Welsh—for it is the Welsh Division (Territorial) we have here— would seem to have lost some of their celebrated skill with the coracle ... I was going, I say, to attempt a picture of all this, when the happy thought seized me that I could convey it far more vividly by sending

c

you a set of photographs. So forth I fared, and to my amazement was told that no one had taken any photographs! 'It was a notion, certainly: but, so far as was known, it had not occurred to anyone.' 'The omission should be repaired ... No, the military authorities would not refuse leave.' I hope the University Librarian will make a note of this. A bound volume of photographs, complete as his well-known enthusiasm can make it, would be at small cost a κτῆμα ἐς ἀεί, priceless in times to come, when the familiar streams flow again, *antiquos subterlabentia muros*; priceless as the *Mercurius Anticus* or Aubrey's Gossip concerning Oxford in the Civil War.

The curfew no longer tolls the knell of parting day. It is not permitted. But when dusk has fallen and the Mayor and Corporation leave the world to darkness and to me, I walk in the Fellows' Garden, carefully hiding the ardent tip of my cigarette (lest it should attract a Zeppelin), and think upon those streams. ... For who doubts they will flow again? 'Not the same' ... No, my dear Dick, I sincerely trust 'not the same!' In your last letter you observed brightly that 'it looks as if, before long, folks would be scrapping in every corner of this blessed planet.' Well, our wise men are already at it here, in corners of *The Cambridge Review*. They are concerned to regulate what is going to happen when the war is over. Well, I do not much believe in cooking an eagle before you have shot him. But suppose him shot ... Do these my reverend co-seniors actually believe that it will be left to *us* to put things right? What, to *us*?—who in our generation, in England and France and Germany, have allowed this thing to come to pass? No, my dear child: that responsibility, with the honour of it, must be yours. It is a heavy one (as a while ago we should have said distrustfully, but now say in solicitude, for the time it will steal from the natural joys of youth): but we left you youngsters to wipe up the mess, and *you* must restore the garden in which we shall walk humbly with you,

—ancients, musical at close of day.

You will come back, and those who return to the University will claim for youth a far larger measure of freedom, as they have earned it ten times over. But as you have always agreed with me that Oxford and Cambridge are two of the loveliest things in the world—each, but for the other, peerless—I can trust you to deal reverently with this one; for she *is* your Mother, after all.

February 24th, 1915

Rex v. Bertrand Russell
June 5th, 1916

The following is an abbreviated account of the trial of Bertrand Russell in 1916, and is the subject of comment in our editorial columns this week. The trial was only briefly reported in the press, and the defence not at all, though it was described in *The Times* as 'a long and elaborate address.' A verbatim account, without comment, was published as a pamphlet by the No-Conscription Fellowship, but this was immediately suppressed and copies of it are very rare. We are indebted to Prof. G. H. Hardy for the loan of a copy from which these extracts were taken.

The leaflet which Russell had written, and which gave occasion for the prosecution, was entitled 'Two years' hard labour for refusing to disobey the dictates of conscience' and dealt with the case of a school-teacher named Everett who, on being drafted by the decision of a con-scientious objectors' tribunal into a non-combatant unit, maintained that his conscience forbade him to participate in any military activity, adopted an attitude of passive resistance, and was finally court-martialled for disobedience and sentenced to two years' hard labour. The leaflet was mainly occupied by a recital of the facts of the case, but in its conclud-ing paragraph denounced the Government's policy and called on the public to support the aims of the No-Conscription Fellowship.

The sequel to the trial is of some interest. Russell refused to pay the fine, and the goods in his rooms in Trinity were distrained upon and offered for public sale, but for the first book a bid sufficient to cover the monies due to the court was entered and the sale terminated abruptly.

THE PROSECUTION

Mr. A. H. Bodkin: My Lord, the relevant words of Regulation 27, under which this summons has been issued, are: 'No person shall in writing, or in any circular, or other printed publication, make state-ments likely to prejudice the recruiting and discipline of His Majesty's forces.'

The pamphlet in question is headed: 'Two years' hard labour for refusing to disobey the dictates of conscience.' It deals with the case of a man named Ernest F. Everett, who was dealt with by a court-martial on the 10th April. To a large extent the history of the matter is set out in the leaflet, but I think it is very desirable that I should remind your Lordship of the terms of the Military Service Act of 1916. Parliament, in passing that statute, recognised that there were certain persons who might be reasonably exempted from its provisions. And I need only mention it to bring it to your mind that tribunals were set up all over the country, composed of popular elements, men selected from each district, to determine, *prima facie*, whether a claimant for a certificate of exemption was entitled to it on the ground of a conscientious objection to the undertaking of combatant service. To those tribunals was entrusted the discrimination between genuine such cases and others in which the conscientious objection was put forward as an excuse for not obeying the law of the country, and not assisting the country at the present time.

That being the law which all of us have to obey—and one would say without fear of contradiction all of us who could, one would think would gladly obey—there appears to have grown up an organisation, called the No-Conscription Fellowship, the objects of which would apparently be to support claims for exemption on alleged conscientious grounds; but whose object was not only that, but to act in direct opposition to that statute, and to undermine its operation as far as possible, to the extent, if possible, of repealing the statute, and of instigating persons to put forward and to maintain their conscientious objections or alleged conscientious objections.

Now I respectfully ask your attention to this [statement by Everett before the court-martial, quoted in the pamphlet]: 'I am prepared to do work of national importance which does not include military service, so long as I do not thereby release some other man to do what I am not prepared to do myself.' Comment upon that is entirely unnecessary. It would be perfectly impossible to tolerate for a moment that a man will select what sort of work he will do, provided that man whose place he takes—whether that man is single or married, making great sacrifices or small sacrifices—so long as he does not do any military service, Mr. Everett is willing to take his place, and do something which he thinks is of national importance—perfectly and absolutely intolerable.

Now, as I said, this leaflet was distributed in various parts of the country, doubtless in large numbers, and under the present defendant's own hand we learn that six men have been condemned to varying terms of imprisonment with hard labour for distributing this leaflet. That was up to the 17th May, and on that morning, in *The Times* newspaper, under the heading '*Adsum qui feci*,' the following letter appeared:

'Sir—A leaflet was lately issued by the No-Conscription Fellowship dealing with the case of Mr. Everett, a conscientious objector, who was sentenced to two years' hard labour by court-martial for disobedience to the military authorities. Six men have been condemned to varying terms of imprisonment with hard labour for distributing this leaflet. I wish to make it known that I am the author of this leaflet, and that if anyone is to be prosecuted I am the person primarily responsible.

Yours faithfully,
BERTRAND RUSSELL.'

It was determined without the smallest hesitation that if persons were dealt with in different parts of the country for its distribution, it would have been a failure of duty on the part of the authorities if, when an anonymous circular was acknowledged, its author should not also be brought before the Court for that Court to pass judgment on his conduct.

It is for you, my Lord Mayor, to form your judgment upon the leaflet, but our submission is that throughout in its terms, and especially in the comment at the end, the effect it would have would be to prejudice both recruiting and discipline; and coming from this organisation which is supporting those who find that their consciences permit them to take advantage of the security of the country, but refuse to permit them to do anything which tends to secure the safety of the country, that it has the tendency of preventing recruiting for that reason, and is eminently likely to discourage what is so essential, the full and complete embodiment of the manhood of the country in the forces of the Crown at the present time. And so the matter is put before you for your consideration and judgment.

THE DEFENCE

The Defendant: My Lord Mayor, I do not propose to call any witnesses, as there is no dispute in regard to the facts. The facts are plain and are admitted. I wish to suggest to your consideration that this case raises an issue of very considerable importance in regard to the legal limits of political agitation at the present time. We have been repeatedly assured in Parliament that political agitation against conscription is not illegal. But if such a leaflet as this which is before you to-day is to be held contrary to the Defence of the Realm Act, it is not easy to see how any political agitation can possibly be carried on. It would seem to follow, if this view is upheld, that although we may state as a bare fact that we are not in favour of conscription, we shall be precluded from stating any of the grounds upon which that opinion rests, and I submit to you, my Lord, that an opinion in favour of which it is illegal to state any arguments is rendered impotent; and, in fact, if the view is upheld the supposed political liberty becomes a farce.

The legal position—as it appears to the Government—in regard to prosecutions of this nature, was explained recently in the House of Commons by Mr. Herbert Samuel. He said:

> 'It is one thing to advocate repeal of the compulsory Military Service Act. It is another thing to advocate resistance to its provisions.'

In view of that answer everything turns upon the question: What is considered to be advocacy of resistance? Is a conscientious objector advocating resistance if he says: 'I intend not to perform military service, even if the tribunals should fail to grant me exemption?' Or if, having failed to obtain exemption, he states that he, as a conscientious objector, cannot conform to that decision? Is he in saying that advocating resistance? I do not think that that view can be held.

A conscientious objection is by its very nature one which cannot be overridden by any decision of a Court of Law. It cannot therefore be said that a man is advocating resistance by a mere statement that he himself does not propose to perform military service, even if he should fail to obtain exemption. I think some such statement he is bound by law to make when he comes before the tribunals, because if he were willing to obey the decision he would not be a genuine objector, and would not be entitled to the exemption of the Act.

Now I should like to take a step further. If a man has a right to state that he himself cannot obey the law under certain contingencies, and that right is accorded by the conscience clause, it cannot surely be against the law to state that there are such men? If indeed that were against the law, I submit that Mr. Herbert Samuel infringed his own regulations. He said in his speech:

> 'I can understand the individual conscientious objector saying as an individual: "Whatever happens to me I do not care. I hold certain doctrines, and no human power can ever compel me to

form a part of a military organisation." Such a man can be respected.'

Those are Mr. Samuel's words. But, my Lord, it is the very thing which I said in this leaflet, in effect the same sentiments.

All human institutions are liable to error, and it is possible for a tribunal to decide erroneously either as to the genuineness, or as to the nature, of a man's conscientious objection. Now what is a man to do in case such an error occurs? Is he to break the law, or is he to violate his conscience? There is no third alternative open.

I am charged with making statements likely to prejudice recruiting and discipline. No evidence has been adduced, and I submit that no evidence can be adduced, to show that such an effect is likely to follow from the distribution of this leaflet. I think that the authorities wish the sentences which are inflicted upon conscientious objectors to be known as widely as possible in the Army, and as little as possible in the civilian population; and I wish to suggest that what is objected to in my leaflet is not any effect which it may have upon recruiting or discipline, or within the Army, but the effect which it is thought likely it may have in producing sympathy in the civilian population for the sufferings of the conscientious objector, and the belief that the conscientious objector is a genuine person, and not the shirker he has been represented as being.

I do not think there is any evidence possible to adduce, and no evidence has been adduced, in favour of the view that this leaflet prejudices recruiting. At the time when it was issued, single men were already subject to conscription, and therefore any supposed effect would have been only in regard to married men. Now, the married man who contemplates voluntarily enlisting is *ex hypothesi* not a conscientious objector. The leaflet informs him that if he chooses to pose as a conscientious objector he is liable to two years' hard labour. I do not consider that knowledge of that fact is likely to induce such a man to pretend that he is a conscientious objector when he is not.

I come now to the question whether this leaflet is likely to prejudice discipline. The purpose of the leaflet is to make it known that a man is liable to two years' hard labour for refusing to obey discipline. Does this knowledge encourage a man to resist discipline? Surely such a contention is preposterous. If the authorities are right in stating that this leaflet is prejudicial to recruiting by making the sentences known, they must have been wrong in inflicting the sentences. If they were right in inflicting the sentences—right from the point of view of promoting discipline—they must be wrong in saying that the leaflet is prejudicial to discipline by making them known.

It is true that the leaflet does not confine itself to a mere statement of facts. There is in the last paragraph a criticism of those facts. It may be said that discipline is endangered by this phrase: 'Everett is now suffering this savage punishment for refusing to go against his conscience.' But the belief that Everett's sentence was excessive was not confined to the writer of this leaflet; it was shared by the authorities. Soon after the leaflet began to be distributed his sentence was commuted from two years' hard labour to 112 days' detention. In view of this fact we must suppose that the authorities felt that their action in inflicting such a sentence was indefensible. If the punishment did not deserve criticism, why was it commuted? If it did deserve criticism, with what justice, with what face, can the prosecution object to that criticism being uttered?

I would say, my Lord, that whether I personally am acquitted or condemned is a matter of no great importance, but it is not only I that am in the dock; it is the whole tradition of British liberty which our forefathers built up with great trouble and with great sacrifice. I think that under the stress of fear the authorities have somewhat forgotten that ancient tradition, and I think the fear is unworthy, and the tyranny which is resulting will be disastrous if it is not resisted. I would say to them: 'You cannot defeat such men …'

The Lord Mayor: I have allowed you a good deal of latitude because you are not an expert. Really now you are making a political speech.

The Defendant: I wish to say that the only way in which discipline can be preserved is not to punish these men, but to let them go.

THE JUDGMENT

The Lord Mayor: I have given the fullest consideration to Mr. Russell's argument, but it has failed to convince me. I fine him £100 and £10 costs, or in default of distress 61 days, and I give eight days in which to pay the penalty.

March 1st, 1940

A letter from the Western Front

J. M. G.

Things have really 'hummed' in the trenches this spell in. We had a reasonably quiet time the first four days, but there was a good deal of noise the last four. We went in on April 12th. The weather was beastly then, and it remained beastly the whole time we were in. There was water in the trenches when we came in, and it got knee-deep by the time we went out. On Palm Sunday night, April 16th, we began to 'strafe,' and the Boche and we between us kept it up till Thursday night. We set the ball a-rolling. The programme started with a mine. As a matter of fact we knew the Boche was mining us, and that he had nearly completed the job. Our mine was a purely defensive one to stop his games. In addition to exploding the mine we had a party to raid the German front trench to try and collar a prisoner. Your beloved son had to provide a covering party on the left flank; there was a similar party on the right flank, and another in the centre to cover a party which was to dig a new trench on the lip of the prospective crater. The mine was timed to go up at midnight. As a matter of fact it went up eight minutes earlier. At the moment I was down near the spot calling in some sentries to keep them out of the way of falling débris. The ground literally rocked, and if I had not clung on to a traverse I should have come off my legs. For what seemed ages the air was full of chalk and stones. When the stuff had stopped falling I saw the most extraordinary sight. The whole ground had changed. A bit of our trench had gone, and in its place I saw a huge white mound (the lip of the crater) some 20 ft. high. The mound had formed only 15 yards from where I stood. Apparently the Boche charge was laid and we exploded it with our own. The engineers said that we had fired our charge none too soon; it was only a matter of half-an-hour to two hours before the German had set his mine going. The result was that a bit of our front line was taken, and it became necessary to dig a new trench round our side of the crater. The Germans had a small advanced trench just about thirty yards from our front line. Unfortunately the mine had not caught this, and they thus had a clear way up to their lip of the crater. It became our business to rain rapid fire on this to stop them coming up. Our artillery let loose at once on the explosion of the mine, and every rifle and machine gun in the neighbourhood joined in the chorus. In nine minutes the Boche gunners were replying. As we were only 60 yards from the Boche our shrapnel burst immediately over our heads. The Boche shrapnel burst in the same place, and some of their 'whizzbangs' knocked in our parapet. The flame of shells was so great that the whole place was lit up for quite a minute at a time. Meanwhile our raiding party had rushed the German advanced trench; found nobody there—probably in anticipation of their own mine—and though only a dozen strong headed straight for the Boche front line. They found the place alive with men, and could make no prisoners. They inflicted a respectable number of casualties and drew off, losing only the officer in charge, slightly wounded, and he got safely back.

Shortly after the raiders returned, a party of Huns tried to come round the crater on my flank and bomb the digging party. I at once manœuvred a machine gun and a party of bombers into position, but the sight of several live Huns was too much for one of the men nearest the spot. He was out and over the parapet in two shakes, and threw two bombs straight into the middle of the party. This made the Germans' minds up. What was left of them retired hurriedly, and we were never troubled on my flank again. Some little time after this a report came down to me that the officer in charge of the digging party in the crater had been hit. As nothing was then doing where I was, I left a sergeant in charge of my party and went off to the crater. It was a curious sight that I saw. The Germans kept sending flares up, which lit the whole place up. They then turned machine guns on us. Round the crater itself it was raining bombs. On the top of our lip I could see silhouetted our covering party blazing off their rifles. Down below was the digging party, digging for dear life to get down under cover. Almost immediately after I got there the sergeant in charge of the covering party—as fine a type of N.C.O. as you could meet—was shot through the head, and I climbed up the lip to direct the fire. The crater was an enormous width, some 30 yards in diameter, and its depth was quite 30 feet in centre. I could see spurts from Boches' rifles on the other lip of the crater, and periodically a bomb came over.

For the next five hours I had a sample of what 'consolidation' means. We had to finish our trench, and make a bullet-proof observation post on the lip which could command the crater on all sides. I had been promised a relief at daybreak as the men were dog-tired, but the relief did not come. Our position was at a salient in our lines, and the result was we could be enfiladed by rifle and machine-gun fire on both flanks as well as in front. When day broke the machine-guns spotted us and got to work. More than once we had to hug the ground hard whilst they played over us. We could only crawl on our stomachs; any man who got upright was instantly hit. Lying prone we had to scratch out the earth and put it into sandbags, and then push them into position on the breastwork. As I did some of this work I can tell you how fatiguing it was. Some of the men who had been digging eight hours slept over their shovels. Altogether it was a weird experience. On the far side of the crater I could hear the Germans at work. From the front and each flank came bursts of machine-gun fire spitting all round us. Now and then there was a groan as one of my men got hit. Once I heard a Boche shout as if he was hit. On the top of the lip were a few men crouching and keeping a look-out over the crater. The men were dead beat, but did not shirk their work. I am conscious of trying to cheer them up with a few feeble jokes; they needed cheering up, for it was drenching with rain. By 9 a.m. we had so far dug ourselves in in two spots that men could lie flat and observe with periscopes. That is to say, the position was consolidated and I could withdraw the covering party.

At 6 p.m. on the last night our final mine went up and was followed by an hour's intense bombardment. This was further to our left, and very little came our way. That night we were relieved and paddled out of the trenches. We got some hot drink behind the firing line, and were then shipped on to 'busses' and came back to where we are now. We arrived at 6.30 for a lovely Good Friday morning. The women of the village were returning from Church, and must have been astonished at the unshaven, bedraggled, and foot-sore crowd they met coming into the village. It was a pleasant contrast to see this peaceable sight after what we had been doing for the last eight days.

May 31st, 1916

KEYNES AND THE SLUMP
i. Keynes on Money

MAURICE DOBB

The unknown apparently fascinates grown-up as much as ungrown children. Wherever the field of experience is uncharted, the worshippers of magic can withdraw and hold their sway. Hitherto in economics the theory of credit has been such a field. The classical theory of money was built when the modern credit system was still in a primitive stage; and subsequent treatment of the subject did little more than revolve within the limits of the classical framework: at least, it did little to invent an improved analytical technique. The credit mechanism was left with a serious unexplained *hiatus* where mystery reigned and 'currency-cranks' rushed in to produce from its darkness some universal talisman. And when the rapid passages of war and post-war finance revealed this unmapped region as the junction of the most important causal trains of events, the need to end this mystery became imperatively clear.

This Mr Keynes has at last done for us in this impressive treatise,* eagerly awaited by economists for some time past, and in the future likely to represent as bold a milestone as some of the leading contributions to the subject in classical political economy. The chief limitation has hitherto been that the older theories of money provided us with an equation of identity, establishing for us a static equilibrium, but telling us little or nothing about the causal sequence once that equilibrium was disturbed and affording no means of forecasting the degree and nature of such a disturbance once movement had started. Moreover, in Mr Keynes' opinion, the older theories were further handicapped by imperfect clarity as to the meaning and significance of the concept, 'the value of money' or 'the general level of prices.' These deficiencies the novel approach and original treatment of this treatise goes a long way—perhaps it will prove the main part of the way—to repair. The argument begins with a careful and illuminating discussion of different types of index-numbers, in the course of which the concept of 'purchasing power of money' (assigned a new and somewhat difficult

* *A Treatise on Money.* By J. M. Keynes.

definition) is singled out and distinguished from numerous alternative types of price-level appropriate to their several particular contexts. This is followed by what will soon be the famous new 'Fundamental Equation,' which differs from the older formulations in relating the value of money, not merely to monetary circulation and the supply of goods, but also to the ratio between saving, investment and the output of finished consumption goods (as distinct from capital goods, such as machinery). In this way more complex and dependent variables are reduced to more primary terms, and an important shift of emphasis is achieved in the approach to the causal problem of price changes. This equation by itself is also no more than an equation of identity, providing us with the conditions of static equilibrium. But it is supplemented with a number of additional propositions which go a considerable way towards providing a causal sequence of dynamic processes. (The most interesting, perhaps, of these, even though it be admittedly no more than a tautology, is that which relates one of the terms of the first equation to the level of 'efficiency-earnings.') It is characteristic of the author's lucid treatment of a somewhat intricate subject that he is not content merely to present us with his own contribution: he is careful also to reduce his equations and his predecessors' to a common denominator and to show us the precise relationship in which they stand.

In the final hundred pages of Volume One the Fundamental Equations are combined and utilised to form a theory of the 'credit cycle.' Wicksell's fruitful concept of 'the natural rate of interest' is expanded into the central proposition that the credit cycle acquires its rhythm from a disequilibrium between 'savings' and 'investment,' which produces a change in the price-level of consumption goods. This occurs when the market rate of interest diverges from the 'natural rate' (or the rate which will leave the terms of the Fundamental Equation in equilibrium). From this emerges the highly important practical corollary that it is within the power of the Central Bank to control the credit cycle—to control credit and price fluctuations and their related fluctuations in industrial activity and employment—by controlling the market rate of interest through its own discount rate. The general theory, applicable to internal equilibrium within a 'closed system,' is extended to deal with the terms of 'external' or 'international equilibrium' and the causes of departure from it; and the first volume closes with an interesting chapter treating among other things of the topical reparations transfer problem, which prepares the ground for the suggestive concluding chapter of Volume Two, entitled 'Problems of Supernational Management,' where the possible extended functions of the Bank of International Settlements are discussed.

The second and separate volume is designed to carry over the propositions of the pure theory into an 'applied theory of money.' This volume is rich in historical illustrations of the main theme, in analysis of the mechanism of the present credit-system in this and other countries and in suggestions for change and improvement. In the course of it there emerges much that is of considerable theoretical significance as well as of practical interest—for instance, the concept of 'working-capital' and of 'productive and unproductive consumption' (which Mr Keynes advances as a rehabilitation of the classic Wages-fund), the theory of stocks and of 'open-market dealings.' But the very breadth of scope and richness of detail of this second volume precludes any adequate description of it in a short review.

And the fruits—do they surpass expectation or disappoint them, after the zest of struggle with so imposing a fund of new analytical material? That needs time and experience to show. Perhaps the value of its immediate practical fruit will exceed its value in enlarging our *organon* of knowledge; perhaps the converse may prove true. Whichever it be, the work seems likely to leave a permanent trace, possibly a deep one, on the future history both of monetary theory and of monetary practice. And even if the work was less fertile by a half, its influence would doubtless exceed that of books of equal stature to this one, because of the directness of thought and language and the lucidity of exposition of which Mr Keynes is probably foremost among his contemporaries as a master.

November 28th, 1930

ii. A Letter to the Editor

Sir,—It is not surprising that, in a bewildered attempt to make some contribution towards solving the country's difficulties, many individuals and institutions should at the present time be turning towards economy—thus offering the sacrifice which Authority would, by precept and example, appear to be demanding from them. The parallel of the War is constantly being brought to mind. We wish to

suggest that this parallel, superficially so convincing, is not only misleading, but dangerous.

The present situation is wholly different from that which existed at
the beginning of the War. It was then necessary for us to economise in
order that we might set free men and resources to fill other and more
urgent needs. To-day no similar necessity exists. In fact, the characteristic feature of the present situation is the failure to employ fully the
men and the resources at our disposal. To release by private economy
more men and more resources can only aggravate that situation. It will
add to the present volume of unemployment, without increasing either
our present or our future wealth.

Many persons and many institutions will, of course, have to economise because, for one reason or another, their incomes have been
reduced. In their case some reduction of expenditure is, we recognise,
inevitable. A wise husbanding of resources may in some cases be
desirable. But personal economy, although it may be dictated by individual necessities, is not a patriotic duty. For many of us there will be
a conflict between our desire to economise for personal reasons and our
duty to spend for national reasons. We must recognise this conflict. In
particular we must refrain from attempts to justify, under the cloak of
patriotism, an action dictated by personal interest.

May we suggest, therefore, that members of the University should
not rush heedlessly into extravagant economies, and so add to our
existing difficulties? Ostentatious expenditure may at the moment be
more than usually undesirable, but wise expenditure is a patriotic
duty that we ought to show good cause for refusing.

Yours, etc.,

C. W. GUILLEBAUD
H. C. B. MYNORS
E. A. G. ROBINSON

October 23rd, 1931

iii. Lament for the Gold Standard

JACQUES RUEFF AND J. M. KEYNES ATTEND A MEETING OF THE MARSHALL SOCIETY

Talking last Monday, before a meeting of the Marshall Society, the French and the Anglo-French Societies, and after emphasising that while he enjoyed a good point of observation in the French Embassy in London yet all his opinions must be taken as purely personal, M. Rueff began by praising the London money-market as practically a perfect economic institution, in its mechanism for tenders and treasury bills, unique in a central bank that does not discount, but only rediscounts bills, in a treasury which until recently was alone in publishing weekly statements, and finally unique in a government that thinks economic reasons are worth applying to daily life or have anything to do with politics, and which asks Royal Commissions for reasons for changes that it contemplates. He quoted Mr Ramsay Macdonald and La Fontaine in an attempt to prove that the English are a logical people, as such method of action would seem to suggest.

The chief economic difficulty of our time is the change from pre-war to post-war conditions. Before the war equilibrium of the balance of accounts was obtained through the gold standard by changes in the price level, but in the heedless rush to buy during the war the combatants lost that balance and readjustments were necessary when the exchange machinery was restored after the war. Loss of gold, entailing lower prices and reduced lending abroad was the natural result, but attempts were made to prevent these painful processes of adaptation from taking place. One method, favoured in Central Europe, was stabilisation of prices, but it was observed that wherever legal maximum prices were established an inadequate supply was found to ensue, as proved by food queues in some countries and the shortage of flats in France which is being cured as the rent restrictions are gradually raised. Britain and Germany also witness to the hardships caused by attempts to hinder the adaptation of the price level. France and America have pursued the same policy, especially in the matter of agricultural prices.

The working of the gold standard would have brought about equilibrium of the balance of accounts, but the British policy of open market dealings since 1928 has hindered it. (M. Rueff agreed with Mr Keynes' theory of the relation between price level and gold movements: that gold has to be exported when high prices cause exports to drop, because imports are comparatively unaffected). And although the Board of Trade returns indicate that the money to spare for lending abroad has diminished considerably the amount of the loans has not in fact decreased. The American open-market policy (which M. Rueff thought did not work as it is commonly described) which sterilized gold just after the war in an attempt to stop the results of the rapid inflow, had the same results. Again, large holdings of foreign currencies by central banks have been used to maintain the position, especially of East European countries, but this also makes the exchange market less sensitive. Bad effects have also attended the movements of credit without corresponding movements of gold, particularly during the period of extensive American loans to Europe, and the scarcity of gold due to maldistribution (for the gold holdings of the world's central banks doubled from 1913 to 1930) is due to the mechanism of the gold standard not being allowed to work. Here, in passing, M. Rueff mentioned the charge that France has been obstructing better distribution of gold. He thought that possibly the French discount policy might have been more liberal, but there had been no actual obstruction; indeed France had not the means for so doing; the increased reserve of the Caisse d'Amortissement (which has now been reduced again) had but little effect.

The system of credits made in order to be re-invested in the lender country has enabled double credit moves, and has led to inflation. The American Federal Reserve bank increased its discount rate, partly in an attempt to help the pound at a time when it might have been better to stop the boom, which from 1927 to 1929 was allowed to go too far and has resulted in a deeper depression which is again prolonged by the hindrance of adaptation of prices to the cost of production. That adaptation has even been made impossible in some Central European countries except through depreciation of currency, a dangerous method, though one which has spread even to Britain.

This method of seeking equilibrium by revaluation of money is an important factor in our new economic world. There is no certain way of adaptation now that we have broken with the past and suppressed the free working of the gold standard without substituting a managed monetary policy. Either of these systems is logical and justifiable

D

(although he thought the second too complicated to be practicable) but to have neither is absurd.

There then followed a discussion, where Mr Keynes agreed with M. Rueff's arguments, but not with his conclusions (in reply to the accusation of logicality he pointed out that we pride ourselves on reaching the right solution in the wrong way). He described the pre-war monetary system as not automatic, and as a sterling, not a gold, standard. It had broken down in becoming a dollar and a franc standard. The system had broken down on a small scale in the early '90's, and had never been faced with such a task as now. The system had never been so fluid as M. Rueff suggested, and the gold standard was demanding now from the social organism a degree of self-adaptation never before thought of. M. Rueff in reply claimed that the wage and cost of production movements from 1921 to 1923 did testify a very fluid state of affairs but the levels have been held rigid since then. The pre-war gold standard was managed according to the banks' reserves, now it is according to the bankers' ideas; a managed policy has always bled the central banks after a few months.

May 20th, 1932

The Economic System in a Socialist State

JOAN ROBINSON

In the ideal system depicted in the text books of economics, the free play of private enterprise, under competitive conditions, produces the maximum possible material welfare from the productive resources available to society. The consumer is free to buy what he chooses, and lays out his income in such a way as to obtain the greatest possible benefit for himself; the producer is free to supply whatever will yield the greatest profit to himself; prices reflect demand, demand governs profit, and the interaction of individual decisions works out in such a way that the available resources are steered into the uses which yield the greatest benefit to society. A comparison between the ideal system and the actual operations of capitalism reveal striking exceptions to the text-book rules. Extreme inequality in the distribution of income, the frequent occurrence of unemployment and the prevalence of monopoly are obvious blemishes in the actual system, which notoriously falls short of the text-book ideal. Many writers, impressed by the beauty of the ideal competitive pricing-system, advocate socialism as the best method of bringing it into actual existence. If private enterprise were abolished and all production controlled by a central plan, it would be possible to reproduce by artificial means the workings of the ideal competitive system, and to achieve the results which the actual system has failed to bring about. Mr Hall* is, in general, of this school of thought, though he presents his case temperately, and must not be classed with the fanatical *laisser-faire* socialists. He sketches the competitive system, shows how modern capitalism fails to resemble its flattering portrait, and then proceeds to discuss what devices a socialist system could use to remove the blemishes from capitalism, and model itself upon the text-book plan.

But it is necessary to inquire how far the ideal competitive pricing system really does provide a working model which the authorities in a socialist system could use in framing their plans. There are many decisions, as Mr Hall is ready to admit, which they would have to make without any guidance from the text-book system.

First of all, there is the question of distribution of income. The actual distribution of wealth (which largely governs the distribution of income) in a modern community is a legacy from the remote and the immediate past, shaped by the accidents of history. It follows no rational scheme, and claims no moral justification. The text-book system throws no light on it, for the text-books discuss the distribution of the production industry between the factors of production, not the distribution of factors of production between individuals. As Mr Hall points out, costing under socialism can be divorced from actual payments, a purely book-keeping value being attached to the factors of production. The actual incomes of individuals under socialism must be decided, presumably, by a mixture of expediency and rough justice, without any assistance from the text-book scheme.

But this, so far as it goes, is a justification for the point of view represented by Mr Hall. Inequality of income, it has always been recognised, constitutes a fatal objection to the contention that the system of private enterprise leads to maximum social welfare. The freedom of the consumer is at best only freedom to spend his own income, and a system

* *The Economic System in a Socialist State.* By R. L. Hall.

under which incomes are widely different, so that some individuals live in luxury and some on the edge of starvation, is wasteful of resources and uneconomic in a crude and obvious sense. Under social-ism, it may be argued, the range of differences in income would, to say the least, be narrower than at present, the major departure of the actual from the ideal system would be removed, and the vaunted freedom of the consumer could at last be allowed to come into its own.

But there are other important questions which the text-book system cannot help the socialist authorities to answer. All strategical problems, under any system, must be solved by authority, not by the interplay of individual decisions. And these problems concern not merely the allocation of resources to defence, but the whole policy of national self-sufficiency; they ramify, indeed, into almost every department of economic life.

When these questions have been decided, another major decision remains to be taken by authority. This concerns the question of saving —of foregoing present consumption for the sake of future wealth. Under private enterprise there is a chronic tendency (at least in modern times) for the interaction of individual decisions to result in an attempt to save more than, under private enterprise, it is profitable to invest in real capital. The result is unemployment and a widespread waste of resources. This waste would be eliminated under socialism, and it might be argued, once more, that socialism could beat capitalism at its own game.

But supposing that full employment of resources is guaranteed, the question still remains open how far they should be employed in capital accumulation, as opposed to current consumption. It is idle to argue that individuals should be free to decide how much they wish to save, the authorities making it their business merely to see that what is saved is invested in the most useful forms. For the state, even if it does not regard itself as immortal, at least has a longer expectation of life than the individual, and must attach greater importance than the individual to future benefits. The authorities would not be justified in allowing themselves to be guided blindly by individual decisions, and no amount of mathematical ingenuity can provide a criterion for deciding between the interests of one generation and the interests of its grandchildren. Investment does not cease to be useful to society until capital equip-ment is so plentiful that the rate of interest has fallen to zero (this is a point which Mr Hall fails to bring out) and the ultimate objective is clear enough, but the rate at which the goal ought to be approached can only be determined by an arbitrary decision.

In the large-scale decisions, therefore, the text-book system is of no assistance. At best its usefulness is confined to the narrower sphere of the detailed allocation of resources between particular types of goods. But even here it is very deficient. There are many instances to which the criterion of the ideal competitive system fails to apply, simply because in them competition cannot prevail. All transport facilities, all public utilities, such as the provision of water and gas, all production for narrow markets (as in a sparsely populated countryside), all manufactures where the economies of large-scale require a single productive unit for efficient organisation (and these grow more common as modern technique develops) are monopolistic by the nature of the case. In many of them, even to-day, a compromise has been patched up between control and private enterprise to save the consumer from blatant exploitation. Here there is no question of imitating the simple workings of ideal competition, and a far more complicated system of ideas must be called into play to achieve the theoretical maximisation of welfare.

These defects in the text-book system are formidable enough, even if we accept the text-book assumption that the individual consumer, given his income, allots expenditure between different goods in such a way as to get the greatest benefit from it. But this assumption admits of well-recognised exceptions. Not to mention the drug-fiend and the sot, it is generally admitted that the individual is inclined to spend less on education than is desirable on general grounds. Certainly, few children would freely spend on education as much as their parents think right, and if the parents may coerce the children, it is difficult to argue that the state ought not to coerce the parents. The same argument is admitted to apply to the question of medical services. And health is affected not only by sanitation and bottles of medicine, but by diet, housing and clothing. The authorities under socialism, guided by scientists, can make wiser decisions for the individual in all these matters than he can make for himself.

The sphere of action of the competitive pricing system, once all these exceptions are admitted, has been greatly narrowed. And it must be still further whittled away. For it is obvious that in reality advertisement, fashion and the custom of society dictate the actual expenditure of individuals far more than the text-book principle of 'equalising marginal utilities,' and if individuals, left to themselves, allot their expenditure between goods under influences which have no ultimate rational justification, it seems hard to maintain that the socialist authorities ought to be guided by the decisions of individuals, reflected in the pricing system, rather than by any other plan which may recommend itself to them.

It is desirable, no doubt, that the individual consumer should not be coerced in such a way as to rouse his resentment, and in matters of minor importance the pricing system, no doubt, would still be useful under socialism. When the major decisions have been taken which affect defence, health, education and the provision of capital, the next task must clearly be to produce an adequate supply of what everyone regards as basic necessities, and so long as it is a question of providing the whole population with food and shelter a general commonsense view of what is needed will provide at least as good a guide as the workings of a pricing system imitated from the text-books. When all these problems have been solved, and the question comes up of choosing between one kind of luxury and another, the free choice of the consumer may well be allowed to come into play.

February 26th, 1937

Thoughts on War Thought

G. KITSON CLARK

The urgency of public danger, the high emotional tension, the restless desire for action which press on men's minds in time of war, naturally affect among other things the kind of statements they are prepared to publish. Since men's hearts and minds are often more open in wartime, in many ways the effect of war on public discussion is good; but it is not altogether good. Men in war seem to speak more loudly, to think more loosely, to snatch at catch-phrases more eagerly than they would have done in time of peace, with the result that there can remain afterwards a mass of promises and declarations some of which come to seem, very soon after peace is signed, to be impracticable, some repugnant, some even actually unintelligible—as did the pledge to hang the Kaiser very soon after the last war. A great

deal of the talk produced is entirely ephemeral and becomes when war
is over little more than a historical curiosity, but it sets the tone of
public discussion, it affects the language of the day and therefore the
language, and still worse the promises, of statesmen; and it is going to
be a very serious thing for the world if the men who are going to be
set the very difficult task of making peace should come to their task
embarrassed by too much queer luggage which eager publicists have
thrust into their hands. Therefore to criticise what we say in time of
war is perhaps even more important than to try to remember in time
of peace why we said it, and just as difficult; and it may be useful to
attempt to consider two possible tendencies in wartime thought.

One wartime habit is a continuous indulgence in moral condemna-
tion. War is amply justified from a moral point of view if it saves
humanity from intolerable evil, but that does not satisfy a great many
people, particularly if they are Englishmen and Americans. They wish
it to comply with the moral pattern for the world with which they are
still most familiar, the pattern of moral retribution, of guilt, crime,
and punishment. They are uncertain about the relation of moral retribution to the domestic justice inflicted in their own law courts, many
of them claim to be uncertain about the application of a code of fixed
morals to their private lives, but when they come to consider the
behaviour of nations they appear to be filled with a new eager confidence. In wartime the theory of the Guilty Nation, which one would
have thought was in many ways one of the most difficult, if not disputable, of historical conceptions, becomes a commonplace. It is
responsible for the writing of a great deal of rather queer history to
prove that one nation has always been wicked, or at least inimical
to the peace of Europe. It prescribes the form in which a good many
people think about the war and its causes, and the danger is that it
should rise to the council table to turn the decisions of the statesmen
making the peace into a moral judgment inflicting a punishment
on a transgressor, a conception likely to be drowned by a warm flood
of pity and sympathy for the vanquished—at least in Anglo-Saxon
breasts—as soon as the sentence begins to take effect.

The history of the Treaty of Versailles, particularly the history of
the popular estimation of it, might suggest the question whether this
process is wholly desirable. At any rate it may be worth while to
question—now rather than later—the conception behind it. It is true
that if ever we can detect moral evil in our fellows we can detect it in

the men who have gained control of Germany: it is also true that that evil corresponds with an ugly strain in German history and German thought, which prepared the way for them. It is our part to defeat those evil men, to check the results of that strain, and, if we can, to eliminate it from the Europe it has devastated. But perhaps we ought to pause before we feel capable of estimating the moral guilt of the individual German, affected as he may well have been by historical accident, by ignorance, by a sense of national peril, bad leadership, bad training, or plain brutal compulsion. Some may have been guilty, others not so guilty, some quite innocent, but to punish the whole nation is to punish them all, and their posterity with them. For the sake of the peace of Europe we must wish to recommend to the Germans better ideas, democracy (if we believe in it), Christianity (if we believe in that), freedom and mercy, and respect for other peoples. But those ideas will not recommend themselves very warmly if our moralising in their name is always to be associated in the German mind with hostility to the German people, and also with the bitterness of defeat and a sentence pronounced on them by a victorious adversary. We are fully justified in doing all we can to break Nazi tyranny, and in taking any steps we think fit to prevent its recurrence, and in believing in the exalted nature of that duty. It is hard not to express our disgust at the deeds done in Germany's name. But when we have done these things it may be desirable to exercise what self-restraint we can, to give morality a rest, and to leave the attribution of moral guilt to God, or his very humble servants the Historians. We should be perhaps wise if we let our treaty, when we make it, rest on the pragmatic needs of the case, and not on the moral responsibilities of the vanquished, remembering that they must accept it, and we must stand by it this time, if it is to become the foundation of the public law of Europe.

But continuous moralising is not the only danger in wartime thought, there is also the feeling of the certainty of compensation. War is very terrible, it inflicts cruel hardship on humanity and, therefore, by the theory of compensation to which humanity when in agony inevitably but illogically holds out its hands, suffering so awful must win, can only be justified if it does win, advantages as great and good as war is bad. This feeling gives an immediate opportunity to the looser and more sanguine thinkers of the day. Abstract schemes for the regeneration of mankind are not hard to construct, attractive phrases leap readily into the minds of men whose main contribution has been in the sphere of imaginative literature. Plans for what is to happen at the end of the war are difficult to criticise, they cannot easily be brought to the touchstone of what is practical, for they are to be realised in a period which will admittedly be unlike the present, as it will probably be unlike the past, but a period over which now rests the golden haze of the hopes of peace. Consequently it is very tempting for men to lay down what in their opinion must be humanity's reward for so much suffering, indeed they are clearly tempted to go further and to attempt blackmail by saying that unless their ideas are realized the suffering cannot be justified, and they will not support the war.

In this way another difficulty is created for the statesmen after the war. Phrases are born which have not cost their authors much time in the labour of analysis. They seem to be appearing now just as they appeared last time to echo down the wind afterwards with increasing ironic force. 'A war to end war,' 'make the world safe for democracy,' 'a land fit for heroes to live in,' 'industry without profit in future,' 'the abolition of National Sovereignty'—it is a little difficult to discriminate between what appeared between 1914 and 1918, and what has started to appear in 1940. Indeed there is a peculiar danger in 1940, since men are now playing with the idea that Hitler will in the end be defeated by a social revolution on the continent, and one of the most necessary preparations for such a revolution is the promulgation of promises that no man can fulfil. Already the cry has gone up for the definition of War Aims, that is, for our leaders to make promises—sometimes very elaborate and sometimes very controversial promises are demanded— about the arrangements to be made at the end of the war.

But we can know very little about what the world after the war will be like. It will be a mourning world, a dangerous world, a disordered world, but beyond that it is difficult to see anything for certain; and it would have seemed that it ought to be difficult to promise much for that world for certain either. To promise more than you can be sure of performing may seem at times politically desirable, but it is after all dishonourable, and may be unwise. Consider the case of the Americans in the last war. The Americans had completely adequate reasons for fighting in the last war. It was necessary for them to stop the outrageous attacks made by Germans on their shipping; even then, though less than now, a German victory would have been a danger to them, and by fighting and helping to win the war they did make the world safer for democracy. But they were led to believe that

by their fighting they ought to secure a much more extensive programme, and when the task of peacemaking came, and the difficulties
of this programme became apparent, together with the further responsibilities it would lay upon them, they shrank back aggrieved, and ever
afterwards rather unjustly they felt they had been deceived by the
statesmen of Europe, a feeling which helped to poison their minds at
times when American help and American sympathy might have been
all important to the peoples of the world. Nor was the poison of disappointment confined to the Americans alone. Disappointment that
you do not immediately receive what you have been promised at the
end of a cruelly hard struggle is a very bitter feeling, and it served then
and it may serve now to divide men and nations at a time when their
co-operation is of urgent necessity. Perhaps by promising less this time
we may gain more for everyone in the end.

For the theory of compensation rests upon a fallacy, and a peculiarly cruel fallacy. The immediate object of war, at least of war as
waged by peace loving nations, is not positive, it is negative, and yet
it can completely justify war. Our immediate object is to prevent the
Gestapo and the Storm Troopers from entering this country, and our
proximate object must be to remove those dreadful things and the
power that spawned them from the face of the world. If we do those
two things, and fail to do anything else, the war will be completely
justified whatever resurgent pacificism may afterwards say to the
contrary. We have no right to believe that after the victory Utopia
will be thrown in as a bonus. Of course we ought not to be content
with a negative end. A better world and a better Britain should be the
desire of any man of good will. We ought certainly to try to think
ahead in order to understand the needs of such a world, and we ought
to have a better chance of achieving what we desire when freed from
the menaces, and it must be added from some of the cant, which have
haunted us of late years. But with our thoughts must be mixed the
realisation that these things must be secured after the war, and will not
come as a result of the war alone. Further effort, further sacrifices will
be necessary. Nor will the form of these better things necessarily be
what the imaginations of Anglo-Saxon publicists now picture. Theirs
are not the only brains, and, stranger still, not the only consciences in
the world. Nations now dumb in slavery must have their chance to
speak before anything is settled, men now under arms must say their
say. There will be controversy, there will be disagreement, differences

of opinion which it will be no service to mankind to ignore. But the task will be a worthy one, and we shall approach it with the greater chance of success if we do not approach it having pledged ourselves to prejudge all its issues, if we have not been too generous in our moral condemnations, and if our feet are not too much entangled by the loose phrases which afterwards we feel sure that we never meant.

October 11th, 1940

Letter to a Friend

GERALD BULLETT

Yes, the atomic bomb gave every one a shock. And, as shocks so often do, it caused a great deal of unthinking vociferation. The best comment, which expressed every one's first feelings about it, was the one attributed to an anonymous American citizen: 'This is either the end of war or the end of the world.' The worst, by which I mean the shallowest, was to the effect that with the invention of the atomic bomb war has become so wicked that we really must see it doesn't happen again. 'Wicked' is the word I quarrel with there. Whether or not war is wicked is an arguable question, and a question quite un-affected by the choice of weapons. Morally, it is no worse to kill a hundred thousand people with one bomb than to kill a hundred thousand people with five hundred bombs, or with heavy artillery, or with machine guns, or with bows and arrows, or with a child's cata-pult. And it seems to me—but not apparently to you—that it is better to bring a war to an end by an act that incidentally involves killing a hundred thousand at a stroke than to achieve the same purpose slowly and laboriously by the expenditure of, say, a million lives: the net gain in human life is a handsome one. Our use of the atomic bomb was an unspeakably horrible act, but not so productive of human misery as the indefinite prolongation of the war would have been.

You may think it perverse in me to question the proposition that war is wicked. Needless to say, it is no liking for war that makes me do so. I hate it in practice as much as you do, though not perhaps in theory, because I don't believe, as you do, that it is always and neces-sarily the *worst* of evils. But ranting against war and industriously advertising its horrors, of which there was so much in the 'twenties and 'thirties, never got us anywhere except into a state of demi-semi-pusillanimous pacifism which made people ready to applaud the monstrous Pact of Munich and to persuade themselves that what was going on in Hitler's concentration camps was no affair of theirs. War is a colossal human disaster, but the proposition: 'War is wicked,' is altogether too vague, woolly, and undiscriminating. It is wicked for a nation to make wanton war on its neighbour; but it is emphatically *not* wicked for the attacked nation to defend itself or for others to join in the defence. You, obstinately as I think, refuse to admit any distinction between the nations who deliberately and of set purpose force war on the world and those who take up arms against them in defence of certain elementary human liberties. And your dogma that to kill is always not merely a sin, but the worst of sins, prevents your admitting that a society unprotected by law, of which the ultimate sanction is force, would be at the mercy of any homicidal lunatic with a gun. The atomic bomb is not an argument for 'pacifism,' that is for allowing any violent aggressor to work his own sweet will unopposed: it is an argument for the establishment of world unity and a world authority. That can only be done by abandoning the idiotic conception of 'absolute national sovereignties.' I should like to think it will happen, but it seems very unlikely. The event is likely to prove, on the contrary, that we have not enough collective sense to do what would have to be done to save the world from suicide; and I fancy you are over-sanguine in putting the ultimate catastrophe as late as a hundred years hence.

I suppose we all have certain mental rigidities that make us at points impervious to argument. One of yours, if I may say so, takes the form of an automatic recoil from any opinion widely current among your own countrymen. You think our use of the atomic bomb makes it absurd for us to proceed with the trials of 'war-criminals.' I would agree with you that the phrase is a misnomer. The crimes in question have no necessary connection with war. And there is a sufficiently clear distinction between acts of war, however terrible, and the deliberate indulgence in cruelty for its own sake: Belsen, Buchenwald, the Japanese use of prisoners of war for bayonet-practice, the wholesale mutilation and slaughter of Jews as such, the deportation of Polish girls for use in German brothels, etc., etc., *ad nauseam*. For my own part, I would not willingly cause a moment's unnecessary pain even to the authors of these outrages: I would merely kill them with all speed, since their reconversion into human beings is only theoretically possible. Not war, not killing, but the deliberate infliction of pain, is the sin against the Holy Ghost.

But history moves so fast nowadays that many of these considerations seem already a little out of date. And with your main contention, that the release of atomic energy is something we are unfitted to cope with, I of course agree. The new knowledge enables us to make an end of all human civilisation, if not of the whole human species; and the chances are that we shall do just that, sooner or later, through sheer pigheaded incapacity for international co-operation. Clearly the phrase *homo sapiens* is now the best joke in the world, and the bitterest.

November 17th, 1945

Egypt, Great Britain and the American People

D. W. BROGAN

These are times that try men's souls, tempers, judgment. Sir Anthony Eden has shown us—and the world—how foolish were those critics of democracy who have argued that a free government can never act secretly, suddenly, surprisingly. Stalin and Hitler have little on Sir Anthony although, in another mood, he recalls to an historian M. Émile Ollivier rather than more recent political gamblers.

We are in the dark, and much speculation is bound to be futile. But there are some results of the Eden policy (I refuse, so far, to accept it as British policy) which are already evident. And one of these is the deep, lasting, possibly irreparable damage it has done to the close political and ideological alliance with the United States which has been, one had been told, the basis of British policy since 1941. That close connection, the necessary adjustment to the fact that the United States was now so incomparably more powerful than Britain, provoked rancour on the Left, bile on the Right. But our government and our people had, one thought, too much sense to ignore the palpable fact that to American friendship we owed victory in 1918 and survival in 1940 and 1941. To American friendship, trust, belief in a common view of life; for it was the existence of this bias that made possible the intervention policies of Wilson and Roosevelt. Material, geopolitical interests would not alone have done it. It is a childish and bogus 'realism' to doubt this, and if there are still people in this country who think of American policy as merely hardboiled, selfish, based on a desire for markets or on ill-concealed imperialist ambitions, one can only say that there are fools in all ages and in all countries. This friendly bias grew up despite a very powerful historical tradition. The government of the United States dates all important official documents by 'the year of Our Lord and of the Independence of the United States'. The American national holiday celebrates the resistance to British rule, the American national anthem celebrates a British repulse. All Americans, save a few cranks, believe that rebellion against the Britain of George III and Lord North was the necessary condition of American greatness. When we consider how the population of the thirteen colonies has been reinforced by tens of millions of immigrants from countries with no or with hostile memories of Britain, it is surely notable that, in this century, against all the most sacred traditions of policy associated with Washington, Jefferson, Lincoln, the American people has been ready to aid, to fight with, to collaborate with Britain. It has done this continuously since 1940, with wisdom and generosity. It has done it because, basically, it has been led to believe that we and they stood for the same things, that 'righteousness exalteth a nation'.

It has believed, too, that we stood for the same idea of the necessary reorganization of the post-war world. It has felt guilt at its share in emasculating the League of Nations. It has put great, no doubt excessive, faith in the United Nations; and in a war fought, it believes, to preserve the principles of the Charter of the United Nations, it suffered in Korea great and deeply felt losses, went through strains of anxiety and emotional commitment, of which few in this country have any idea or have made any sympathetic attempt to understand.

There have been serious differences of opinion on important matters, over China (not so simple a black-and-white case as we are prone to think). Our immediate short term interests and policies have often differed. There have been clashes due to bad handling of problems of co-operation. There have been many American faults in tact and judgment. I am quite prepared, for instance, to admit that no free state has had a more tiresome spokesman than Mr. Dulles since the days of Sir John Simon. But the Americans believed that we stood for a new world order of which the Korean 'police action' was the price. What can they think now when we assume the role of North Korea and of Mao's China, take the law into our own hands and destroy the whole structure of the United Nations?

We do it, too, in a temper and for motives that recall only too clearly that England of Lord North that the Americans were told was dead. Few things have won us more trust and been politically more profitable than the grace and wisdom we have shown in the face of rising nationalism. India and Pakistan, both choosing to remain in the Commonwealth, have shown another side of our imperialism than that of the old American tradition and have been often contrasted with the disastrous results of the foolish intransigence of the French, with whom we are now partners in crime. That great gain the Eden government has thrown away.

I know as well as most people the vagueness, sentimentality, innocent egoism, ignorance, bad judgment of the average American on many questions, his indifference to problems that do not come home at once to him. There is nothing to choose between Bolton and Indianapolis on such points. The Americans like us are human.

But I know also (as no editor of a great newspaper on the grand tour can possibly get to know) the representative American men and women of the small towns, of the lesser cities, honest, anxious to do their duty by their country and the world, not jingoistic, not complacent, the members of the local Parent Teacher Associations, of the Rotary Clubs, of college faculties, the local editors doing their best to keep alive some interest in the outside world, the candid if innocent supporters of the United Nations, the overwhelmingly generous givers to all good causes who have taken the world for their parish. These people trusted us, refused to believe the propagandists incessantly at work, who told them that England had not changed. These people the Eden government has betrayed, disillusioned, wounded. They deserved better of us and of their candid and too simple faith.

There is another aspect of British (and French) policy that arouses American indignation and alarm and provokes in them the deepest moral disappointment. Again, it is impossible to discuss this point without recalling that the Americans do deeply and sincerely believe that there are 'good' and 'bad' policies, not merely prudent or imprudent, profitable or unprofitable policies. This may be a deplorable fact, like the absence of oil in commercial quantities in England, but it is just as much a fact and as important a fact. Since the end of the war, the Americans have had a 'concern' as the Quakers put it; the war into which they so reluctantly sidled had been represented to them as a war of liberation as well as of self-defence. Its result, complete military victory, was not followed, in their opinion, by liberation in a great part of Europe, but by a new form of enslavement. For few Americans believed in the 'People's Democracies'. There were several reasons for this. But one was that Americans knew too much. They knew too many Poles, too many Magyars, too many Czechs to be taken in by the political Potemkin villages which were good enough for too many of us. They did not believe, could not believe, that the pride, spiritual integrity, national tradition of the Polish and Hungarian peoples had been competently abolished. They thought the trials of priests and dissident Communists alike were frame-ups, crimes. They thought that under the apparatus of police control imposed by the Red Army, fire smouldered, that liberty meant what it had meant until we began to denature the word. They believed, foolishly, in the possibility of real liberation, they believed that the cause that they thought they had fought for was not dead, that, to quote a well-known Cambridge man, its friends were as they had always been, 'exultations, agonies and love and man's unconquerable mind'. They were obviously foolish; they are obviously right. For the peoples officially written off by our realists have stirred, risen, stripped the clothes from the odious Soviet reality, so completely, so suddenly, so heroically, that the *Daily Worker* itself is bewildered, almost silenced, the most foolish and most credulous adulators of the new order suddenly given a chance to show that the old English tradition of freedom is not dead even in the most doctrine-muddled minds. The whole world had its eyes on Warsaw, on Budapest, the monstrous regiment of tyranny was shaken, the nightmare of *1984* shown to be not our necessary doom. At that moment, and perhaps because of that moment, (we do not know, we know nothing), our government has chosen to put itself on the side of the Red Army if not yet of the N.K.V.D. We have relieved the Russian rulers (that is, our government has relieved them) of one of their nightmares, of being alone in a world that saw in them the enemies of the spirit of liberation. They are no longer alone. I know, we all know, that we are different, that we do not wish to impose on Egypt a Nagy, much less a Rakosi, but we flatter ourselves if we think that all the world, above all the African and Asiatic world that was beginning to wonder about its kindly Russian friends and would-be helpers, sees this comforting truth as clearly as we do. Certainly the Americans do not.

For millions of Americans whose kinsfolk have been enslaved in the guise of liberation, the past weeks had given new hopes, new solace; for tens of millions of Americans they gave a promise that the expectations of the last war had not been mere empty words, that 'these dead had not died in vain.' If the rulers of Russia, now emboldened, dare to crush this heroic drive for liberty, we can be sure that the Americans (and not only the Americans) will impute part of the blame to us. We shall be seen as a people that ingeniously and dishonestly identified its own material interests, (they will be seen as simple 'imperial' interests) with those of the great principles of the western tradition of freedom, a people that, at a turning point in human history, played for its own hand and by so doing that revealed how right were those who, in 1939-41, told the American people that they were being played for a sucker, not being asked to defend the 'laws of Nature and of Nature's God'. Those of us who devoted time, energy and good faith to denying those charges are silenced at last.

We shall remain silenced and, what is a thousand times more serious, our American defenders will remain silenced as long as the government of Sir Anthony Eden is deemed truly to represent us. It will be something if that government repents its *coup d'état* and brings forth fruit meet for repentance. But deep, long-lasting, irreparable damage has been done to the trust in us shown by a generous, emotional, in many ways unworldly people who think, now, that we have betrayed not only them, but 'the last, best hope of earth', the creation of an international order based on free and responsible states. That order did not yet exist, but its chances of coming to birth have not been helped by our midwifery. The American people did not forget George III and Lord North, but they were ready to believe them dead as Queen Anne, or nearly so. In that belief the American people gave great and increasing place to 'the close affection which grows from common names, from kindred blood, from similar privileges and equal protection. These are ties which, though light as air, are as strong as links of iron.' Strong as they were, Lord North and his colleagues, ignoring Burke, snapped them. So, to the best of his considerable abilities, has Sir Anthony Eden. There are no doubt as many on the Right as on the Left who resent the realities of the case, who dream

E

of a world in which we need pay little or no attention to the insuffer-
able parvenus across the Atlantic. That world does not exist. We shall
not be able to crawl into our little 'imperial' shell. We shall have to
live in the harsh, now unfriendly, world that will not now pardon us
our many weaknesses, material, moral and intellectual, as it did even
a week ago. We shall seem to stand for nothing but ourselves, our
oil supplies, our standard of living, our sulky *amour propre*. I repeat,
that is not a just picture of even Eden's England, but it is the picture
the world will paint, above all it is the picture the American people
will paint. Because they painted another picture in 1940 our steadfast-
ness then was not fruitless. To-day we shall have fewer friends than
we deserve, and we do not, at the moment, deserve many.

We should have to be much more confident than I am in our
strength, wisdom, unity to risk such isolation with complacency. We
shall have to pay a high price for our government's policy, and it will
be ruinously high if we hide from ourselves what we have done and
blame our closest and most important ally for the bills that not the
United States, but the political nature of things, will send in.

November 10th, 1956

2

History and Historians

Lord Acton: An Obituary

F. W. MAITLAND

It was from the first but a hopeless sort of hope that we had of Lord Acton's return to Cambridge. And now it has passed away. Early in the vacation there came to us the news of his death. Since then we have had time to think of our irreparable loss. The more we think of it, the heavier it seems.

Of it I should not dare to write a word, were it not that when the Cambridge Modern History was hardly yet an embryo, I (being then one of the Syndics of the Press) was allowed the privilege of seeing the great project take shape in the hands of one, who, as I thought then and think now, had at last found a long-sought opportunity of teaching the world some part of what he had learned in the course of a laborious life. Comparing what I then saw and heard with what has since been published in the newspapers, it seems to me that there is some little danger that an imperfect estimate of our misfortune may pass current even in Cambridge.

The learning we may take for granted. All who as yet have ventured to write of it have agreed that it was immense. Whether any other Englishman, whether any other human being, ever knew more of Universal History than Lord Acton knew—in truth it is some such question as this that we are prompted to ask, and the name of the man of whom we ought to ask it does not occur to us. If with a laudable wish to avoid extravagance we recall the giants of a past time, their wondrous memories, their encyclopædic knowledge, we must remember also how much that Lord Acton knew was for them practically unknowable. This is a truth that he was fond of teaching by examples. 'Where Hallam and Lingard were dependent on Barillon, their successors consult the diplomacy of ten governments.'

The immensity of the learning being unquestionable, some disposition to question the use that was—or was not—made of it was to be expected, and has in fact been observed. That 'daily consumption of a German octavo,' did it benefit him and the world, or was it only a stupendous feat of intellectual voracity? Reference to the catalogue of the University Library might give point to the question. One lecture, an inaugural lecture, delivered in 1895, one letter written in 1870, a German letter written to a German bishop—these, so the inquirer might say, appear to be all the published works of John Emerich Edward Dalberg, first Lord Acton. He might also notice that this letter seems to have taken a quarter of a century or thereabouts in reaching our shelves, and might not be there now, had not Dr. Hort acquired a copy. Some want of interest among the generality of Englishmen in a great historic event of their own time, some unwillingness to believe that a German letter to a German bishop could contain matters of importance, might thus be established incidentally; but the main question would not lose its edge. Was ever such disproportion between intake and output?

Now no one who heard him talk or read what he wrote or borrowed a book from the most generous of booklenders would for one moment think of him as reading idly, for amusement, for distraction, to pass the time. It was serious work the reading of history, calling not only for a chair, but for a table, pencil, pen and abundant slips of paper. The day's book was mastered. If it was of any value, certain facts had been ascertained from it, and they had been correlated with countless other facts. And the author had been judged: not vaguely consigned to a class, but judged in a reasoned judgment: often condemned. You had but to ask and you might hear the sentence, plain, decided, not what you had expected, for, though there was reticence, though there was irony, a plain question about book or man brought a plain answer and an unconventional. Once it happened that a solemn filler of many volumes, a German too and an historian, whom I supposed to be highly respected, was dismissed with 'mountainous jackass.' Some years ago an adversary in high place, who feared Lord Acton and his then associates, charged them with 'the ruthless talk of undergraduates.' In the accusation or the compliment there was, so it seems to me, some truth that we here can understand. He could speak straight out, from heart and head. Age, experience and erudition had not taught him to minish and mince. On the other hand, readers of anecdotes will do well to remember that he was by no means incapable of casting a pearl of irony in the way of those who would mistake it for pebbly fact.

No, if the reading had been idler, less purposeful, more might have been written and published. 'Everybody has felt ... that he knew too much to write.' These are words that he applied to Döllinger, his friend and master, and in some sort they were true of himself. But the obstacle did not consist merely in the enormous weight of the mass that was to be moved. Huge it was, but in his hands not unwieldy. There was also an acute, an almost overwhelming sense of the gravity, the sanctity of history. He was not the man wearily to preach upon this or any other text. A little irony, a little raillery would do more good than the set sermon. Yet read the reviews that he signed, read the reviews that he might have signed, and beneath the playful, witty, enigmatic phrases, you see the solemnity of the historian's task. Lord Acton's favourite metaphors came, not from the laboratory, but from the court of justice. It is judicial work to be done without fear or favour in the midst of the subtlest temptations. Not merely is it the historian's duty to see that individual rogues shall not escape, more especially the rogues of his own nation, his own party, his own creed, but there is the universe—nothing less—at the bar of the court, called upon to give an account of its behaviour before an inexorable judge. Even to the verge of paradox—and some would say a little further— he bore the standard of high morality. Once he spoke a light word of 'that rigid liberalism which, by repressing the time test and applying the main rules of morality all round, converts history into a frightful monument of sin.' But, with some theoretical concessions to a 'sliding scale' to be established hereafter by a science 'that is yet in its teens,' and with some (not very much) leniency in the Middle Age, his own precept and practice hardly fell short of this 'rigid liberalism.' 'It is,' he said, 'the office of historical science to maintain morality as the sole impartial criterion of men and things.' We have had other definitions of the historian's duty. This was Lord Acton's.

It may seem to some a plain untruth that he was more deeply interested in certain great problems of a philosophical kind than in any concrete presentment of particular facts. They may well have thought of him as the man who with wonderful exactitude knew and enjoyed all the bye-play in the great drama:—at home, no doubt, upon the front-stairs, but supreme upon the back-stairs, and (as he once said) getting his meals in the kitchen: acquainted with the use of cupboards and with the skeletons that lie therein; especially familiar with the laundry where the dirty linen is washed; an analyst of all the various soaps that have been employed for that purpose in all ages and all climes. Disclaiming all esoteric knowledge and reading only what all may read I cannot think of him thus. When he was observing, recording, appreciating the incidents, the bye-play, he was intent on a main plot difficult to apprehend: 'fatalism and retribution, race and nationality, the test of success and of duration, heredity and the reign of the invincible dead, the widening circle, the emancipation of the individual, the gradual triumph of the soul over the body, of mind over matter, reason over will, knowledge over ignorance, truth over error, right over might, liberty over authority, the law of progress and perfectibility, the constant intervention of providence, the sovereignty of the developed conscience.' Plenty of men are troubled about these matters; plenty of men make theories, 'alluring theories,' about them; but then they are not the men who know the back-stairs or get their meals in the kitchen; not the men who have toiled in the archives, hunting the little fact that makes the difference. For Lord Acton, so it seems to me, nothing was too small because nothing was too large. The whole lay in every part and particle: there and there only to be discovered, there and there only to be judged. A conception of history so abstract and so concrete, so unitary and so manifold, so bold and so minute, would have paralyzed a weaker man. It did not paralyze him. He worked while the light lasted. But to 'seek a little thing to do, find it and do it,' to give all his thought to a century, a nation, a fragment—'no, that's the world's way.'

Of this, however, I am very sure, that when all has been collected that can be collected, and all has been told that ought to be told, it will be clear to the world that the acquisition of knowledge was for Lord Acton not end but mean. The late, the very late, arrival upon our shelves of that open letter to a German bishop—an 'open letter' in more senses than one—should remind us that few indeed are the men in Cambridge or in England who have even a rudimentary acquaintance with what was no episode but perhaps the chief theme of his earnest life. Some day the story may be told. His friends have no cause to fear the truth. If there was failure, surely it was heroic failure; and the end is not yet. Really one must live in Little Pedlington and never transgress the parish boundary if one is to inform the British public that Lord Acton and his 'hoarded knowledge' counted for nothing in the Europe and Christendom of the nineteenth century.* That was not the judgment of those who had crossed swords with him in a world-wide arena and had felt the strength of his wrist. Deeply con-

* See a letter in the *Daily News*, of July 8, 1902.

vinced that the history of religion lies near the heart of all history, he was isolated from the bulk of his fellow-countrymen by religious and from the residue, or the bulk of the residue, by historical convictions, and, this being so, he was not likely to find or to seek an audience in the market-place. Nor was it given to him to beat the big drum outside the patriotic show and call that historiography. Moreover he had home-truths to tell, and they could best be sent home by a few words written for the few. But it is safe to say that there are, for example, some forty pages in the *English Historical Review* for 1890 which will still be shining when most of our justly applauded histories have sunk beneath the horizon.

Opportunities were taken when they were offered. Friends were lavishly helped. This man who has been called 'a miser' was in truth a very spend-thrift of his heard-earned treasure and ready to give away in half an hour the substance of an unwritten book. A journal was edited; it was dreaded and denounced. A great deal of reviewing was done, and reviewing of so admirable a kind that the review has become, for all wise readers of the book, an indispensable appendix. And at last came the great opportunity: at last and too late. We saw with wonder how eagerly it was seized, and how a project that might have been pedestrian took horse, took wings and soared. All modern history—the scheme was large enough. Twelve stout volumes—there would be room for minutely truthful work. Stored knowledge, big thoughts, an acknowledged primacy, polyglot correspondence, ramifying friendships, the tact of a diplomatist, the ardour of a scholar, all were to be subservient in a noble cause, to the greater glory of truth and right: to the greater glory, be it added, of a Cambridge that he had learned to love. It was Napoleonic. I know no other word, and yet it is not adequate. I felt as if I had been permitted to look over the shoulder of a general who was planning a campaign that was to last for five centuries and extend throughout the civilised world. No doubt there was some overestimate of health and endurance and mere physical force, some forgetfulness of the weight of accumulating years. We feared it then; we know it now. But of such mistakes, if mistakes they be, the brave will be guilty. And about mental power there was no mistake. With whatever doubts I had gone to his rooms, I came away saying to myself that if contributors failed, if the worst came to the worst, or perhaps the best to the best, Lord Acton could write the twelve volumes from beginning to end, and (as the phrase goes) never turn a hair. But it was too late: too late by ten or fifteen years.

The execution of his project in his large spirit is the memorial that he would have desired. Our best have undertaken the task. At this moment it would not be right to say more than that we are deeply grateful to them.

Another memorial might be thought of. Those who sat or stood in the crowded Divinity School can never forget the majestic act of pardon and oblivion which was the preface of the inaugural lecture. 'At three colleges I applied for admission, and, as things then were, I was refused by all. Here, from the first, I vainly fixed my hopes, and here, in a happier hour, after five and forty years, they are at last fulfilled.' As it is written, *Lapidem quem reprobaverunt aedificantes, hic factus est caput in angulo*. Those who most revere these words will be the last to say that they teach no practical lesson. Well, intolerance is a foolish thing, and an apology based upon unintended consequences is an apology of just the sort that aroused Lord Acton's indignation. Still to some of his hearers must have occurred the thought:—'Were you not the gainer by our churlishness? Had Cambridge then received you, no doubt you would have been a very learned man and by this time Regius Professor. But would you have been quite such a master of contemporary history, quite such an impartial judge of modern England, so European, so supernational, so catholic, so liberal, so wise, so Olympian, so serene?' And even now, so I cannot but think, the pride and sorrow with which Cambridge writes Acton's name on the roll of her illustrious dead is not unalloyed by an uncomfortable suspicion that just those qualities that were most distinctive of his work and most admirable, are but exotic flowers in our Cambridge garland. An effective resolve that never hereafter shall there be cause for such an abatement of our pride is the debt that we owe to his memory. Meanwhile a little remorse will do us no harm. The pardon was freely granted. We have yet to earn it.

October 16th, 1902

Acton on the French Revolution*

J. H. CLAPHAM

Fourteen years ago I came out from Acton's lecture on the Flight to Varennes with a friend who said—'That is the most dramatic thing I ever heard.' At his request I went as ambassador to Trinity. Was there any chance that the lecture would be printed so that we could read and keep it? 'You can tell him,' said Acton, 'that an American journal has been worrying me to give them something, and if I give them anything it is more likely to be that lecture than another?' Every one of the series now open to us shares the magnificent dramatic quality of that lecture which we longed to possess and the Americans never secured; and I know of no book on the Revolution that is at once so learned, so moving, and so just.

The judgment is terrible as the theme demands. Executed with impartial restraint on statesman and historian, it is most often implied, not formally recorded. 'I shall endeavour,' he said, 'to spare you the spectacles that degrade, and the plaintive severity that agitates and wearies.' This was after one solemn denunciation of political crime and of historians, apologists of crime. 'The strong man with the dagger is followed by the weaker man with the sponge. First the criminal who slays; then the sophist who defends the slayer.' Now and again the clowns are set down, as in the last words of the lecture on Robespierre —'the most hateful character in the forefront of history since Machiavelli reduced to a code the wickedness of public men.'

Sentences in the earlier lectures are packed close with the political learning that was Acton's own. Such is the sentence which traces backward the masters of Rousseau. But learning is relieved with aphorism and humour, even—and conspicuously—in the fragmentary lecture on the Literature of the Revolution, originally delivered as an introduction and printed by the editors in an appendix—a shattered masterpiece of criticism and method. Very characteristic is the discussion of American influence, with its central aphorism. The Americans 'resolved to give up everything, not to escape from actual oppression, but to honour a precept of unwritten law. That was the transatlantic

* *Lectures on the French Revolution.* By Lord Acton. Edited by J. N. Figgis and R. V. Laurence.

discovery in the theory of political duty, the light that came over the ocean.' As the action of the Revolution itself unfolds learning is subordinated to movement, and critical discussion is so used as to help, not to obstruct the flow of narrative. We see the picture of the past based on infinite study in the hands of a man who trusts both his own judgment and his own reconstructive imagination, become no gray uncertain thing. Scattered throughout the narrative lie the scraps of decisive knowledge directly acquired that lit up all Acton's treatment of the most modern history. He did not state his authority for the story that made him reject, almost with contempt, efforts to rid Danton of the responsibility for the September massacres—the story that Danton claimed the responsibility in conversation with Louis Philippe. In fact he had it—like Tarvic before him—from Louis Philippe's son, across a dinner table. From the same source comes the account, admirably employed to close the lecture on Valmy, of Dumouriez 'gesticulating on the pavement at Hammersmith' when he heard the news of Waterloo.

It would be easy to arrange a whole gallery of decisions and phrases that should become a permanent heritage—Fénelon, 'the platonic founder of revolutionary thinking'; 'the appalling thing in the French Revolution is not the tumult but the designs. Through all the fire and smoke we perceive the evidence of calculating organisation': the Declaration of the Rights of man, 'this single page of print, which outweighs libraries, and is stronger than all the armies of Napoleon,' yet 'is not the work of superior minds, and bears no mark of the lion's claw': 'a King at low pressure, such as had been invented by the Whigs': the Republican calendar which signified 'the supremacy of reason over history, of the astronomer over the priest.' Perhaps a few isolated decisions of fact might be disputed even by those who are in full sympathy with Acton's position. More will no doubt be criticised adversely by adherents of that politically dogmatic treatment of revolutionary history which is not yet extinct—which in France, at least, can hardly die. But the book will stand as a last monument of Acton's greatness, both as scholar and teacher. The Cambridge historical school may feel proud that these lectures were produced in it and for its sake, and will be very grateful to the editors for their now finished work.

December 1st, 1910

Maitland and his Work*

G. R. ELTON

To be presented, sixty years after his death, with another 500 pages of Maitland's writing is an event indeed. Though these letters do not amount to another *Domesday Book and Beyond* or *Canon Law in the Church of England*, they are immensely well worth reading. Thanks to Maitland's enforced annual flight, they contain a good deal about the parochial events of Cambridge, though here it would have been more useful to have the letters Maitland received, especially from Henry Jackson who kept him abreast on the questions of the hour (no more, but also no less, significant than those that convulse us today). As Maitland grew older and became known, and as his correspondents started keeping his letters, a fair sample of the historians of the day make their appearance in these pages; and it is particularly pleasant to note the contacts with America. Though he never visited that country, and though visits to Europe seem to have been less commonplace for American professors than they are today, the professionals at Harvard and Yale seem to have been quicker than his colleagues at home to recognise his real greatness, as indeed they today preserve his memory and influence a good deal more purely. The letters throw much light, among other things, on the history of the Selden Society; especially they reveal the sad tale of its first secretary who shot himself after apparently embezzling its funds in the service of his amours. The Society was saved by Maitland, with the ponderous assistance of some of Her Majesty's judges.

And, of course, there is F. W. M. himself. The letters enlarge the familiar picture without adding anything substantial to it, but they bring out his swift mind, insight, generosity and sweetness. His humour —good humour and sharp humour—comes through, though less plentifully than one had hoped. Maitland was not one of the world's great letter writers; he was, one suspects, too busy with less ephemeral things. Now and again there are disconcerting minor prejudices and reminders that a man whose work had rendered him in effect timeless to the reader was yet naturally, very much of his own age. The facts of that age unhappily include the absence of the private typewriter:

* *The Letters of Frederic William Maitland.* Edited by C. H. S. Fifoot.

there is no Maitland archive with copies of out-letters, and the 501 letters here recovered (and very competently edited) must represent a poorish rate of survival.

Of course, the book tells much of Maitland's life—working, walking, suffering—and of his mind. It may seem odd that this man, whose twenty years of active life produced the largest output of great works ever achieved by any historian writing in English, should constantly lament his idleness or doubt his powers. But this is as it would be. To the true scholar it is never the achievement behind him but always the unresolved challenge ahead of him that matters. At the same time, these letters underscore one reason why Maitland, despite illness and the absence of Xerox machines, completed so much. There are references to lectures (treated, it has to be admitted, as rather a nuisance) but none to students, undergraduate or graduate. This is not to blame Maitland. He returned to Cambridge as a reader and was soon a professor; he was never in the way of serious undergraduate teaching. Worse, the whole structure of English academic life, especially at the old universities, at the time operated against the systematic organization of research and advanced teaching. And legal history, to top it all, has always been the preserve of the few—the bane of supposedly 'wider' historians, and merely the amusement of lawyers who too often practise it pretty badly. And so Maitland had no pupils: nothing like Tout's school or even Pollard's could grow up in the Cambridge of the 'nineties.

This fact has been tragic for English historical studies, for (as the letters to friends and colleagues demonstrate, and as Buckland's memoir in the *Cambridge Law Journal* shows even more clearly) Maitland would have been the ideal master of a band of disciples. Deprived of this, the Cambridge history school has since his day drifted away from his main inspiration, preferring the history of diplomacy, economics and especially ideas. All these admirable disciplines engaged Maitland's interest, but he brought to them a firm foundation in record study and a ranging concern with the people of the past which have been less conspicuous in men whose influence has been much greater. Maitland was not, of course, without influence: his books saw to that. But that influence was never institutionalised, and so perpetuated, in a tradition of teaching and research, nor did it ever amount to the transmission of attitudes and methods. To some extent at least Maitland is unique because he never trained anybody.

So he remains admired and little followed. What he would have said about the smiles which nowadays greet any suggestion that historical studies, even among undergraduates, must be rigorous to benefit the mind, or about Tripos proposals which promise to eliminate his beloved middle ages, despise his recognition of the law as the best guide to past societies, and would replace analysis by evocation, may be imagined. He knew that the historian's graces, which he possessed so fully—absence of pedantry, a sense of life, subtlety and an imaginative understanding—can come only out of hard work, hard thought and narrowed search. There is no other way to those stars. But Maitland is dead, and we who are left are too few and perhaps too incompetent to resist the tide of philistinism as it advances under the tinsel banners of social service and consumers' demands. History at Cambridge is about to take the wrong fork in the road, has perhaps already taken it. Maitland beckons down the other turning, one which no doubt looks less easy and attractive but actually leads somewhere.

May 22nd, 1965

Mr Belloc on Medieval History*

G. G. COULTON

This breezy book will bring back to readers of George Eliot a pleasant whiff from the parlour of the Red Lion at Milby, where Lawyer Dempster held forth with such inexhaustible lungs to an audience convinced that ecclesiastical history is a matter of ingenious guesswork. The capital letters and the stentorian dogmatism of his first few pages are rather overwhelming: but we soon find ourselves on familiar ground. We discover that we can know nothing about the Middle Ages until we have first learned how little the Cabinet knew about the Great War, in comparison with Mr Belloc. 'Small wonder,' he concludes, 'that the Cabinet at Westminster hesitated!' Small indeed; the real wonder would have been if Mr Belloc had hesitated; yet even this marvel of marvels confronts us on p. 27. By this time his main thesis is developed; good and Catholic peoples are of the Ancient Roman stock; bad and non-Catholic peoples are not. But unluckily

---

* *Europe and the Faith.* By Hilaire Belloc.

England (here classed among the Romans) is bad, while Ireland, the non-Roman, has remained good. It speaks volumes for Mr Belloc's essential honesty that he has not attempted to juggle with these difficulties. He might so easily have put England on the non-Roman side, and thus have won the obsequious assent of Academic Pedants, Protestants, Men in the Street, and other hydra-heads of modern corruption. A little manipulation, again, might have made Ireland essentially Roman; and then his thesis would have gone happily on all fours. But Mr Belloc has the courage of his prejudices; he would rather put his money frankly on the wrong horse than back even a winner from the Augean Stables of Protestantism. The Roman ancestry of England is maintained, therefore; but she became bad by 'accident': Ireland, again, has remained good by 'an accident inexplicable or miraculous.' The still more remarkable exception of Poland—one of the few really Catholic populations of to-day, and yet less Roman than Ireland—seems to transcend even this explanation. We can trace, in fact, a most interesting crescendo. Most historical problems, impenetrable to others, yield to Mr Belloc's private key. Ireland is inexplicable even to Mr Belloc; here we must bring in the master-key of miracle. With Poland comes the super-miracle; Mr Belloc is positively reduced to silence.

Yet all his wild words about Roman and non-Roman amount to little more than an excuse for indulging in a temperamental dislike of everything non-Catholic. Under cover of this Roman theory, he can hug himself and flatter his friends with such a sense of superiority as the ancient Jew felt towards the Gentile; and he can allure the proletariat by promising them economic salvation if the Pope came in again. He does not realise, even remotely, the complexity of the problem before him. Where a little patient thought is needed, 'I will not waste the reader's time in any discussion' (p. 280). The most delicate questions, and the most important to modern civilization, are settled by bidding us note two (or three, or five) points which unless we hold fast we shall without doubt perish everlastingly. On p. 300 we are thus bidden to 'pay special attention' to 'three things,' of which the first and third are false, while the second (admittedly of minor importance) is only doubtful. Upon these three things he builds a whole fabric of figments about the Reformation. His two brief allusions to later monachism (pp. 271, 306) not only ignore the tale told by the most important contemporary records, but imply ignorance of their very existence.

The Eastern Schism itself is 'an accident, largely geographical' (p. 290). It would be difficult to find any dozen pages without some blunder of this sort, commended to us with arguments worthy of my Lord Peter. 'The Catholic alone is in the tradition of Europe; he alone can see and judge in this matter'; 'a Catholic … is not relatively right in his blame; he is absolutely right' (pp. 5, 14). Why, after all, should Mr Belloc trouble his head with actual medieval records, when he knows that all appeal to history against the voice of his church is a treason and a heresy? For him, the Middle Ages exist only as he chooses to imagine them; only as his hatred of modern thought demands that they should be; he is a typical illustration of Bossuet's warning: 'Le pire dérèglement de l'esprit, c'est de croire les choses parce qu'on veut qu'elles soient; et non parce qu'on a vu qu'elles sont en effet.' When he undertakes to paint the Middle Ages in detail, his figures resemble the originals as a plaster statue of St Augustine in an image shop resembles the author of the *Confessions*.

This apotheosis of the past, however false to history, may be palliated on the plea of charity, or at least of natural party-patriotism. But the latter excuse has little place, and the former has none at all, in the stale falsehoods which Mr Belloc repeats about Protestantism. 'Today, outside the Catholic Church, there is no distinction between opinion and faith, nor any idea that man is other than sufficient to himself' (p. 68). It is strange that one who must have known many Catholics and non-Catholics familiarly should not hesitate, on the very threshold, before venturing to restrict self-sufficiency to those outside his own communion. *Ignorantia plures habet superbos quam humiles*; these are the words of a great medieval Abbot, quoted by one of the greatest of Catholic historians in self-defence against those who would have blustered him down with their superior orthodoxy.* Moreover, to go deeper into Mr Belloc's accusation, it ignores the crucial fact that the Protestant acknowledges a responsibility to God for his opinions at least as complete as that which the Catholic acknowledges to his Church. Every sincere Theist, whether within or without the fold, feels himself responsible to God for every thought of his heart; and Catholics who choose to ignore this are as ignorant or as reckless as the Protestants who choose to see nothing in the Roman system of Indulgences but a traffic in sin-licences. Scarcely less perverse is Mr Belloc's sneer at the Bible as 'the Hebrew Scriptures' (311; cf. 323). In his

---

* Mabillon, *Traité des Etudes Monactiques*, pt. 1, ch. 13.

F

calmer moments, he must realize that the New Testament is more truly Greek than Hebrew—indeed, he shows a faint consciousness of this on p. 46. Bible ignorance is, of course, endemic in his communion. Of all his Catholic readers, how many will be able to quote the three familiar Pauline passages which give the lie to his contention that the Romans under the Empire 'would never have regarded the legal distinctions between slaves and free as a line of cleavage between different kinds of men'? (p. 58). The story of the official revision of the Roman Vulgate text, from the 9th century until this actual moment, would be one of the comedies of history if it were not at bottom so tragic. In the palmy days of Sir Thomas More's father, before the axe had been laid to the root of the medieval Church, there were pious English gentlefolk who would have been shocked and incredulous to hear that the Virgin Mary was of Jewish birth. Mr Belloc's affectation of contempt probably covers a lurking and uneasy sub-consciousness of these things; he talks loudly because he is braving the matter out before his own friends.

That, indeed, is what explains much that is otherwise inexplicable; this book springs from a religious sect, and is written mainly for sectarian readers. It is one of the many Roman Catholic books of our day which enable us to realise poor Cardinal Newman's despair at the impossibility of getting his co-religionists to write true history. Mr Belloc, too, despairs of all help from his fellows; 'the Catholic reader of history... has no Catholic history to read' (p. 27). Nor can he have, in the nature of the case, until his Church formally abjures those retrograde principles of censorship and persecution which are still an integral part of Canon Law. Mr Belloc, of course, may write practically what he pleases; he is an unofficial layman, earning his living mainly in other fields than history; and this irresponsibility enables him to say things freely which would have made faggot-fodder of him in the 13th century. But there are small chances for real history when a man's freedom to speak is strictly proportionate to his irresponsibility.

October 22nd, 1920

The Dawn of Modern Politics

G. KITSON CLARK

It cannot be said that this book* is well described by the title
which its author chose for it. It deals with the development of political
parties and political creeds in a period stretching roughly from 1765
to 1850. It treats with the emergence of political parties in something
like their modern form, with the partial reconciliation of English
statesmen to the principles of democracy, and with the growth of a
doubt as to whether the state's functions were adequately fulfilled by
conceding bare freedom to all. This period is too long and these issues
too varied and too vital to be usefully attached to the two statesmen
on the title page. It is to be hoped therefore that many will penetrate
beyond the threshold and discover how useful and comprehensive a
book it is.

Of course the subject is by no means new, a thousand busy pens,
bulging note books, and restless printing presses seem to testify every
day to the interest rightly taken in it. But that need not detract from
the value of Professor Davis' work. For the subject is not only important; it is dangerous. Unless bad history is to be written about it,
it requires qualities not always, alas, to be found in Historians. For one
thing, when men are dealing with political opinions and their application to politics they are apt to find that the opinions are much more
easy to discover than the applications. In consequence they can very
easily slip into the habit of spending most of their time resurrecting
obscure Radicals or criticising the resolutions of rightly evanescent
political clubs while they leave the doings of Kings and Cabinets,
Courts and Parliaments crammed uncomfortably into a very small
corner of the picture. And obviously when an exciting period is in
question, whose issues are very often substantially the same as those of
modern politics, whose parties are connected by direct lineal descent
with political parties which still exist, there must be a danger of bias.
There must be a danger that the story of politics at the end of the 18th
century and during the first half of the 19th will be used not as a

* *The Age of Grey and Peel*, being the Ford Lectures for 1926. By the late H. W. Careless
Davis, Regius Professor of Modern History in the University of Oxford, with an Introduction by Professor G. M. Trevelyan, C.B.E.

reservoir of facts but as a magazine of projectiles, and that it will be described, not by sober Historians, but by a hungry crowd of Whigs, Social Reformers, Liberals and Labour men, and not least of all young Tories, screaming defiance at one another, and all anxious to provide themselves with political principles for the use of their friends and pathetic instances to be launched against their enemies.

It is therefore of peculiar importance that the period should be reviewed from time to time by some man with cool judgment and a sense of proportion—qualities which Professor Davis possessed to a very remarkable degree. Through the whole book his independence and impartiality stand out—particularly perhaps in his treatment of the popular societies at the end of the eighteenth century and of what has been called 'Pitt's reign of terror'; or again in his criticisms of the Whigs during the last stages of the war against Napoleon. Moreover his sense of proportion is also very evident in the book. He tells how the Whigs were translated from the groups which surrounded the Dukes of Newcastle and Bedford or the men who followed Rockingham and still shrank from Parliamentary Reform, to Lord John Russell and his colleagues who had passed the Reform Bill and were almost preparing to accept the doctrine that the State had other duties beyond those of defending the liberty of the individual and the rights of property. And he tells this story with discretion, economy and completeness. He shows the same qualities when he describes those various streams of revolutionary or Reforming opinion most of which flowed at length into the great river of nineteenth century optimism, philanthropy, and democracy. Especially well is justice done to a set of men who have sometimes received a good deal less than justice, that is the able Dissenters who wrote on politics at the end of the eighteenth century—such as of course Priestley, or that Dr Price upon whose back Burke ploughed such long furrows.

Even the Tories have a chapter devoted to their ideals, at a time at which some might declare that it would be difficult to fill half a page on the subject. But is that really enough? It is one Chapter among XIII. Of course some Tory statesmen are dealt with elsewhere, Peel even enjoys a chapter to himself; and no doubt the Whigs and Radicals had the handling of the most important ideas of the time. But the Tory Party governed the country for so long and contained within itself so much of the political life of the time, that it does seem that a truer picture would have been drawn by devoting a little more space to them. For instance both as pioneer critics in one way, and as partial opponents in another, of laissez faire, some Tories played a part not easily gathered from this book. For one thing it seems possible that if factory reform were mentioned at all there ought—say, to be more than a passing reference to Michael Sadler as the predecessor of Ashley. About Huskisson the only thing to be gathered is that though a Canningite he was an obstinate Tory. Professor Davis intended to show how certain principles effected politics. He took count of the Tories, indeed he included one of their leaders on the title-page. Yet his book might easily give the impression that their contribution to the application of important ideas to practical politics was a great deal less than in fact it was.

The truth is that it is not easy to be just to the Tories. Their principles seem often sterile, their arguments weak, their prejudices intolerable; while the tone of Eldon's whinings would get on any man's nerves. Professor Davis is often remarkably fair when talking of their fears— but even he does not seem to realize how constantly after the French Revolution they all felt that there was a fiend at their heels. Nor is the path well beaten by other researchers for the minor figures among the Tories before the Young England movement have received but little attention. But the Tories were important, and, stranger still, some of them had something to say. One special difficulty stood in Professor Davis' way to being just to them. When he criticises their major figures such as Peel and Liverpool he is often criticising the actions of politicians struggling with the immediate exigences of very difficult politics. It is not easy to do that fairly without giving a complete picture of the political situation of the moment. For instance such a picture is necessary in order to test Professor Davis' criticism of Liverpool for not retaining the property tax after the wars, or of Peel for staying in office to pass Catholic Emancipation. Of course Professor Davis had not room to do what justice required; but if he was to treat of these things at all they should have had fuller and fairer treatment. Probably the best solution of the difficulty would have been for him to have reserved this volume for the Whigs and to have devoted a future volume to the Tories—in which he could have put among other things the admirable remarks which he here makes on the importance they gave to the Church and his comments upon Coleridge and Southey.

But alas! that volume would never have been written, and it is impossible to speak of this book without speaking of the loss which

Historical studies have suffered. There were those who regretted that Professor Davis should leave the middle ages and come into the over-crowded paths of the nineteenth century. And there is much to be said against the present concentration of interest on that perplexing period. But the sense of justice, the powers of criticism, and, above all, the powers of selection which Professor Davis possessed were just the qualities which are valuable above price in a period likely to be swamped by research. Undoubtedly his untimely death deprived us of work much more valuable than published lectures can ever be. Neces-sarily limited in space, necessarily broken in plan, lectures can only pretend to be the beginning of wisdom. Admirable and useful as this book is, it cannot be said that it is equal to the large and lasting books which Professor Davis would certainly have given us—if fate had been more kind.

November 1st, 1929

The Legacy of Napoleon

G. M. TREVELYAN

Mr. Butterfield presents us with Napoleon* in the series called *Great Lives*, to wit, small biographies. There are only 143 pages of about 240 words each. Mr. Herbert Fisher's *Napoleon*, in the *Home University* series, was so good that another book of the same size on the same subject, if it is to count, must not only be good in itself, but must have something new to add to the pre-war view of Napoleon's career as it appeared to Mr. Fisher in 1913. I think that these conditions are fulfilled and that any one of us would gain fresh light by reading this new book. It can be done in an hour in these busy times, and leave us with matter for hours of subsequent sad rumination. Sad, I fear it is likely to be. I once came across the following item of intelligence, while turning over the files of an English newspaper of 1793:—

Lieutenant Buonaparte has been killed in one of the recent encounters before Toulon.

* *Napoleon*. By Herbert Butterfield.

My regret that the news proved inaccurate has been increased by reading Mr. Butterfield's book.

The book contains a number of good points, new or newly put; for example, the gradualness and opportunism of his conception of his Empire; the origins and nature of his military methods; the strain of somewhat melancholy fatalism that constitutes his belief in his 'star.'

It was Napoleon's view that Destiny laid a hand on him and drew him to Russia. He afterwards seemed to think, perhaps not entirely without justice, that in going to Moscow, even to meet tragedy, he had somehow increased his grandeur ... At any rate as we watch him move to Moscow we may feel not that he was gloriously defying Providence, but that he was cheerlessly following his fate, not knowing whether it led to triumph or overthrow. (pp. 117–118)

That the Corsican cared more about his own greatness in history, and even about the fortunes of his family, than about France, was the tragedy of France and of Europe. Supreme efficiency was linked to supreme selfishness.

'Hugest of engines, a much limited man,'

as Meredith wrote of him.

But the chief interest of this little book is the light it throws on the origins of the present disastrous condition of Europe. Possibly, indeed, the industrial revolution, machinery and improved locomotion would in any case have produced the totalitarian state and totalitarian war. But, politically speaking, it was the French Revolutionists and Napoleon who started these delights. Such at least is Mr. Butterfield's thesis. For some years past I have always said that the best parallel for the ideas and methods of party rule as perfected by Bolshevists, Fascists and Nazis is to be found in the short-lived French Jacobinism of 1793–4. Mr. Butterfield goes further and sees a definite causal connection. It is best to let him speak for himself.

'The principles of 1789,' he writes, 'spring from a philosophy so liberal, an enthusiasm so sympathetically human—and the rights of man were so trumpeted in the early days of the French Revolution—that Mazzini was able to look upon this period of history as a fulfilment of Christianity, the triumph of individualism. It is strange, therefore—it is a comment on the waywardness of our historical development—that the Revolution itself should have quickly produced an engine more dreadful than any of the absolute monarchs had had at their command for the repression of the individual, inaugurating a type of policy more formidable as an organ of power than ancient feudalisms and ill-jointed dynastic systems could ever have hoped to achieve. Beginning with views much too doctrinaire in their liberalism—beginning with supreme faith in an elected legislature, and showing at the same time an undue distrust of the executive, because the executive power was still lodged with the King—the French Revolution led quickly to a rule by committees, to a government that was almost entirely executive in its concentration of power ... It produced a state more calculated for efficiency, more highly organised, more wide in its competence, more terrifying in its power than any which then existed; and it made government more irresistible from the fact that henceforward government was to claim to be the incontrovertible agent of the new god, the organic people. It is in this sense most of all that Napoleon is the heir—if he is not the logical conclusion—of the French Revolution.' (pp. 13-15)

'Besides creating the modern state, the French Revolution became the mother of modern war. The age of deified peoples supervenes; the conditions exist for the intensification of modern nationalism ... It heralds the age when peoples, woefully ignorant of one another, bitterly uncomprehending, lie in uneasy juxtaposition watching one another's sins with hysteria and indignation. It heralds Armageddon, the giant conflict for justice and right between angered populations, each of which thinks it is the righteous one. So a new kind of warfare is born—the modern counterpart of the old conflicts of religion.' (p. 16)

I well remember a day, more than forty years ago now, when Lord Acton said to me that States based on racial unity would prove more dangerous to liberty than racial conglomerates like the Austro-Hungarian Empire. Thus, while he was all for Italian and German liberty, he was no enthusiast for Italian or German unity. Perhaps this view was academic and impractical, but, as subsequent events have shown, it was certainly not untrue. When his mature wisdom thus admonished my green youth, I thought him strangely wrong: I don't now. But no rule is absolute. France is based on race, but she has got rid of the worst parts of the Jacobinism and Napoleonism which she bred, and she counts as a free country.

But let us get back to Mr. Butterfield. Here are the reasons why he thinks Napoleon was a disaster:—

'It was as though Europe had been lying there, a sluggish and amorphous mass, waiting for the French Revolution to bring fire and an organising principle. For well over a century that continent has bitterly suffered, and is groaning still, because too much happened in the period between 1789 and 1815—the processes of change too wilfully congested there, and fateful movements too drastically telescoped; with cataracts, stampedings and violent uprootings to fret and flurry the path of progress. Europe has to be plagued with monsters that the eighteenth century never contemplated, because at the crucial moment one man was brilliant enough to exhaust the possibilities of exploitation that were implicit in the system of things. Where Napoleon carried his dominion he produced or he precipitated what we might call a geological subsidence; ... Liberalism and nationalism may be wise and enriching if they have blossomed naturally without the generation of great pressure; but we have learned now not to be happy, as our forefathers were, when sometimes these things have appeared too hurriedly and too soon. If Napoleon may claim to have carried something of the results of the French Revolution throughout Europe, if it may be said that his tyranny provoked amongst the nations movements more portentous still, we may hesitate before we count it to him as virtue that he tore his way into the ancient fabric of the European states, and so mangled the processes of historical change.' (p. 96)

'Mangled the processes of historical change' is a forcible expression and gives rise to thought. Some people might say that most 'processes of historical change' are mangled, one way or another, by the folly and violence of men; and that it is often difficult to distinguish between the 'historical process' itself and the accidental 'mangling.' For example, was the English Civil War a 'mangling' of the 'process of historical change' in our constitution, or was it the most essential part of the process itself? I am sure I don't know. But certainly our post-Cromwellian constitution had better luck than post-Napoleonic Europe.

January 19th, 1945

Europe 1848–1918:
The Balance of Power

DENNIS MACK SMITH

The unification of Germany and Italy meant 'two great causes of disturbance got out of the way': so thought John Bright at the time; but then he hardly understood the workings of the balance of power. Europe was continually threatened with instability between 1848 and 1918, and this makes the subject of Mr A. J. P. Taylor's latest book.* It is a detailed study which could have been written only by someone who combined great learning with tremendous confidence in his own judgment. There must be few people who could not learn a great deal from it. The narrative is tightly packed, full of wise remarks, common sense and subtle interpretations. The author has a good eye for ferreting out the curious, the paradoxical and the ignoble. Even though the demands of accuracy may inhibit his more brilliant and exciting sallies, he manages to be as provocative as his material will allow. The result on a cost-page basis is extremely good value for 30s., though hardly recommended for consecutive reading.

It is refreshing these days to find a historian who shows so little hesitation in leaping to his conclusions. Mr Taylor knows that 'if he waited until he possessed all the evidence, he would never write at all —a doctrine [?] favoured by some scholars.' This is forthright history, direct and pungent in its views, at its most characteristic when stated didactically. There can be 'no doubt' about 'the precise responsibility' for war in 1914; and so forth. Sometimes, one must admit, the most dogmatic statements seem to conceal the author's weaker points. Sometimes, too, his argument would have seemed more convincing if he had allowed us to share the inner doubts through which he must once have gone himself. But if little doubt is allowed to show, neither

* *The Struggle for Mastery in Europe.* By A. J. P. Taylor.

at the other extreme is there any overriding thesis to which facts are systematically adjusted. There is no special pleading here for any plot, rhythm or predetermined pattern. Nor is there even any very obvious scale of values running through the work. Occasionally the author is shocked by political deceit, but elsewhere if he criticises the Machiavellians it is for not being Machiavellian enough. This relativism of judgment is perhaps in keeping with his subject matter. So is what might otherwise have seemed an undue preoccupation with the crimes and follies of mankind. Mr Taylor does not find many people to admire. It might even be said that he maintains an impatient attitude towards his characters, and shows for them an absence of enthusiasm which is bound also to infect his readers.

It is to be hoped that other volumes in the Oxford History of Europe will cover aspects of this period which Mr Taylor has had to exclude. His book is not a history of the various states of Europe, but only of the relations between their governments. Even so, Spain, Switzerland, Holland, Belgium and Scandinavia appear very little. International movements, whether socialist, catholic or humanitarian, have to be almost entirely ignored. The Great Powers are assumed to be organisations for war, not for welfare. But the theme is not even war itself, only rumours of wars. It is a story of negotiations and treaties, only on rare occasions interrupted by battles (which usually 'confirm the way that things are going already'). Little time is wasted on the balance of power inside countries, or on changes in the stability and internal cohesion of states, and sometimes the power-complex behind diplomacy is thus left conjectural. The book cannot afford much space for railways and coal, nor for finance and public opinion as determining factors in politics. The concentration on power also excludes consideration of culture in any form, and of religion. No single Pope is mentioned by name, and the fall of the Temporal Power in 1870 is passed over without mention or comment. By this self-denying ordinance Mr Taylor manages to obtain a high concentration upon the diplomacy of the five Great Powers. Even human personality has had to be very largely cut out in the process. Each new statesman comes on to the stage unheralded, unarticulated, one more wooden puppet to play his stilted role in the human comedy.

Diplomatic history, thus limited in scope, provides a brilliant intellectual exercise, a fine training in mental agility. It is an unpopular vein these days, largely because it is such an exacting test of historical scholarship and needs such hard and unrewarding work to get it straight. Only a broad and well-trained mind can focus all the factors in the balance of power and present them plausibly in all their twisting and variety. One must not, however, expect too much from this kind of history. Mr Taylor honestly apologises for the unreality of the counters he is obliged to use—he must talk of 'France' and 'Germany,' but may mean 'literally only two or three men' altogether. Diplomatic history, moreover, is essentially a piecemeal study, where long-term themes and development are often hard to seek. It deals with a world where values and human feelings have little place, where there are few ideals in any idealistic sense and little nobility of conduct and character, and where the only aesthetic pleasure is in admiring a virtuosity of technique. This severe preoccupation with diplomacy gives us a surprisingly limited insight into modern society. The chief characters so often seem to be the funny little men of H. G. Wells making irrelevant comments on the margin of events; or humourless, incalculable machines, without personality, but with an inset affinity for wickedness and deceit. The stake they play for is always human lives and happiness, but the masked men around the Green Table evidently treat this stake with callous indifference. Surely the concentrated study of such a subject would colour one's whole view of human nature and one's way of seeing history at large. What is gained in technique may be lost in judgment and psychological perception.

It would be easy to quarrel with this book over many small details of fact and interpretation—the remarkable thing would be if one could not. On a more general level, one is at once tempted to quarrel with the challenging claim on the dust cover that it aspires to be literature as well as scientific history. In fact, there are many examples of a certain lack of fastidiousness in writing ('French ambitions in Morocco are often ascribed to economic motives; the opposite is the case'). Putting aside his usual coruscating and allusive style, Mr Taylor has chosen a clear but bloodless narrative prose, dry and compact, tautly spun, relentless and unrelaxing, with no concessions to literary artifice or to grace and charm. The whole text is strung at precisely the same continuous tension, never varying to build up a climax, and easing only for an occasional anti-climax. Nor is there enough dramatic or architectural organisation in the book to make up for this. Its drama is episodic, its structure is not symphonic but a monotonous succession of studies in strict counterpoint. It is a hard style of writing, like a hard wine that will never come round. The meaning is always perfectly clear, and that is rare enough nowadays; but we are still left waiting for a Maitland who will make diplomatic history readable.

A noteworthy characteristic is the author's habit of exaggeration for effect, and his reluctance to admit uncertainty. There is something to be said for this, especially in a textbook (though he insists that this is not a textbook). He is often enviably sure about which wars were aggressive, which defied 'international law,' and which elections were honest. We are assured that in 1858 'the French middle classes were discontented for the first time since 1851'; and that 'no Frenchman thought seriously of recovering Alsace and Lorraine'; and, later, that 'the French had ceased to be a warlike nation.' A similar certainty of conviction allows him to be the exception to his own rule that one should not speculate about the might-have-beens of history, and to make further exceptions to his other rule that no war is inevitable until it breaks out. He readily generalises about national characteristics, about the sharp practice and bad temper of the Russians for instance; and Italy is always faulted, whether she does anything or nothing, cowardice and vanity being her motives either way. An invariable touch of banter and ridicule about Italy can always be relied on for some very necessary light relief, even if at the cost of distortion and factual errors. This connects up with an admiration of the strong and a contempt for the weak which seem to be among the more consistent features of this book.

Most people will gladly allow Mr Taylor his bias for the sake of those quirks of fancy which keep his narrative continually on the boil. He loves to search out the little ironies of history, to show how treaties produce quite different results from those intended, and how formal alliances can be directed more against their own members than against a presumptive enemy. Wherever possible a traditional judgment will be turned upside down in a paradox, and this treatment can be most successful when dealing with a paradoxical figure like Napoleon III. The Crimean war is thus converted into a decisive event in history; but Louis Napoleon then frittered away his 'hegemony' over Europe. It is baldly stated that he was more interested in helping Italy than in acquiring Savoy or the Rhineland; and that he, rather than Bismarck, was the man responsible for any decline in international morality. It was Napoleon who wanted war in 1870, whereas Bismarck was actually taken by surprise. Indeed, the idea of a German-dominated

continent was abhorrent to the German chancellor. All these statements are calculated to make people think, even if they are true only
in part.

The origins of the First World War give plenty of scope for such
shock-treatment of accepted views. William II, though himself a large
shareholder in Krupps, was less bellicose and anti-British than his
subjects, and the object of his Tangier visit in 1905 was really 'to get
on closer terms with France.' Likewise Lloyd George's Mansion
House speech in 1911 was really directed against Caillaux, and was
meant to promote reconciliation with Germany. In the end the generals
swept aside both William and Bethmann Hollweg—Bethmann, ' "the
good German," impotent to arrest the march of German power,
deploring its consequences, yet going along with it.' By 1914 both sets
of alliances were precarious. They were maintained intact ultimately
because the Central Powers were aggressive, whereas 'the Powers of
the Triple Entente all entered the war to defend themselves.' This may
be too simple and convenient a conclusion, but it is at least a conclusion, and that is more than the safety-first historians would have dared
to give us.

November 6th, 1954

Classical Education

M. I. FINLEY

It is a source of unceasing wonder how successfully scholars, even
in the well populated disciplines, often avoid some of the most
obviously important and interesting subjects. Here is a striking
example, and it was left to a Sorbonne professor of early church history
to write the first systematic modern account of education in classical
antiquity, from Homer (for M. Marrou deliberately and correctly
ignores the Minoan-Mycenaean world) to the end of the fifth century
after Christ.*

M. Marrou is too modest, and his preface overstresses the need to

---

* *A History of Education in Antiquity*. By H. I. Marrou, translated from the 3rd ed.
by George Lamb.

provide a survey for 'our students' and the educated public. That he has certainly done, and much more, for he is master of his subject, down to the most recent papyrological and archaeological finds, and he has written a most intelligent book, filled with original ideas and insights, plainly spoken in its value judgments, and (in the original) attractively set forth. To uncover admirable qualities in Isocrates ('the reader will surely understand that I am pleading out of professional duty and against my own inclination') or to write with such historical and psychological understanding and yet with such common sense on 'pederasty as education' is, in the light of M. Marrou's own faith and sentiments, an achievement of real quality, moral as well as intellectual. To hold the reader's interest in the notebooks of Greek children in Roman Egypt, while we examine the methods of teaching the alphabet, is also no small achievement, intellectual as well as aesthetic. And with it all there are massive references to the sources, many quoted in translation (including a welcome number from the more recondite writers), and a critical guide to the scholarly literature.

'Education' is, of course, an unhappy and imprecise word. The subject of the book may be more accurately defined, in the author's own terms, as the history of ancient 'culture', its norms and values, its variations and transformations according to the shifting social relationships of antiquity, the institutions and techniques by which it was fostered. M. Marrou restricts 'culture' to its 'specifically French sense', the *personal* form of the life of the spirit', something very different from the German *Kultur*, which is synonymous with 'civilisation'. (*Kultur* is aggressively value-loaded, and on that subject we are well provided, with respect to ancient Greece, with Werner Jaeger's *Paideia*. M. Marrou is extravagant in expressing his debt to this work, and I find that puzzling. Despite Jaeger's great erudition, his three volumes are a storehouse of meaningless rhetoric—'the eternal knowledge of truth and destiny'—of the kind which so often passes for philosophy; and there is none of that in the volume under review.)

At one pole is the culture of the noble warrior, at the other the culture of the scribe. M. Marrou imagines the history of ancient education to be a slow, uneven, sometimes rather turbulent movement from one to the other, not completed until the end of antiquity, when 'the Christian faith decided to organise culture and education around the Book par excellence, the Bible.' As metaphors, perhaps even as ideal types, the concepts of the warrior and the scribe are useful. They repeatedly help to illumine one or another facet of the picture: the subtle changes in the position of the aristocracy or in its self-image, for example, or the complicated and often equivocal role of physical education. (M. Marrou is very good on such matters as *kalokagathia* and *mens sana in corpore sano*, chopping away both the clichés and the cultism which adhere to them in so much modern writing.) But as basic analytical concepts they are far from sufficient, as the author is well aware. Early Rome, for example, had neither culture: her ideals were those of the peasant (rich, no doubt, but a peasant nonetheless), not of the noble warrior, and when, after many centuries, Rome at last found a poet to serve as her Homer, he drew much of his inspiration from Hesiod, that curious, isolated figure in Greek history who refuses to fit any pigeon-hole into which he may be pushed.

Fortunately, M. Marrou does not play too much on the warrior-scribe theme, despite the way he opens with it as a key generalisation. He has another, more important theme, which makes his book particularly exciting, and which invites earnest and extensive debate. The ancient world produced 'only one coherent and clearly defined educational system', and that system was not achieved until a 'comparatively late date, which I place after the decisive contributions of the two great educators,' Plato and Isocrates. 'This need not surprise us … A civilisation must attain its proper form before it can create the education which will reflect it.' But what, apart from educational systems, came immediately after Plato and Isocrates? The end of the independent *polis* and the dominance of the autocratic Hellenistic monarchies; the end of the great creative period in Greek literature and philosophy and the rise of the compiler and the pedagogue; the triumph of the isolated individual (whether he sought salvation in *ataraxia* or Tyche or Mithras is irrelevant) over the ideal of the rational *zoön politikon*. What M. Marrou must consider, therefore, is not merely a civilisation which 'created the education' that reflected 'its proper form', but also a civilisation which died at that very moment, so that the education which lived on (for 700 or 800 years) inculcated and transmitted the ideals and norms of a society which was no longer there. But he himself tells us that 'education is not an element that can be detached from one civilisation and borrowed by another. It is the concentrated epitome of a culture and as such it is inseparable from the form of that culture, and perishes with it.' On M. Marrou's own excellent presentation of the evidence, it may be argued that the fully developed educational system of the post-Alexandrian world was in fact the proper reflection of *that* world, not of Plato's world, and surely not of Euripides' world, though many of the tools which were used—Homer and Attic Greek and the orations of Demosthenes and so on—were borrowed from an earlier age.

M. Marrou is not naïve, and he is cognizant of the difficulties in which he has placed himself. His efforts to extricate himself are serious and subtle, and more than once (as in the justification I have quoted for his defence of Isocrates) he seems unsure of their success. It would require an extended essay, at the very least, to develop the difficulties and objections I have suggested. This much may be said here. M. Marrou's paramount interest is in the continuity of the European tradition, in which the scholars and pedants of the Hellenistic age performed one indispensable service: they preserved and transmitted the material elements of the classical culture on which that tradition rests. We may join him in expressing our thanks. But must we admire the vessel along with the wine, the wireless (and the directors of the B.B.C.) along with Beethoven's Eroica, Aristarchus along with Homer? Isocrates triumphed over Plato, and rhetoric, not philosophy, became the centre of higher education. M. Marrou's defence of rhetoric (and of pedantry) is attractive, and up to a point even sound. But surely he will be the first to agree that it is no concern of rhetoric (or the rhetorician) whether the values it serves are ethically defensible or not, so long as they wear elegant dress.

Clearly this book should be made available to a wider audience, and an English translation is a commendable idea. The one we have been given, however, is a dubious service to either 'our students' or the general public or the author. The translator obviously knows nothing at all about the subject and not enough about the French language. The numerous mistakes range from such silly howlers as 'B-linear writing' to blunders which destroy the sense: *nos étudiants* are not 'students of history', an *homme lettré* is neither a 'literary man' nor a 'scholar', *De la pédérastie comme éducation* (a chapter title) is not the same as 'Pederasty in Education', and so on and on. (My quotations from the book are all based on the French text.) M. Marrou's skilful and rather free translations of sources are re-translated from his French, with the expected results. When the French translation of a modern English book is cited, we are sometimes given a re-translation of the title,

G

which of course comes out wrong; sometimes the French version with its page references; and, in at least one instance, the correct English title with the page references of the translation. And, finally, the translator has an unerring ear for the banal, the long-winded and the inelegant. I gave up after one chapter and read the original (priced at 27s. 6d.).

November 3rd, 1956

The Originality of the Namier School

HERBERT BUTTERFIELD

This study of English politics from the fall of Walpole to the firm establishment of the Pelhams★ approaches the form of political history more closely than most of the work of the school of Sir Lewis Namier. The narrative of the period is re-told with denser documentation and a closer dove-tailing of multiple sources than ever before; and the result is sometimes a tightness of texture never hitherto attained. What we call 'the structure of politics' is in something more like its proper place at last; because if it is not always introduced merely as an instrument for the interpretation of the political history, it gives greater fulness and precision to the background of the story. It is not used as a substitute for the political history, or as an excuse for the re-deployment of the familiar results of repetitive analysis.

It is true that the imposing episodes—even such things as the fall of Walpole or the crisis of 1746—could bear a more dramatic treatment and a more vivid 'resurrection' in the manner of the great narrators. A powerful writer may some day make more of the portraits and descriptive scenes, or may do more clever work with the staging of the whole story. Though Dr Owen's manuscript sources add points even to the diplomatic side of the history, the work is chiefly pre-occupied with those problems of political mechanics which have caught the interest of the present day. A fuller history of England during the same years would, for example, make much more of what was happening in the field of foreign policy and war, and, of course, much more

★ *The Rise of the Pelhams.* By John B. Owen. Methuen. 30s.

of the 1745 rebellion. This is academic writing—not at all history in the grand style; yet Dr Owen, addressing the scholar, possesses not merely preciseness and austerity but sometimes a certain beauty as a writer. And in the early chapters, as well as in some of the later episodes —and particularly in many passages where he is writing further away from the raw materials of history—he gives his account or unfolds his exposition with a certain artistry.

Because bad history often has a wider and longer currency than good history, it is possible to exaggerate the novelty of this book, and particularly of its more general political analysis. The strategic lines of the picture which the author provides—including some of the things particularly noted (as showing the results of the modern method) in Sir Lewis Namier's review in *The Spectator* for February 15, 1957—produce a general pattern which in many respects is surprisingly familiar. In Volume VI of the *Cambridge Modern History*, which appeared in 1909, there is a racy chapter on 'The Age of Walpole and the Pelhams' which, now that it has been vindicated by Dr Owen, stands out as easily the most remarkable contribution to that whole volume. When Dr Owen tells us that 'The Court and Treasury Party' numbered at the time of Walpole's fall 'only slightly more than 100', he is repeating practically the very words of Temperley, who, however, noted that the reliability of the men in question might depend on the existence of a good understanding between the King and the Treasury. Temperley held that, though direct bribery has been proved against Walpole in a few cases, 'the evidence suggests that it was not common, and most of Walpole's "corruption" consisted in the use of indirect means of securing party allegiance which every parliamentary leader employs.' He added, however, that 'in the imperfect state of parliamentary discipline it would seem that indirect bribery at any rate was a necessity.' In all this he anticipates again one of the structural themes and some of the interpretations in Dr Owen's book. He realized the existence and the importance of that considerable number of independent members which the House of Commons contained— another of the points which are emphasized and expanded in the present work. He declared in an unequivocal manner—though, here, even he was by no means original—that the political world of Walpole's time is not to be interpreted in terms of the modern party-system. Finally he criticized one of the most consistent traditions in English historiography—a view that provided the basis for the predominant interpretation of George III between 1800 and 1914. He firmly attacked the notion that, in the time of the first two Georges, the monarchy had been under eclipse—enslaved by the oligarchical Whigs. He even anticipated Dr Owen—and if he differs from the latter in his way of approach, I am not sure that he is not the wiser of the two—in reducing the constitutional significance which had traditionally been imputed to the crisis of 1746. If D. A. Winstanley, in the years immediately after 1909, had taken Temperley's hints or followed his clues he would have been forced to make an interesting qualification of his thesis that George III set out to rescue the monarchy from its enslavement to the Whigs. And he would have saved himself from his greatest howler, for it was just his belief in the water-tight efficiency of corruption that made him follow Acton at his worst, and assert that George III came to achieve a control over Parliament which nullified the effect of the Revolution of 1688.

Since the world has become so unscientific and uncritical in its measurement of what is original or what is new, it might not be out of place to recall that, in the *Quarterly Review* for 1914, Harold Temperley, writing of the ministry of North—a ministry which he regarded as having brought about an increase of corruption—still declared that 'royal influence and parliamentary corruption' are 'explanations which satisfied the Whigs but must not deceive the historian.' And anybody who is interested in those mental transpositions which are now regarded as necessary for the student of eighteenth-century politics (and which are sometimes thought to be newer than they really are) will find some of the important ones—including some of Dr Owen's—in Laprade's Introduction (e.g. pp. ix–x) to *Parliamentary Papers of John Robinson*, which goes back to 1922.

The story of the election of that parliament of 1741–47 with which Dr Owen's book is concerned cannot be properly envisaged or fully understood without a more adequate picture of the dramatic events in diplomacy and in war which were taking place at that time; and it has become a defect of writers on English history in this period to neglect unduly the repercussions of diplomacy on home affairs at a time when diplomacy was so admittedly royal in character and the connection with Hanover made the issue so delicate. Dr Owen's study of the election contains surprisingly little that is new, confirms the accounts as they have long been accepted, neglects the examination of the strategic episodes—Cornwall, Scotland and Westminster—and could be improved by the methods of the narrative historian, interested in enquiring, for example, whether it was true that Walpole let the business slide through over-optimism or indifference. The stimulating account of the same election by Vaucher in 1924 is not superseded and is more useful for the student because, apart from being based on closer documentation and a wider range of sources (some of which the Namier school unwisely neglect), it examines the strategic points in the story and embraces wider considerations. This work had already shown that at least the Duke of Newcastle had not been inclined to let the business of the election slide. Dr Owen, who is a wise historian, admits (on p. 34) that his explanation has been made 'from a purely mechanical point of view'.

The criterion of novelty is not everything, and Dr Owen's account of the election is succeeded by an analysis of the position and the fall of Walpole which must rank as one of the finest pieces of exposition ever produced on the subject of eighteenth-century politics. Yet here again the general thesis is not new, and is contained in Vaucher, who, also, says that Walpole was a new kind of Prime Minister, ruling only because he had the confidence of the King—the King, however, being incapable of supporting a mere favourite, because his confidence 'ne pouvait se justifier que si elle allait au ministre capable de rallier autour de lui la majorité parlementaire.' This chapter and this whole book confirm the suspicion that the Namier school are over-contemptuous in regard to their predecessors; and that though they may be right in reacting against the earlier Whig historians they have overlooked some excellent work that has intervened. Dr Owen is clearly unaware of the fact that Vaucher tracked down a mis-dating of the letter from Chesterfield to Dodington which he quotes at some length on pp. 16–17. This would suggest that in their almost total withholding of acknowledgements to their predecessors (or to anybody save one another) the members of this school are acting out of neglect, perhaps, rather than policy. Furthermore, this book, especially when taken along with the recent work by Mr Brooke on *The Chatham Administration*, confirms the view that, so far as political history is concerned, the work of the Namier school is shaking down into something less novel than was at one time claimed. The effects of structural analysis on our interpretation of the actual narrative is less revolutionary if one sets it, not against the writings of the Whig historians, but against the work that was produced between 1909 and 1929. After the severities of

England in the Age of the American Revolution Dr Owen (in a passage curiously parallel to that of Winstanley, *Lord Chatham and the Whig Opposition*, pp. 13–15) even sets out (pp. 127–29) to rescue the Duke of Newcastle from the slanders of preceding writers.

In his account of the famous crisis of 1746 (and his interesting exposition of its antecedents pp. 272–73), it is not clear that Dr Owen does not represent a retrogression, or at least a nearer approach to the attitude of the Whig historians, in spite of the novelty and the value of some of his arguments. Temperley, too, had discovered that, of the ministerial resignations at that time 'some ... were calculated, others spontaneous.' He asserted that the constitutional importance of the affair had been exaggerated; and this is a point on which it would perhaps be difficult to overthrow him. At any rate it takes time to decide whether a successful stroke of policy is going to turn into a constitutional precedent or will come to be regarded by the future as an act of usurpation. Dr Owen's account of the episode, and indeed his whole book, is a criticism of the view that a king could just choose any minister or adviser he might like—a point to be borne in mind if it is ever suggested that George III had such a right or was to be regarded as immune from challenge on this issue. The author of the present work not only sees George II as defeated in the attempt to follow an irresponsible Closet adviser but considers that the King was foolish in ever undertaking the duel with the ministry. When the Pelhams resigned, the Closet adviser, Granville, proved unable to form a ministry because he lacked support in the House of Commons; but, granted the general unpopularity of the man, I am not convinced that the influence of the Pelhams had nothing to do with the hopelessness of Granville's position, especially as 'the King still looked on the Old Corps as the essential basis of his Government.' Though the episode itself was of less constitutional importance than has often been assumed, we must not forget that the legend of it proved to be of considerable moment: both George II and George III held that the monarchy had been put in bondage to the politicians. In this sense the occasion had a genuine significance; and one could have wished that Dr Owen, who so clearly has the power of handling more than the 'purely mechanical' parts of history, had dealt more spaciously with this matter.

Even where Dr Owen picks up the old issues and confirms the older counts of the general strategic situation, he brings everything into better focus, now giving the points greater precision, now more definitely establishing the case; so that his book has undoubted value. Part of his distinction and charm lies in the quiet methods by which he has achieved his object, and the absence of cliquish arrogance or vulgar contentiousness.

May 25th 1957

What Is History?

HERBERT BUTTERFIELD

Even those who do not normally care for works about the nature of history are likely to be interested in Mr E. H. Carr's George Macaulay Trevelyan Lectures.* If its exposition of theory had been less skilful than it actually is, his book would be valuable as the self-examination and confession of a distinguished practising historian. We do not find him with his feet caught in the strings of his balloon, and sailing up into the sky, as Collingwood so often did. Perhaps at the same time he does less than justice to the Positivists, and, while not being a Positivist myself, I should like (if he would feel it not too unfitting on my part) to note that the virtues of these estimable people are too easily overlooked. He is best of all—and most central—when, on pp. 22–23, he describes in a concrete manner his own procedures as a writer of history, or when, on pp. 10–13, he makes his beautiful examination of the Stresemann documents.

We must watch him very carefully when he tells us that 'the historian is not really interested in the unique but in what is general in the unique.' Ranke makes the highest possible call for generalisation, but at the beginning he actually loves (for their own sake) the curiously shaped pebble, the rose that he holds in his hand, the old personality, and just the thing that is unparalleled in a specified conjuncture or historical event. When happenings or people are seen in their uniqueness we have the kind of history with which there is nothing that one can do except to narrate it. Mr Carr must not exclude from

---

* *What is History?* By Edward Hallet Carr. The George Macaulay Trevelyan Lectures delivered in the University of Cambridge, January–March, 1961.

his definition of history the good story, the depiction of its back-ground, the portrayal of a person, or the attempt to discover whether St Peter went to Rome.

He does not deny chance or personality or unique events (which in a sense are all connected) but it is to the interest of his doctrine to deprecate them somewhat. These things do not exhaust the com-mentary that we can make upon the past; but, once their role is con-ceded at all, is it not clear that, from a certain point of view, they are omnipresent? Mr Carr thinks that their role is over-stressed by his-torians who want comfort for their minds—want to explain away their own misfortune and misery. But surely these things give equal ground for hope to those other people who are optimistic and glad. Their existence merely implies that the historical process is more subtle and complicated (and, also, more *sui generis*)—with many more varieties of possible futures ahead—than if the meaning of history were ex-hausted by sociological explanation. It has become fashionable to argue that the individuals who make history are themselves first of all the product of their age. We must remember, all the same, that human beings are sometimes particularly the product of an intense local environment, as well as of the general one. Also, they may differ greatly in their reaction to their environment. The influences and ingredients which they receive can be so churned over and re-mixed inside them that each person becomes in a certain sense a separate source of action, a separate well of life.

I wish that Mr Carr, when he is at a loss for an argument, would not go on reiterating that the rest of us, in a period of gloom, have taken to dejected views of history. It would not be less plausible to argue that, if ever this country becomes desperate and depressed, there will be a wild rush to the Marxist interpretation of history. At the particular level which is here in question, I have always been an unblushing disciple of Ranke; and it is nonsense to suggest that Ranke's view was composed in a period of dismal recession and retreat.

Mr Carr is really leading up to the thesis (p. 60): 'the more socio-logical history becomes ... the better ... '; and one can be interested in the sociological approach while still feeling that, in this, he is narrow-ing historical science. One effect of such a tendency has generally been to produce an appalling thinness and crudeness in ideas about human moods and motives. I wonder if there could be a better example of this than the mechanical reiteration of Mr Carr's explanations of those historians who happen to differ from him. An imputed sociological explanation can too easily become the substitute for a serious enquiry into the matter. Mr Carr takes the line (p. 58) that 'if the evidence is not clear whether Richard III murdered the princes in the tower' we might enquire 'whether it was the habit of rulers of the period to liquidate potential rivals.' I ask myself if this would not serve as a parable—a hint of the dangers of sociological history.

The lectures form a most interesting book, but behind them there is a distinct tendency, and it operates to undermine the status of history as an autonomous science. I see no reason to give up my view that it is the function of history to establish things by historical evidence— my view, that, indeed, nothing is historically established unless demonstrable in a coercive manner, demonstrable to Catholic or Protestant, Whig or Tory, Muslim or atheist—irrespective of any particular theories that they happen to hold. For Mr Carr, 'objectivity' exists (p. 117) when the historian 'chooses the right facts, or, in other words ... applies the right standard of significance.' He means, when the historian has 'the capacity to project his vision into the future.' I wonder if he is right in his suggestion that those historians have proved most durable who had this kind of vision of the future. I wonder if he is right and wise to say (p. 102): 'Besides the question, Why? the historian also asks the question, Whither?' The truth is that, in all this, history is being tied more closely to topical issues—brought more than before under the dominion of present-day ideas. Mr Carr certainly puts his finger on an essential point when he says (p. 38) that 'the historian who is most conscious of his own situation is also more capable of transcending it.' We can never have perfect history, but it seems to me that much less attention is being paid nowadays to that discipline which meant training oneself to transcend the present as much as possible.

There are even resources in the nature of historical scholarship itself which can be used to assist this kind of discipline; and I am not sure that Mr Carr is not being misled because he is a special case—a pioneer in a field that is to a considerable degree unworked, (besides being fairly recent and particularly appropriate to a sociological method). A person who enters the field of Lutheran studies inherits a long tradition of scholarship which, as it reaches him in 1961, does not merely reflect the ideas of 1961. It holds some sort of deposit from the views of 1561, 1661, 1761 and 1861; and many students coming into this field will find problems to hand—problems which arise from the present state of Lutheran scholarship. It is true that they will hardly be able to avoid inserting some of the ideas of 1961 into their view of the problems in question, or applying new methods of enquiry. But a scholarly book does not cut away the whole inheritance, and is rather kept in balance by it. One can easily distinguish such a work from the more topical production which merely draws straight lines from Luther to the present day. In any case, there is an interest in history which is a true historical interest—not arising out of present-day issues, but out of curiosity about, say, the Renaissance, for its own sake. I think that my teacher, Harold Temperley, was right when he once said that the coming popularity of history was going to be a danger. It introduces so many other factors to dilute or divert the interest in the past as such.

One can feel with Mr Carr (p. 150) that, in our time, the 'subordination of reason to the assumptions of the existing order' (indeed just the *fear* for that order) has become what he would call a distrust of progress and what I should call a distrust of Providence. I personally feel that it has disastrously curbed and stifled all radical thought in our time, both in conservative and in socialist, both in politics and in religion, both in Anglicanism and in nonconformity. I regard Marx as one of the very very rare figures in the history of historiography who have been original on a magnificent scale. I shall shock Mr Carr if I say that I think he discovered the things which Christians ought to have discovered, which Christians would have formulated more satisfactorily if they had discovered them, but which Christians failed to discover because they crippled their thought by tying it to existing régimes. If I think Ranke greater, though he lacked what Marx possessed, it is because in Marx there are defects which produce a monotony in the total result. I think Ranke has the greater catholicity and comprehension in spite of obvious defects, and shows something like a Shakespearian mind. But Ranke's system left these possibilities open to him. We are now being confronted by views of history which are too exclusive.

Mr Carr (pp. 35–36) has challenged me in such a provocative manner, that it would seem like defeatism if I reviewed his book without comment on the matter. In 1931 I published a criticism of a particular fallacy which I regarded as underlying both the Whig and the Protestant versions of history. It happened that in 1938, when I was invited to lecture in Germany I was asked to proceed one step further and talk about the history of the Whig interpretation. In 1944, that lecture appeared, with little alteration, in the first chapter of *The Englishman and his History*—really an essay on the Whig political tradition. I carefully collated this work with the former one, and indeed added some trip-wires for the careless reader—including p. 3, a menace to those who thought that the criticism of the Whig historians involved an attack on the Whig political tradition. I added all the safeguards I could think of—the view that the Whig interpretation, which later became an obstacle to historical understanding, was at first an advance; the view that it contributed to our appreciation of one side of the story, while cutting the effort of understanding short, and refusing it to the other party. I drew attention to the fact that wrong history might be beneficial in its political results—that the myth of Magna Carta helped the cause of liberty.

The most acute of the critics of my *Whig Interpretation* was a Cambridge Conservative who saw that I was no conservative but was merely anxious to have the Whig historians more liberal-minded. He said that the book ought to have been entitled 'An Appeal from the Old Whigs to the New.' But many critics complained that I had chiefly attacked the Protestant version of history. And even Mr Carr cannot claim that I became a Protestant nonconformist since 1931. He provides, however, a species of sociological explanations for an alleged liberal conversion of mine which he sees as a result of the Second World War, though if there were the slightest grain of truth in the suggestion, the thing must have occurred by 1938. 'My purpose,' he says, 'is merely to show how closely the work of the historian mirrors the society in which he works.' He would come nearer to the truth if he could persuade himself that, precisely because I am a Protestant, I would like to see Protestants training themselves to transcend private opinions and topical prejudices when they come to technical history.

December 2nd, 1961

Tawney, Trevor-Roper and the Gentry

PETER LASLETT

With the publication of *The Members of the Long Parliament** another piece of Fabian masonry crumbles and falls. It is not a very good book and it is not a very profound one, but it is undoubtedly important, and for anyone who has followed the fortunes of the Fabian view of English society and its development it is a very interesting one.

The late Douglas Brunton and Mr D. H. Pennington have assembled all the evidence they can find on the 827 men who sat in the Long Parliament from the time of its first meeting in 1641 right through the war of Royalist and Roundhead, with its exclusions and its purges, down to the final dissolution of the assembly in *annus mirabilis* 1660. Of this formidable number, 552 were originally elected to the body which argued and fought the issues of the Great Rebellion up to 1645, and 275 were men recruited after that date to fill the spaces left in St Stephen's Chapel by the departure of the Royalist members to Oxford and the King's army. They have analysed all this material in the first place in accordance with the classical canons laid down for the history of Parliament by Sir Lewis Namier and Professor J. E. Neale. So we have something of an equivalent for the mid-seventeenth century of *The Structure of Politics in 1760* and of Neale on Elizabeth's Parliaments.

All this is valuable, but it does not get very far. This is understandable because the Long Parliament presents a problem of quite a different order from the Parliaments of Elizabeth, and its detailed analysis on these lines would be an enormous undertaking. But it is difficult to resist the conclusion that the authors of this book did not get beyond the preliminary stage of this enquiry because their attention was diverted by the possibilities their material presented to them for a second sort of analysis, a study of social movement. So instead of a detailed account of how parliament and politics really worked in the age of Cromwell and Clarendon we have a quasi-statistical com-

* *Members of the Long Parliament.* By D. Brunton and D. H. Pennington.

mentary on the Marxian and post-Marxian thesis about the under-lying character of the Puritan Revolution.

If it is true that they were seduced into writing this sort of book, it must be admitted that the temptation was exquisite. In its crudest form the thesis they comment upon states that the Puritan Revolution was 'the story of how one social class was driven from power by another.' Although Professor Tawney says in his introduction that 'only a char-latan will dogmatise on the welter of conflicting motives which find their agonising issue in the choice of allegiances in a Civil War,' it is also true that in recent years many historians have come out with just such a dogma, either in the pure Marxian form just quoted, or in the more cautious form which is usually, and correctly, associated with Tawney's own name.

Right, say the authors of this book, let us look at the men who actually did the talking and fighting. What should we expect if this thesis is true, that the Royalists or Parliamentarians should be the older? Surely only the younger generation could be expected to attach themselves to the new ideology. In fact, however, it was the Royalists, the backward lookers, those half living in the Middle Ages who were the rising generation; there were twice as many of them in the crucial age group under 30 than there were of their opponents. Who were the merchants? They were on both sides, perhaps slightly more Royalist than otherwise. Who were the lawyers? They were on both sides too, and though more inclined against the king than for him, not so much so as to make for a correlation between Parliament and the law. Where were the new families? Everywhere, on both sides—in fact, so many were 'new' that if they had been all against the king, there could have been no Civil War.

And so it goes on. Perhaps the most novel and unexpected of the conclusions they come to is that the whole movement of the land of England from the old families to the new in the period 1540–1640 can be explained in terms of births, marriages and deaths. To explain the passing of the old social order there is no need to invoke the forces of capitalism, or the inexorable demands of economic law. It was the mild and simpering figure of 'the heiress, and more particularly the co-heiress,' which was 'the most powerful element in breaking up old estates and founding new families.' Now this may turn out to be so, but it can hardly be claimed that the conclusion is demonstrated in this book. To do that it would be necessary to calculate what were, in fact, the expectations of life and prosperity of families in the society of that era, and then try to show whether or not what did happen was different from those expectations. This would be a complicated and difficult manoeuvre, and our authors can hardly be expected to undertake it; to be fair to them it must be said that they do not attempt to build anything on the supposition that the calculation had been done. More impressive is the proof that the men elected to replace the Royalists in and after 1645 were of almost exactly the same sort as those originally elected, in spite of the fact that so many of those who might otherwise have stood were debarred by the circumstances and that many of the elections took place in areas under military control. Here is no evidence of a Revolution going inexorably to the Left, no convincing sign that it was towards the smaller gentry and the bourgeois townsman that the political balance was swaying.

At this point the thesis presented in criticism of Professor Tawney last year by Mr Trevor-Roper* gets caught up into the discussion, though it seems that his tract had not been published in time to be taken into account by our authors. In so far as Mr Roper identifies himself with Professor Tawney's general position in the highly deferential overture to that essay, which reads a little oddly in that somewhat acerbic style, he, too, comes under the criticisms already described. Indeed, he may feel himself galled by Tawney's own remark, for he also has been guilty of confidently suggesting, if not pronouncing dogmas about, the reasons why men took up arms in the Civil War. But in his two major positions Mr Roper may feel himself triumphantly vindicated. The evidence that Brunton and Pennington have seen convinces them, as it convinced him, that it was *office* which was the really important source of wealth and power in that society, and that if a family enjoyed the Royal favour, or could capture or buy a nice fee-producing sinecure, for a generation or better for two or three, then it did rise, it did succeed in establishing itself, it did become a candidate for the landed interest of later times. This is provided, of course, that it was lucky enough to be on the right side of the vital statistics, that it did not perish for want of heirs, and its daughters married into families where the sons all got smitten by the plague or sunk in a naval expedition.

But Mr Roper's thesis is not all a matter of the insolence of office. His second great source of wealth and success was commercial and

* *The Gentry 1540–1640.* Supplement to the Economic History Review.

mineral wealth, and here, too, the evidence on the families of those who sat in the Long Parliament bears him out. 'Merchant wealth is so common in families that survived that we begin to wonder whether a landed estate could last more than a few generations without being subsidised through commercial or professional fortunes, or through the sale of new lands acquired by marriage.' Here, then, they are all on common ground, and on ground which can no longer be occupied by Tawney and his followers, though always with the proviso that everybody's position is insecure for so long as the actuary's task for the society in question remains undone.

The coda to Trevor-Roper's essay is the suggestion that the Independents were the falling gentry, those out of office, those who weren't in commerce and coal. This is in itself a little trite, because it suggests that all that has to be done is to take the given pieces on the board and arrange them in a different way. If a rise of the gentry won't explain everything, and particularly the causes of the Civil War, then it must be a fall, if not of all then of some. If extreme Puritanism won't do as the rationalisation of economic progressivism, as the Marxists have implied, then it must serve as the rationalisation of political failure and economic decadence, which is useful in another way too, since it brings in the Catholics who were also recusants and also political outs. Brunton and Pennington do not confirm Trevor-Roper's inspired guesswork here because though they reveal the extent to which enjoyment of office and commercial privilege tended to put men on the side of the King, they do not present a picture of the Independents as small scale gentry on the downgrade, and they make it impossible to think that the men who benefited from the war by getting into Parliament were likewise the smaller, rural and provincial ones.

Nevertheless, the relation between the two cases remains obscure because no concerted attempt is made in the book to sort people out on the basis of religious conviction. Occasional reference is made to religious convictions in the rambling survey of all the members and their family connections by county and by region which forms the body of their text. Difficult reading this makes, and confusing too. It is based on published sources only, and it cannot be relied on as a reference source since it has to be selective and superficial, whilst it is only occasionally relevant to the general theses which they present to begin with and which they reiterate at the end. That latter function is much better filled by the admirable tables printed at the end. But it would be

natural to expect that in a war which was fought, so the fighters themselves said, primarily over religious matters the thing to find out would
be what men belonged to what religion. It hasn't been done. We don't
know even roughly how many Puritans fought for the King, or how
many Anglicans supported Parliament. We are left with no idea if
there was any correlation at that time between what a man believed
and what position he occupied in society.

What then of the relevance of this book, and of Roper on Tawney,
to historical interpretation in general? Does it make what has been
called the Fabian view of the development of English society invalid
in general because it can't any longer be applied to the Civil War? It
can be said at once that whatever happens to the economic historians,
so predominantly Fabians for so long, the Marxists will soon find their
way out of it. If you hold a view as rigid as they do on economic substructure determining the behaviour of religious, intellectual and
political superstructure, the breakdown of the detailed interpretation
of one political change, however important, cannot matter for long.
After all this was not the only occasion, in the Marxist view, when the
bourgeoisie rose. They had risen under the Tudor despotism with its
new men and its commercially conscious landlords, they were to rise
again in 1688, and again in 1832. All the Marxist need do is to put his
figures into different places on the ladder. This is for him just one more
instance where the application of general sociological law does not
issue as easily into specific social and political event as had been thought.
This historical instance will not lead him to modify his sociology; no
historical event could do that.

There are two possible lines of defence for those with less rigid
convictions. In the first place they can take the view that the Parliament is not the nation, and that the process they believe in was taking
place in society, although it did not show itself in the membership of
Parliament. Brunton and Pennington themselves seem to take that
view at one point, and Tawney refers to it. It is rather an uneasy
position however. If the House of Commons cannot be taken as a
fairly representative sample of the people who ruled society at that
time, what body can be? No one supposes that they represented the
nation as a whole—not since the glorious days of the Whig fallacies
that is—but it seems difficult to believe that if any body more powerful
than those they did represent had existed at the time, the Civil War
would not have had a different course. These people, whoever they

were, would presumably have intervened to dispose of both Royalist and Parliamentarian as soon as their quarrel had become a nuisance. The second defence might use the considerable number of points of detail which do in fact bear out the conventional thesis and which the two authors do not, perhaps, weigh as they should.

The true position may be that we need a new model for seventeenth century society. We need an account of the social structure in its own terms, one which avoids the anomalies of classes rising and falling. We must strive to develop a picture which will allow of conflict going on not between the governing stratum and something above it or beneath it, but within the stratum itself. We ought to provide ourselves with a method of criticism which makes it possible to give weight to all the reasons for complex conflict at this time, everything from the growth of a wage earning proletariat in the mines to the anarchy of views on the proper organisation of the Christian Church. In the references it makes to the social system of this society, in its emphasis on family and on county, this book makes some approach to a view of this nature. To work it out further than they have gone would take far more than a critical review of a short pamphlet and a slim book.

May 8th, 1964

Christopher Hill and the 'Intellectual Origins of the English Revolution'

QUENTIN SKINNER

Mr Christopher Hill must undoubtedly be regarded by now as one of the foremost as well as one of the most prolific of practising historians. He received the accolade from English historians in 1962 with the invitation to deliver the Ford lectures at Oxford. A much expanded version of these lectures has now been published as *Intellectual Origins of the English Revolution.** This book will in many ways confirm Mr Hill's high reputation both as scholar and writer. The learning is vast. It would be an impertinence to praise it, were it not that historians with such a command of highly specialized information are

* *Intellectual Origins of the English Revolution.* By Christopher Hill.

so often accused of shirking 'the wider issues.' Mr Hill's work very effectively gives the lie to this sort of philistinism. He has read with tremendous zest in the secondary sources, particularly on science (a bibliography would have helped here). He has also read in the literature of the period with a sensitivity and a grasp which seem to be rare among historians, and which yet provide countless illuminations of historical points. The style, too, remains as crisp as ever. Lovers, say, of Tawney's thundering periods will feel able to fault Mr Hill when his briskness leads sometimes merely to ambiguity (what can one make, for example, of remarks *tout court* like Ralegh 'enjoyed shocking parsons'?). But the general effect of Mr Hill's prose is brilliantly direct, the general level of the writing very high.

A small quibble is in place here, for Mr Hill's merits and especially the speed of his output are not without their cost. There are some signs of hasty composition. In the Conclusion, where Mr Hill promises to tie up the strands of his thought, we are presented not with a finished account but with a number of new suggestions—all of them interesting, but not one of them followed out. Throughout the book there are too many small slips. There is also rather a lot of repetition. Mr Hill states and re-states his theme, not always in the same form. He even re-states some of his points: information on p. 2, for example, appears again on p. 209; information which first appears on p. 137 appears again on p. 150, again on p. 205, and yet again on p. 276.

Mr Hill's work, as he says himself, is nothing like an intellectual history. Its concern is to argue one point, or rather aspects of a single theme. Its method is to a great extent biographical. Mr Hill's concern is the sociology, the ideological relations, of the scientific revolution in England. The thesis which claims to unite scientific with political revolution is that 'the ideas of the scientists favoured the puritan and Parliamentarian cause'. It is somewhat difficult, however, to hold in the mind the exact nature of the relationship which this is claimed to suggest. It would not, I think, be malicious to add that the argument derives some of its plausibility from the fact that all the correlations are put forward very tentatively, in a variety of forms, and never strictly in the language of historical proof. It is also difficult to remember what is thought to be relevant. Sometimes Mr Hill wants to exclude puritanism altogether from his story. Sometimes he suggests merely that 'the triumph of science' was 'brought about' with the success of the Parliamentarian revolution. Yet he still regards puritanism as 'the most important complex of ideas that prepared men's minds for revolution'. And the bulk of the work does claim to trace links between all three of the movements, puritan,Parliamentarian, scientific —links which are described at different points as being close, very tentative, and on the whole arguable. The chief protagonists then singled out to illustrate the various possible links are Sir Francis Bacon and his popularisers among the London artisan-scientists; Sir Walter Ralegh and his circle of scientific and literary friends; and Sir Edward Coke, 'the myth-maker.'

One of the correlations between these three factors which Mr Hill's account frequently claims is that if you were a puritan and a Parliamentarian, you were (thereby, apparently) likely to approve of the new science and of the men who patronised it. Thus Bacon was spurned by the Court, Ralegh as a patron of science became a 'Parliamentarian and puritan hero', while with Sir Edward Coke 'the struggle of common lawyers as Parliamentarians was given historical significance and dignity'. One of the reasons for such approval, Mr Hill often asserts, was that 'puritans and scientists had long had enemies in common'. This is hardly a respectable argument. One might equally well point out, say, that fascists and communists have enemies in common: to do so is certainly not to establish any relationship of affinity between the movements. Another reason, Mr Hill argues, was that the inspiring ideas of Baconian science and of puritan ideology were analogous. The concept of knowledge for the relief of man's estate made science, to the puritan, 'positively virtuous'. This is ingenious, but the argument has to depend in turn on unstated assumptions about the character of puritanism. If it was 'puritan' to approve of science because it was useful, puritanism must have been a much more worldly sort of religious ideology than is commonly supposed. This was, of course, the thesis advanced by Mr Hill in his previous book (much cited in the present work) on *Society and Puritanism*, in which puritanism was treated as the characteristic ideology of 'the industrious sort of people.' This view, however, can be damagingly criticised for ignoring the important—and politically ambivalent— contributions of the noble and gentry classes to the puritan movement. It is perhaps a weakness of Mr Hill's present work that it has to rely on taking a previously quite tentative suggestion for an established truth.

Another correlation which Mr Hill frequently claims is that if you were a scientist and a Parliamentarian, you were likely to be a puritan. It is important to discriminate this argument (more, perhaps, than Mr Hill does) from the previous one, which tended to assert that puritans and Parliamentarians—though not necessarily scientists themselves—would approve of the new science. This argument, on the contrary, tends to assert that the patrons and practitioners of science were themselves likely to be puritan. It leads Mr Hill to sketch puritan affiliations for both Ralegh and Coke. The investigation is directed in particular to showing that both can be regarded as 'economic liberals.' For Coke this is done mainly by use of Wagner's well-known essay—though characteristically Mr Hill touches in many extra details with much greater erudition. For Ralegh it is done by some very fascinating interpretation of the *History*.

This scarcely substantiates the case. The argument has to depend on assuming a close relationship between puritanism and capitalism. But it seems somewhat old-fashioned to write as if this leaves no room for debate. The argument also depends on assuming that both of these phenomena can similarly be linked to the new science. But the alleged relationship between puritanism and science is even more in debate, although Mr Hill will not deign to answer the arguments of the many scholars who have cast doubt on it. Mr Hill, moreover, himself uses this argument in a markedly peculiar manner. The usual line is to stress the driving force of puritanism, and this is the theme of all the material Mr Hill cites. But his own argument seems to put the correlation back-to-front. It seems a rather weakening ambiguity that the evidence used by other scholars to establish the scientific commitment of puritans is assumed to work equally well for discussing the puritan commitment of scientists.

Mr Hill's further efforts, moreover, to demonstrate Coke's and Ralegh's 'puritan' affiliations strike me as the weakest part of the argument. If we merely consider one other equally plausible candidate on this 'side,' any strict correlation can immediately be falsified. Consider Ben Jonson, for example, who holds all of Mr Hill's cards—member of Ralegh's circle, anti-Spanish, teacher at Gresham College. Yet it is for the puritans that Jonson in his plays reserves his most malicious scorn. With Ralegh and Coke, in any case, Mr Hill has a hopeless task. With Coke he has to content himself with citing his 'puritan' relations. With Ralegh he hopefully suggests that 'allegations that he was an atheist may have been put about in the fifteen-nineties in order to discredit a man who had close connexions with the puritans'. But he eventually has to give the game away and admit that he 'seems to have had the sort of tolerance born of indifference which finally triumphed in 1689'.

The main correlation, however, with which Mr Hill's book is concerned is simply that if you were a scientist (which turns out to mean a Baconian) you tended to be a Parliamentarian. In two Chapters (II and III) Mr Hill seeks to link anti-Court, anti-Spanish, eventually revolutionary political radicalism with the work of London artisan-scientists—with their vernacular scientific literature and their technological skills, with Bacon to turn their popular attitudes into an intellectual system. In a further Chapter (the longest and the most ambitious, and a magnificently fruitful piece of research) Mr Hill similarly links political radicalism with the historical researches of Ralegh and his followers—their abandonment of historical discussion in terms of divine causes, their insistence on investigating secondary causes, 'to take arbitrariness out of history, to replace God's direct intervention by the idea of historical law.'

Mr Hill concedes, of course, that there is nothing necessary about this alleged link. This also means that he is not as impressed as he perhaps ought to be by the prominence of the counter-examples—by the fact, for example, that Harvey, perhaps the greatest 'Baconian', remained a staunch Royalist, or by the fact that William Prynne, one of the most prominent puritan Parliamentarians, remained both ignorant and contemptuous of the new science. The connexion is 'less direct'. But there does seem to be a real point here. It would, I think, be perverse not to allow that Mr Hill has suggested, however loosely, a very plausible relationship, that he has done so with telling erudition, and that his point will now need to be seriously considered in any attempt to explain the division of seventeenth-century society.

Mr Hill's evidence about both 'Baconians' and 'Parliamentarians' is nevertheless much more equivocal than his conclusions seem to suppose. It is not at all clear, in the first place, what it means to be a 'Baconian.' If the title can be extended to place a man like Sir Edward Coke on the same side, it begins to seem an extremely slack shorthand for describing men with 'scientific' interests. Mr Hill's own procedures, indeed, for establishing Bacon's 'influence' seem far from strict. To be a 'Baconian,' in nearly half of the cases cited by Mr Hill, means to have been claimed and discussed as a 'Baconian' by some modern scholar.

But this is no longer to conduct a properly historical argument. For someone, moreover, as censorious as Mr Hill can be about the presuppositions of other scholars, this is to rely on other scholars' work to an extent very difficult to justify.

It is also not at all clear, even with the confessed 'Baconians,' even with Bacon himself, how meaningful it is to claim them as 'Parliamentarian.' Consider, for example, the case of that prominent 'Baconian' Sir William Petty, cited by Mr Hill a dozen times as a man with all the elements of a 'Parliamentarian,' cited with John Graunt as 'puritans and Parliamentarians as well as Baconians and Fellows of the Royal Society.' One still needs to know, to put it crudely, what any of this could possibly have to do with the Parliamentary 'side' of the English revolution. Petty was still a boy when the Long Parliament met, and anyway spent the time of the civil war abroad. The 'puritan' Petty, moreover, was educated by the Jesuits and died something like a sceptic, while the 'puritan' Graunt was a roman catholic.

Most disturbingly, the alleged 'Parliamentarian' commitment does not seem to hold even for Mr Hill's own selected figures. Bacon makes an odd member of the Parliamentarian 'side' in the Revolution, since he was all his life (as he remarked to James I) a 'perfect and peremptory' royalist, and anyway died fifteen years before the outbreak of the revolution. Ralegh (who died even sooner) makes an even odder candidate. He may well, as Mr Hill claims, have been associated with the alchemical tradition which may in turn have had radical political affiliations. But this is hardly to provide proof of political (still less, one might feel, of 'scientific') commitment. He may well have attacked monopolies 'on several occasions.' But this did not prevent him from holding some of the most notorious monopolies himself.

It is difficult in general to feel at all convinced by Mr Hill's claim that Coke, Bacon and Ralegh have 'curiously much in common'. Only Bacon was a practising scientist. Bacon hated Coke, and got him dismissed in 1616 from King's Bench; Coke hated Ralegh, and attacked him bitterly in 1618 at his trial. They seem to me, on the contrary, three extremely odd heroes to bracket together on the same 'side' in anything, let alone to help explain anything as momentous as the upheaval of English society.

As an attempt to explain the ideological component of the English revolution Mr Hill's work strikes me as slack and partial. As a pioneering attempt, however, to suggest the methods and the significance of such a general study it must be regarded as an important as well as a courageous undertaking. There is pioneering in the whole conception of the book, which synthesises and makes relevant an enormous amount of detailed findings by many scholars in fields too often left in isolation. There is pioneering in many of Mr Hill's own discussions, which keep showing how much work is still to be done. Discussions about London science, for example, are still hampered by the fact that there is no modern history of Gresham College. Discussions about Ralegh's work are similarly hampered as there is still no critical edition of his works, no guide for distinguishing what is genuine among the vast corpus of work attributed to him. The merits of Mr Hill's study may not be those of careful proof, but he has all the merits of a daring pioneer, and they are undoubtedly more exciting. He raises more points than he begins to answer, but he does so with an enthusiasm which demands further and serious discussion of the claims he makes, and with a range which guarantees for his own contribution a place of paramount importance in any such discussion.

May 22nd, 1965

3

Philosophy and the Social Sciences

Sidgwick and the Old Ethics

G. E. MOORE

The attentive reader of this book should be convinced that almost all the principles, which have been enunciated with the greatest emphasis by Green, and Spencer and Martineau, are either false or utterly unfounded.* As much as this Professor Sidgwick proves conclusively. Unless, however, the reader is very attentive, he will probably be convinced of nothing. And, even if he has been convinced of what Professor Sidgwick proves, he will be left in great perplexity. If what Professor Sidgwick says be true (and it is true), what are we to think of the ethical works of Green, and Spencer and Martineau? Can those works have any value whatsoever?

Miss Jones tells us in the Preface that 'Professor Sidgwick came to regard the Transcendentalist and Evolutionist schools as the principal rivals in contemporary English Ethics of his own system,' and that the lectures on Green and Spencer 'are an examination, expository and critical, of the views of Transcendental or "Idealist" and Evolutional Ethics, as put forth by their most distinguished exponents.' Now there can be no doubt that these two schools are those which have now-a-days the greatest number of followers; nor that Green and Spencer are at all events *among* their most distinguished representatives. We might, therefore, hope to discover from these lectures what are the views which distinguish the two great schools of modern Ethics, and why we ought not to hold those views. But what we do find is only that we ought not to hold a number of views to which Green and Spencer give prominence; and that Professor Sidgwick is right on a number of points on which they thought him to be wrong. That all these details have *some* bearing on moral philosophy we may see for ourselves: but what bearing they have, how they are related to one another, and which among them are the most important, Professor Sidgwick scarcely helps us to see at all. That we must not hold certain views which Green and Spencer *thought* to be important is plain

---

* *Lectures on the Ethics of T. H. Green, Mr. Herbert Spencer and J. Martineau.* By Henry Sidgwick.

enough; but whether, in spite of this, Evolutionism and Idealism, or even Green and Spencer themselves, may not be right on points that are *really* the most important, we are given no means of deciding.

Professor Sidgwick takes in succession the main divisions of the works criticised, and points out many things that are ambiguous and doubtful and false in each division. He does thus shew us incidentally what is the right view on almost every single point that is likely to occur to the student of Ethics—the more as well as the less important. It *does* follow from what he says that Green, and Spencer and Martineau have not given a single sound reason for believing any ethical proposition: but he has not shewn that this follows.

The book was not prepared for publication by Professor Sidgwick himself. It merely consists of the lectures which for some years he used to deliver annually as his course on Ethics.

November 20th, 1902

Principia Ethica*

AN UNSIGNED REVIEW

Mr Moore's book, short as it is, has an importance which is in no degree to be measured by its bulk. It is written throughout in a simple style, unencumbered by technical terms, and so lucid as to be intelligible to every educated person. Except in a few controversial passages, no previous knowledge of philosophy is required of the reader. But in spite of this, no question is shirked, and the fundamental problems of Ethics are discussed with a thoroughness unsurpassed in the literature of the subject. Mr Moore has inaugurated a revolution, as salutary as it is important, by abandoning the usual resolve of philosophers to uphold, at all costs, some sweeping general principle which is to be adapted to the facts by more or less legitimate ingenuity. Instead of this deductive and dogmatic system-building, the reader will find here a careful and constant questioning of common sense, a deference in detail to ethical intuitions, which render this work extraordinarily living and real.

* *Principia Ethica.* By G. E. Moore, Cambridge.

On the title-page there is a motto from Bishop Butler: 'Everything is what it is, and not another thing.' This simple truism is shown to have been violated by the vast majority of ethical writers, who have been unable to believe that good is really good, but have thought that it must be something else—pleasure, or the life according to nature, or self-realization. They have thought that in so defining *good* they were giving the actual meaning of the word, and have failed to perceive that, if they were right, it would be an empty tautology to say that the things in question were good. This mistake is called by Mr Moore 'the naturalistic fallacy.' From the long list of those who have committed it, Professor Sidgwick forms an exception: he recognized that good must be indefinable. Mr Moore reinforces this position by many interesting and convincing arguments, and is able, by means of it, to demolish most of the reasons which philosophers have given in support of their beliefs.

Professor Sidgwick held, nevertheless, that pleasure can be seen to be the sole good, though he disagreed with most Hedonists in recognizing that this could not be proved. Mr Moore undertakes to refute this doctrine, by pointing out that it has consequences repugnant to common sense and not explicitly accepted by advocates of the doctrine. To those who are at the beginning of ethical speculations, the doctrine that pleasure alone is good *per se* is very plausible; but the more its implications are developed, the less plausible it becomes. The habit of defending a system, however, so quickly deteriorates the power of seeing facts, that it is very difficult to shake the beliefs of those who have become accustomed to view everything through the distorting medium of theory, and this makes Mr Moore's book more difficult to trained philosophers than to unbiassed readers.

Mr Moore's discussion of Ethics in relation to Conduct turns mainly on the distinction between means and end, between what is good for its own sake and what is merely a cause of something good. We are all so much occupied with practice and with reflection on the consequences of our acts, that it becomes difficult to make the mind dwell upon the things that are good merely because they are good, and not because of any ulterior effects. Most people, in praising anything, feel bound to point out that it is beneficial, *i.e.*, that good things other than itself will be brought into existence by it. It is part of the business of Ethics to direct our attention to the things that are good on their own account, and to make us realize that right conduct is that which is likely to have the results which are intrinsically the best. It is true that some conduct is good as an end; but it would seem that such conduct can always be defended as also a means to good. It may be doubted, however, whether Mr Moore is right in saying that what we ought to do is always what will have the best consequences. If we have no means of knowing that one course will have the best consequences, while all the knowledge we can have points to another course, then, though this other course should in fact prove disastrous, it seems that we do right in adopting it. Mr Moore objects that it can never be a pity for a man to do his duty, and certainly to say that it can is a paradox. But the paradoxes resulting from his view are apparently still more shocking.

Perhaps the best chapter, and certainly the most interesting, is the last, on the Ideal. Mr Moore explains that he means by the Ideal all those things which are good as ends in a high degree. He holds that, of the things we know, the best are the enjoyment of beauty and the personal relations of admiration and affection. Many people would be inclined, perhaps rightly, to place certain virtues, and even certain kinds of virtuous action, quite on a level with the goods which Mr Moore thinks the best. It is always difficult, however, in the case of virtuous actions, to separate clearly our admiration of the action from our admiration of the state of mind which it indicates; and the greatest virtues appear to consist of the love of things which are good in them-selves. Nevertheless, when all due allowance has been made for this source of confusion, there seems still to remain a great good for which not enough place is made in Mr Moore's enumeration.

Apart from this objection, it is impossible to praise too highly the subtle and yet lucid analysis of the various elements in the value of the goods discussed. Great use is made of a principle called by the author the principle of 'organic unities,' without which no theoretical views as to the relative values of different good or bad things can avoid being plainly erroneous. According to this principle, the value of a whole is not necessarily the same as the sum of the values of its parts. For example, a beautiful object unseen has little or no value, and admiration of an ugly object, even if the emotion is exactly like admiration of a beautiful one, is on the whole positively bad. Thus in the admiration of a beautiful object, which is certainly good, it is neither the object nor the emotion which makes the whole good: it is the whole as such, namely, the emotion towards an appropriate object, which has value.

It would seem even that dislike of what is ugly is rather good, although in this case both the dislike and the ugly object, if not in themselves indifferent, are rather bad. This explains why people prize good taste, even when they admit that it does not increase the enjoyment, or diminish the pain, to be derived from works of art or from barrel organs.

Thus it is essential to the excellence of aesthetic emotions that they should be directed towards objects which have beauty. Mr Moore discusses the effects upon the value of the whole which result from adding a true or false belief that the object is beautiful, and here he distinguishes two possible kinds of error, namely (1) the belief that the object has qualities which are beautiful, but which, as a matter of fact, it does not have; (2) the belief that qualities which it does have are beautiful, when as a matter of fact they are ugly. Of these errors the second is the more lamentable. Mr Moore also discusses the effect on value of a true or false belief that the object exists; this is a most interesting question upon which turns the relative value of nature and landscape-painting, or of history and romance. From all these discussions it results that the very high value we attach to knowledge of the truth is to be justified, not chiefly by the intrinsic value of knowledge *per se*, but by the fact that knowledge is an ingredient which adds greatly to the value of some of the best wholes, whereas false belief will often render otherwise excellent wholes worthless. The whole discussion of this and kindred topics is beyond praise; and it is very much to be hoped, for the sake of the educated public, that it will not fail to become acquainted with Mr Moore's brilliant and profound inquiry.

December 3rd, 1903

On Logic, And How Not to Do It

LUDWIG WITTGENSTEIN

In no branch of learning can an author disregard the results of honest research with so much impunity as he can in Philosophy and Logic. To this circumstance we owe the publication of such a book as Mr Coffey's *Science of Logic*: and only as a typical example of the

work of many logicians of to-day does this book deserve consideration.* The author's Logic is that of the scholastic philosophers, and he
makes all their mistakes—of course with the usual references to
Aristotle. (Aristotle, whose name is so much taken in vain by our
logicians, would turn in his grave if he knew that so many logicians
know no more about Logic to-day than he did 2,000 years ago.) The
author has not taken the slightest notice of the great work of the modern
mathematical logicians—work which has brought about an advance
in Logic comparable only to that which made Astronomy out of
Astrology, and Chemistry out of Alchemy.

Mr Coffey, like many logicians, draws a great advantage from an
unclear way of expressing himself; for if you cannot tell whether he
means to say 'Yes' or 'No,' it is difficult to argue against him. However, even through his foggy expression, many grave mistakes can be
recognised clearly enough; and I propose to give a list of some of the
most striking ones, and would advise the student of Logic to trace these
mistakes and their consequences in other books on Logic also. (The
numbers in brackets indicate the pages of Mr Coffey's book—volume
I.—where a mistake occurs for the first time; the illustrative examples
are my own.)

I. [36] The author believes that all propositions are of the subject-
predicate form.

II. [31] He believes that reality is changed by becoming an object
of our thoughts.

III. [6] He confounds the copula 'is' with the word 'is' expressing
identity. (The word 'is' has obviously different meanings in the propositions—

'Twice two is four'
and 'Socrates is mortal.')

IV. [46] He confounds things with the classes to which they belong.
(A man is obviously something quite different from mankind.)

V. [48] He confounds classes and complexes. (Mankind is a class
whose elements are men; but a library is not a class whose elements are
books, because books become parts of a library only by standing in
certain spatial relations to one another—while classes are independent
of the relations between their members.)

* *The Science of Logic*: an inquiry into the principles of accurate thought and scientific
method. By P. Coffey, Ph.D.

VI. [47] He confounds complexes and sums. (Two plus two is four, but four is not a complex of two and itself.)

This list of mistakes could be extended a good deal.

The worst of such books as this is that they prejudice sensible people against the study of Logic.

March 6th, 1913

Bergson on Metaphysics and Intuition

BERTRAND RUSSELL

This little book is a translation, revised by M. Bergson, of an article which appeared in the 'Revue de Métaphysique et de Morale' in 1903, before 'Creative Evolution,' but after 'Matter and Memory.'* The translation is excellent: so far as I have verified it, I have found only two points in which it differs from the original, namely, on p. 5 the translation has 'extraordinarily simple' where the original has merely 'simple,' and on p. 77 it has 'infinitely simple' where the original has 'simplicity itself.' The work well deserves translation, since it affords an admirable 'Introduction to [M. Bergson's] Metaphysics.'

The one topic dealt with is the nature of 'intuition,' and the way in which it differs from 'intellect.' In the first paragraph we are told that there are 'two profoundly different ways of knowing a thing. The first implies that we move round an object; the second that we enter into it.' The difference between the two lies chiefly in the fact that the first involves analysis, while the second does not. Analysis, according to M. Bergson, consists essentially in the mention of qualities which the object analysed appears to share with other objects, whereas, since everything is in truth unique, description by qualities which may be shared is description by what is external and not really characteristic. Although it is, of course, true that every object is, in a certain sense, unique, the use which M. Bergson makes of this fact to discredit analysis does not seem justified. Like most enemies of analysis, and like

---

* *An Introduction to Metaphysics.* By Henri Bergson, Member of the Institute, Professor at the Collège de France. Authorised Translation by T. E. Hulme.

I

the older empiricist supporters of analysis, he invariably assumes that in analysing no account is to be taken of the *relations* of the parts.

'Suppose I am shown,' he says, 'the letters which make up a poem I am ignorant of. If the letters were *parts* of the poem, I could attempt to reconstitute the poem with them by trying the different possible arrangements, as a child does with the pieces of a Chinese puzzle. But I should never for a moment think of attempting such a thing in this case, because the letters are not *component parts*, but only *partial expressions*, which is quite a different thing.'

But as an argument against analysis, this is wholly fallacious. A complete analysis would mention also the *order* of the letters, and then the difficulty would disappear. The letters A, R, T, for example, do not constitute a complete analysis of the word 'art'; they may equally form the word 'rat' or the word 'tar.' But if we are told further that A is to come before R, and R before T, the analysis is complete and the word is no longer doubtful. Exactly the same answer applies to M. Bergson's objections to the analysis of motion into a series of positions in a certain temporal order. He assumes always that the analysis retains only the positions, and ignores the time-relations which give the order. Hence he is led to regard motion as indivisible and ultimate, and moving things as fictions. 'All reality, therefore, is tendency, if we agree to mean by tendency an incipient change of direction.' He regards his view as the only alternative to the opinion that rest is more real than motion, that 'there is more in the immutable than in the moving' —an opinion which he attributes to Plato, and regards as infecting, more or less, every philosophy except his own. It is natural to the intellect, he says, to seek out the likenesses among processes, to ignore what is unique and therefore unpredictable, and to divide movements embodying a single impulse into parts which are purely fictitious. If we wish to become philosophers, we must resist this vice of the intellect. 'To philosophize,' he says, 'is to invert the habitual direction of the work of thought.' But if a philosopher is to persuade us of so momentous a thesis, he must first persuade us that he knows what is relevant in 'the work of thought.' M. Bergson does not persuade us of this. The nature of analysis, the mathematical theory of motion, the difference between predication and division into parts, are matters upon which it is vitally necessary to him to understand the best that his opponents can say. So far from such an understanding, however,

we find, in his accounts of the views he is combating, a mere jumble
of antiquated ideas acquired in youth and never revised. It may be that
something could be said for his philosophy even by one who knew
what is to be said against it; but such knowledge is closed to M. Bergson
by the habit of rhetoric and intellectual impatience from which few
philosophers have been exempt.

April 17th, 1913

Whitehead on Nature[*]

J. ELLIS MCTAGGART

This seems to be one of the most valuable books on the relation
of philosophy and science which has appeared for many years. To a
certain extent it covers the same ground as the author's *Principles of
Natural Knowledge*. But there is much that is new, and also the treatment
is rather different. As the writer explains in the preface: 'whereas the
former work based itself chiefly on ideas directly drawn from mathematical physics, the present book keeps closer to certain fields of
philosophy and physics to the exclusion of mathematics.'

Dr Whitehead defines the field of his enquiry with admirable clearness. 'Nature is that which we observe in perception through the
senses.' We can think about nature without thinking about thoughts.
In this case we may be said to think 'homogeneously' about nature. It
is to this that Dr Whitehead confines himself. 'Science,' he tells us
elsewhere, 'is not discussing the causes of knowledge, but the coherence
of knowledge.' And he protests against the bifurcation of nature into
two systems of reality, of which one 'would be the entities such as
electrons which are the study of speculative physics. This would be
the reality which is there for knowledge; although on this theory it is
never proven. For what is known is the other sort of reality, which is
the by-play of the mind. Thus there would be two natures, one is the
conjecture and the other is the dream.'

Dr Whitehead does not exclude the possibility that part of what he
classes as nature may be the work of mind. Or, rather, he only excludes

---

[*] *The Concept of Nature*. (Tarner Lectures delivered in Trinity College). By A. N.
Whitehead, Sc.D., F.R.S.

it from the philosophy of science, as being a question of general meta-physics. His limitation is conscious and deliberate. 'The boundary,' he tells us, 'is set up just where the philosopher is beginning to get excited.' The limitation and distinction appear to me to be extremely wise. The ultimate questions fall—must fall—within metaphysics. But, besides metaphysics, there would also be a philosophy of science. Much con-fusion of thought has often risen by the confusion of the two subjects. It is one of the great merits of Dr Whitehead's work that he separates them so clearly.

I have no space to give even a brief analysis of the book as a whole, and can only make a brief reference to the chapter on Einstein's work. Dr Whitehead accepts the main principles of this, but does not accept 'the theory of non-uniform space on the assumptions as to the peculiar fundamental character of light signals.' He makes a distinction between 'the creative advance of nature, which is not properly serial at all ... which we experience and know as the perpetual transition of nature into novelty,' and any like series. I have a conviction that in this dis-tinction lies the way to a solution of many difficulties which to an amateur like myself appear to beset the theory of Einstein. But Dr Whitehead on this point remains rather cryptic.

I am sure the study of this book will benefit metaphysicians. I ven-ture to believe that it will benefit men of science.

October 21st, 1921

Oakeshott and the Modes of Experience*

R. G. COLLINGWOOD

'*Experience* stands for the concrete whole which analysis divides into *experiencing* and *what is experienced*'; and experience is not mere consciousness, it is also and always thought, judgment, assertion of reality: there is no sensation which is not also thought, no intuition which is not also judgment, no volition which is not also cognition: these, like the subject-object distinction, are distinctions valid in them-selves but erroneous if taken as implying a real division between the

* *Experience and its Modes*. By Michael Oakeshott.

elements distinguished. Experience, thus conceived, may be pictured as an infinite ocean or endlessly-flowing river; and to navigate its waters, conscious of their infinity, is to philosophise; for philosophy, alone among forms of experience, is identical with experience itself, 'experience without reservation or arrest, without presupposition or postulate, without limit or category.'

But experience may be 'modified' by arresting it at this or that point, and there, using the point of arrest as an inviolable postulate, constructing a 'world of ideas' in terms of this postulate. Such a world of ideas is not a constituent element in experience, not a reach of the river, but a backwater of the river, a digression from the unreserved flow of experience; but it is not a 'world of mere ideas,' it is not only coherent in itself but is a special way of presenting experience as a whole: not *a* world, but *the* world as seen from that point of view, and, subject to that qualification, rightly seen. Such a world is a 'mode' of experience. There are many such modes; theoretically their number is infinite; but none is inevitable; every one of them, in so far as the arrest of experience at that point is unjustified, rests on a foundation of error, and the concrete world of experience is achieved by avoiding them all.

Such, though sadly travestied by this clumsy compression of his statement, is Mr Oakeshott's main conception; from which he proceeds to examples by a survey of three modes: history, science and practice. Each of these is a complete and self-contained world; not a part of experience, but experience itself as organised and envisaged under one peculiar category. History is the world *sub specie praeteritorum*: its differentia is the attempt to organize the whole world of experience in the form of the past. Science is the world *sub specie quantitatis*: its differentia is the attempt to organize the world of experience as a system of measurements. Practice is the world *sub specie voluntatis*: the world as a system of acts, each modifying 'what is' so as to bring it into harmony with what ought to be.

I have tried to expound Mr Oakeshott's thesis rather than criticise it, because it is so original, so important, and so profound that criticism must be silent until his meaning has been long pondered. Nor is the thesis an essay in system-building copied (as his modest expressions of indebtedness might possibly suggest) from Hegel and Bradley. It has been arrived at, I suspect, mainly from an intense effort to understand the nature of historical knowledge. Mr Oakeshott writes of history like an accomplished historian who, driven into philosophy by the problems of his own work, has found the current philosophies impotent to cope with their philosophical implications; and in that sense the chapter on history seems to me the real nucleus of his book. Of this chapter, I can, in this brief notice, only say that it is the most penetrating analysis of historical thought that has ever been written, and will remain a classic in that hitherto almost unexplored branch of philosophical research. But the whole book shows Mr Oakeshott to possess philosophical gifts of a very high order, coupled with an admirable command of language; his writing is as clear as his thought is profound, and all students of philosophy should be grateful to him for his brilliant contribution to philosophical literature.

February 16th, 1934

Dialectical Materialism: An 'Official Philosophy'

MICHAEL OAKESHOTT

Dialectical Materialism is described by those who profess it as the official philosophy of modern Communism; and this at once indicates its unique character, and makes any fresh exposition of its principles a matter of some general interest. Professor Macmurray, in one of the essays which compose this attempt to expound once more the notions of Dialectical Materialism,* says that 'there is something fundamental in the philosophy of Dialectical Materialism which distinguishes it from all other philosophical systems which I know, and which establishes a gulf between it and them.' But he understates the case: Dialectical Materialism has more than one characteristic peculiar to itself, and the idiosyncrasy of being an official philosophy is the most peculiar of them all. To anyone who has attended to the history of philosophy this claim to an official character must appear a little naïve; even an indiscretion, when we consider how often the 'reception' of a philosophy has been a symptom of its decay. An official

---

* *Aspects of Dialectical Materialism.* By H. Levy, J. Macmurray, R. Fox, R. Page Arnot, J. D. Bernal and E. F. Carritt.

religion, or an official art, perhaps; these are not absurd ideas: but a received and an official philosophy, surely this is a little too heroic. Yet Dialectical Materialism boasts an imprimatur: and its defenders will not hear of it being anything but a philosophy, *the* philosophy; they will not tolerate the suggestion that perhaps it would be better to describe it as a religious creed.

And this characteristic is not without implications. The reckless courage with which this philosophy is defended, the jealousy with which the teaching of its inspired Early Fathers, Marx and Engels, is guarded against change and contamination, the violence with which all competing prophets are hustled out, like profane hecklers at a political meeting, must make a mere thinker wonder whether his life is not after all too insipid, and a religious fanatic whether he can really be sincere, such is his moderation. It is remarkable how often in these essays a writer will turn aside from argument with the incantation, 'Let us quote the *Communist Manifesto* again' or, 'As Marx himself says.' Mr Bernal's essays might have been written by Engels himself; his exposition is not even fresh in parts, it is uniformly stale. Indeed, the reader is left with the impression that Marx is the only *thinker* who has ever handled this philosophy of Dialectical Materialism; the rest are humble servants of the message of this often ambiguous oracle. In the hands of its expositors Dialectical Materialism is like a theology turned into a gospel, and a gospel turned into a dogma.

It appears to be more necessary that we should believe than that we should understand, and more necessary that we should accept than that we should believe. And this, perhaps, is comprehensible; if one really believed that one was in possession of the truth, it might be difficult to avoid fanaticism. But a philosophy, at once official and fanatical! Is there no refuge from the preacher?

Besides these, Dialectical Materialism, has, I think, three other remarkable characteristics which, if they are not unique, are at least noticeably peculiar. First, it is a philosophy constructed, with the aid of certain borrowed philosophical ideas, by men who were as nearly devoid of the *anima naturaliter philosophica* as otherwise thoughtful and intelligent men could be. Mr Page Arnot, it is true, tells us that 'Marx was the greatest thinker of all time,' and Mr Bernal, that Marx 'was not, in contrast to the founders of most philosophical systems, an ignorant man'; but whatever his greatness and however profound his information, there is nothing in his writings to suggest that he possessed that peculiar, and in some ways lamentable, turn of mind which makes a philosopher.

And he certainly never inspired genuine philosophical thought in anyone else. Some of the authors of this book are, indeed, professional philosophers, but even these (with the exception of Mr Carritt) appear anxious to discard some of the most elementary principles of rational argument. In the main, however, these expositors are amateurs in this difficult and dangerous enterprise of managing philosophical ideas. Secondly, Dialectical Materialism is an esoteric philosophy. I suppose the tendency to make the rules of the game in the course of play is not uncommon in philosophy, and in so far as it prevails in any philosophy that philosophy becomes esoteric. And this tendency is present to a remarkable extent in Dialectical Materialism. It is difficult, moreover, for the detached reader of this, or any exposition of the principles of Dialectical Materialism not to become conscious of the existence of some hidden source of knowledge or inspiration which, if only he were privileged to share it, might make plain much that must otherwise remain obscure. He is, in fact, told that unless he is 'actively participating in the class struggle to-day,' he will certainly fail to understand. This philosophy is one for initiates only. And further, in the actual doctrine of Dialectical Materialism there is a remarkable esoteric flavour; like the 'philosophical' theologians of the Seventeenth century, the expositors of this philosophy seem to move in a world composed of an unbroken system of subtle correspondences. The same rhythmic motion or 'dialectic' governs the history of man, the chemical composition and changes of the world, the properties of numbers and everything else. These writers pass from one region of existence to another to find everywhere the transition of Quantity into Quality, Opposites Interpenetrating, and the Negative being Negated. What happens in one place has its analogue in another; in Dialectical Materialism the primitive passion for analogy is almost unchecked, and the result is a mystical and esoteric philosophy which can be paralleled perhaps only in the writings of the alchemists.

And thirdly, what must already be apparent, Dialectical Materialism is a philosophy more hindered and obscured by jargon than any other in the whole history of misplaced human ingenuity. One of the more critical writers in this book, Mr Levy, remarks upon the 'almost mediaeval language' in which the laws of the Dialectic are described. And it is difficult to avoid the feeling, as one reads these expositions, that, whatever there is to be said for this philosophy, the language in which it is described and defended is hopelessly stilted and archaic. The quaint jargon of Dialectical Materialism is, of all the defects of this philosophy, the one which might most easily be remedied, and is the defect from the remedy of which it would, at the present time, derive the greatest possible benefit. But to relieve a philosophy of the incubus of a jargon and to make it live requires a thinker, and such is nowhere to be seen.

Unlike many expositions of Dialectical Materialism, this book contains two essays in which this philosophy is subjected to something like a critical examination; both Mr Levy and Mr Carritt possess something of the detachment of mind necessary in philosophical argument. But Mr Carritt, at least, does not remain unanswered; for the volume ends with some Notes in Reply to Mr Carritt's Paper, in which Mr Bernal reasserts the pure Marxian principles in the old, decayed jargon and with the old, heroic violence. It seems that it is impossible for an intelligent man to take exception to any of the principles of Dialectical Materialism, because, unavoidably, he will find that what he has been objecting to is not the true doctrine, but merely one of the numerous 'distortions' which the authentic philosophy has suffered at the hands of bourgeois writers who have strayed into the Communist camp. The Marxian principle appears to be not merely that he who is not for us is against us, but also that most of the writers who think they are orthodox have, through malice, inadvertence or ignorance, promulgated a false (that is heterodox) doctrine. *Intelligent* objection is impossible. It is not difficult to understand that a critical attitude to a religion or a political creed is something which may have to be discouraged or even forbidden, but that this attitude towards what represents itself as a philosophy should be discouraged is at once ridiculous and pathetic. And a philosophy, the followers of which spend most of their time and energy merely quarrelling about the meaning of what Marx wrote and said, is one which is difficult to take seriously. For Heaven's sake, the reader gasps, let us have a little more argument and a little less oracular assertion.

Dialectical Materialism is already notorious for the generalisations about the course of history which are imbedded in its doctrines. And more than one of these essays illustrates both the importance of these generalisations to his philosophy and the extreme danger of such an alliance between philosophy and history. The doctrine that every philosophy is conditioned by the general social and economic circumstances in which it is conceived and elaborated, and the doctrine that a 'true' philosophy is that which is most closely tied and tied most consciously to the circumstances of its generation, and consequently that Dialectical Materialism is the only 'true' philosophy to-day, naturally lead those who hold them to issue statements about the course of history. And indeed, this philosophy may be said to be actually based upon certain historical judgments and to stand or fall with this truth or falsehood of these judgments. We are told, for example, that 'the modern European problem is a material problem. At least from the time of the Renaissance, European humanity, as distinct from most other societies at other times in history and in other parts of the world, has had forced upon it for its special task for humanity the solution of the problem of economic production'; and that consequently 'materialism' is the 'proper starting place for philosophy under modern conditions.'

And yet, setting aside the confusion of thought which stands behind this notion of philosophy *conditioned* by economic and social circumstances, how vague and flimsy is this sort of historical judgment. Certainly some of Marx's most profound ideas are concerned with history, but none of these writers show either any considerable knowledge of the history of Western Europe or any grasp of how an historical problem should be tackled. A statement such as, 'if we consider the development of science we shall find that it falls into three successive stages,' if it is intended for an historical judgment, shows all the ineptitude and misconception which might be expected from a philosophaster when he turns to history. The analysis of an idea is substituted for a patient and detailed exploration of a period, and history in any true sense disappears. It is *possible*, of course, to analyse any considerable historical change into the three steps which the Dialectic presupposes, and perhaps it is possible also to find Quantity turning into Quality, and the Negative being Negated, but if you think that in such an analysis you are providing a history, or a substitute for a history, of this change, you must be more than ordinarily foolish. The dialectical materialist would appear to know so much about history and the world in general without recourse to any real study of the facts of the case that it is not, perhaps, surprising that he should treat these facts with some contempt. After all, his business is merely to illustrate his general theory by finding it everywhere exemplified in the world, and in that he can scarcely fail.

This reiteration of the principles of dialectical materialism, then, leaves us with the impression that it is impossible to say anything about them which is at once new and true; it is neither possible nor necessary to do anything but repeat what Marx and Engels wrote. The philosophy is full of ingenious ideas, and imbedded in it are some profound and illuminating *aperçus*; but the whole temper and attitude of its followers is so unphilosophical, so rigid, certain and insensitive, and its doctrines are so full of half-considered information and so devoid of thought, that it must be supposed that the best there is to be said for it remains yet unsaid. Unless it can escape from this temper, from the tendency to descend from argument to authority, from the antiquated jargon in which it is expressed, from the inclination to indulge in the wildest exaggerations, and from certain obvious but disabling errors in its most flourished doctrines, it will never become a philosophical system worth considering. It will remain the creed of a body of men who, not content with doing what they believe will bring the greatest possible benefit to mankind, and regardless of their incapacity, are moved by a fatal urge to construct a theory to explain and justify their activities.

November 16th, 1934

Collingwood's Philosophy of Art*

MICHAEL OAKESHOTT

Since I doubt my capacity to give in this review any adequate and convincing impression of the value and importance of this book, I can do no better than state at once that it is the most profound and stimulating discussion I have ever read of the question, What is art? The field of aesthetic enquiry has not, indeed, been barren up till now, but this book gives us so much that it is difficult for us to persuade ourselves of the value of what we had before. It is the work of an artist and a philosopher; it is written with a charm and a vigour which matches the subtlety and sanity of its doctrine; and it leaves the reader

* *The Principles of Art.* By R. G. Collingwood.

with the impression that he has been in touch with a mind of altogether exceptional learning, tact and penetration. All these are qualities that we have learned to expect from the work of Professor Collingwood; anyone who had read *Speculum Mentis* or *An Essay on Philosophical Method* would open this book anticipating a brilliant performance, but here is something even better than he could have expected. It is a delight to witness the masterly unfolding of its argument; it is equally a delight to follow the author when he steps aside from the exposition of his main thesis to reinterpret Plato's remarks on art, to expose the 'quibbles and sophistries' of Freud's views on magic or to give us his reflections on the condition of art yesterday and to-day.

'The business of this book is to answer the question: What is art?' It is not, however, an attempt 'to investigate and expound eternal verities concerning the nature of an eternal object called Art,' but an attempt to deal with the problems which force themselves upon anyone 'who looks round at the present condition of the arts in our own civilization.' It is the attempt of an artist and an historian, fortified by the critical mind of a philosopher, to make clear to himself the nature of art and the conditions of its life in the world to-day. Anyone who begins to cultivate this field will find in it a luxuriant growth of weeds, and there is plenty of hard hitting in this book; but of carping criticism the reader will find nothing.

The method of exposition, which is also a method of thought, which Professor Collingwood pursues, may be called a Socratic method. First, without any suggestion of a theory, he tries to disentangle what, as a matter of fact, we all know about art, in the belief that the truth is to be found *in* what we all know about it, though often that truth is not exactly what we at first take it to be. This leaves us with a number of philosophical questions to be investigated, because in stating what we all know about art we make use of words and expressions—sensation, thought, emotion, language—which call for analysis. Lastly, there comes the construction of a Theory of Art, a synthesis of the truths which have emerged and established themselves in the earlier discussions. And it may be said that not the least of the delights of this book is its masterly handling of this method.

The argument begins, then, with an attempt to distinguish Art from not Art, to make certain that we know how to apply the word 'art' where it ought to be applied and refuse where it ought to be refused. And it leads to the rejection of certain things which, though they are often confused with art, have a character different from that of art. These are craft or skill, magic and amusement. The confusion of these things with art is dangerous because it has led, in each case, to a false aesthetic theory and to the perversion of art itself. These opening chapters admirably display Professor Collingwood's acute critical mind and are among the best in the book. But destruction is followed by construction, and art proper is shown to have two characteristics: expression of emotion and imagination. And the conclusion of this first inspection of the subject is that 'by creating for ourselves an imaginary experience or activity we express our emotions; and this is what we call art.'

But 'what this formula means, we do not yet know.' And in order to find out we must penetrate a world of philosophical analysis, consider the nature of sensation, feeling, thought and emotion and the nature of language. This, for the ordinary reader, will be the most difficult part of the book; but he need not be afraid of it, for the doctrines are expounded so lucidly that all but the absolutely unavoidable difficulties are absent.

The last part of the book, consisting of three chapters—Art as Language, Art and Truth, and The Artist and the Community—contains the final expression of his theory of art. It would be stupid here to attempt any exposition of the doctrine, and worse to offer any criticism of matters of detail. The value of the book does not depend upon our being convinced by the doctrine (though I myself find it singularly convincing); it lies in the experience it offers of following a masterly discussion of all the fundamental questions which any doctrine must consider. And Professor Collingwood's concluding reflections on the condition and future of art in England are of exceptional interest.

This is not the sort of book that has to be recommended with the qualification that the hard labour entailed in reading it will be rewarded in the end; the reader is rewarded on every page. If there is anyone who, because of the nonsense he has been obliged to read, doubts whether a philosopher can talk sense about art, let him read this book. It has something to offer anyone interested in literature or art; it is a book in which, for example, anyone engaged in the study of literature in a University will find illumination. And it is a book which anyone who can take pleasure in a profound and critical piece of philosophical thinking will find a delight.

June 9th, 1938

Wisdom's Guide on
How to Think

R. B. BRAITHWAITE

Mr Wisdom celebrates his translation from a philosophical lectureship at St Andrews to one at Cambridge by publishing a guide on how to think, in the manner he had learned at Cambridge under Professor Moore, upon problems some of which have particularly interested St Andrews.* As he says in his preface, 'an attempt is made to give an elementary but not too inaccurate introduction to the applications in philosophy of what is now sometimes called the analytic method'; and this is to be done, not 'by explaining the nature of analysis,' but by giving 'elementary examples of its *use*.' He has succeeded admirably in his purpose: in his 200 pages he gives an excellent idea of the method of attacking and type of solution of philosophic problems which have commended themselves to some of the best contemporary philosophers. Mr Wisdom has a gift for expressing abstract matters both accurately and tersely; and he has not disdained to summarise the facts of psychology and physiology which are relevant to the problems he is discussing. [I was shocked to read that there were no *perceptible* changes in sensory nerves in sensation (p. 48) until I discovered that Mr Wisdom meant by 'not perceptible,' 'not visible through a microscope'!]. Thus the book is very well suited for those who come to philosophy for the solution of intellectual problems; and as a primer I class it immediately after Bertrand Russell's *Problems of Philosophy*.

The book opens with thirty pages of introduction in which the differences between analytic and speculative philosophy are illustrated, and in which an 'analytic vocabulary' is introduced. Mr Wisdom uses as few technical terms as possible, and illuminates them by happy examples and metaphors (e.g. 'in the fact the universal colours the particular, and the particular energises the universal.') The next seventy pages deal with the traditional problems of the relation of body and mind with special reference to their treatment in Professor Stout's *Mind and Matter*. Besides throwing light on a very difficult book, Mr Wisdom makes some interesting original suggestions. But I feel that

* *Problems of Mind and Matter*. By John Wisdom.

this is the weakest part of the book, because most of the problems are about the existence or non-existence of causal connexions between body and mind, and Mr Wisdom never discusses the nature of causal connexion in general. This is the more important in that, if Hume's view of causation as merely regular sequence were established, the differences between epiphenomenalism, parallelism and interactionism would vanish. Moreover, until one knows what Mr Wisdom thinks about causal connexion, one cannot rightly appraise the surprising amount of *direct* knowledge he alleges he has on the subject.

There follows a somewhat disconnected chapter on Freewill, which is interesting in showing Mr Wisdom's turn of mind. He propounds the following dilemma: Either A's act of will is never ultimately determined by purely external circumstances (e.g., by heredity or by Calvin's God) or A cannot be blamed for making that act of will. Mr Wisdom grasps the first horn of the dilemma, and consequently maintains that A has pre-existed from the beginning of the world. An ethical naturalist would prefer to grasp the other horn, and would meet Mr Wisdom's dilemma with the reply that no one does or consistently should blame in the far-reaching sense required. But Mr Wisdom has certainly propounded a 'teaser' for absolutists in ethics— or at any rate for absolute blamers.

The last part of the book deals with some problems of cognition. After mentioning alternative theories of the relation in perception of the sense-datum to the physical object perceived, he defends the simplest view, sometimes called 'naïve realism,' according to which the sense-datum directly seen is identical with part of the surface of the physical object perceived. Like other naïve realists Mr Wisdom has to complicate his theory in order to escape from its critics. He is forced to maintain, for example, that when I see a 'double image' of my finger, what I am immediately seeing is the physical object which is the background appearing fingery in two places. This implies that I can make my finger transparent by an act of will! And he completely ignores the difficulty raised by the fact that the physical event perceived temporarily precedes my perception of it. In the following chapter on our knowledge of material things, Mr Wisdom seems to have been taken in by Russell's specious argument that the material world, whatever it may be, must be similar in structure to the world given by sense. [Russell's argument deceived us all until it was exposed by Mr M. H. A. Newman (*Mind*, 1928), who showed that all that similarity of structure in the abstract entails is that there should be as many physical causes as sensible effects, which tells us nothing about the physical causes themselves.]

The final chapter—on Judgment and Truth—also advocates what seems to me too simple a solution of the problem. Mr Wisdom introduces the central question of philosophy in the most admirable manner by shewing that we must steer our way between the 'error against which Oxford logicians fought so long'—that of 'supposing that a proposition has a peculiar specific form of *being*'—and the 'error against which the Cambridge logicians fought'—that of supposing that the proposition is a particular event in my mental history. He explains that the question at issue is the analysis of judgment-facts (e.g. I judge that Cameronian beat Orpen). But he goes on to maintain that the analysis can be given in terms of the relation of the *order* of the elements in the judgment-fact to that of the elements in the fact judged, adding the surprising remark: 'It must be understood that the elements in a fact are numbered from left to right'! From which it would appear that Mr Wisdom is thinking of the sentence (in English?) by which the fact happens to be expressed; and that he is engaged upon what seems to me the hopeless attempt, at present all too fashionable, to deal with the problem of judgment by reference to only the *external* features of the symbolism in which the judgment is expressed.

The fact that Mr Wisdom sincerely believes and ingeniously defends what seem to me too simple solutions of some of the problems of philosophy is a positive merit in this book. For it is much better that students approaching the subject should have one doctrine presented to them clearly (provided it is done tentatively and undogmatically) than that they should be overwhelmed with a multiplicity of alternative solutions. Taken as the last word on the problems with which this book deals, it would be very inadequate; but as the first word which should be considered by all serious students, it is quite excellent.

February 8th, 1935

'Paretology'*

JOSEPH NEEDHAM

The *Treatise on General Sociology* of Vilfredo Pareto has recently been attracting attention in much wider circles than those of professional sociologists and economists. It has been described as a work of genius which should be read by all who take an interest in human affairs and human relationships, whether politically or from the point of view of the pure spectator. As introductions to Pareto's work the two books here considered may be highly recommended, though whether they will predispose many to acquiesce in a very favourable verdict may perhaps be doubted.

Pareto was born in 1848 in Paris, where his father was in exile on account of revolutionary activities in connection with the party of Mazzini. It was against this revolutionary atmosphere that Pareto was in rebellion throughout his life. He shared in the disillusionment which followed the victory of the Italian national cause in 1866, but instead of being driven away from the ideals of his father's generation, he retained to the end a positive hatred for them. He is continually attacking humanitarianism, the 'god of progress,' etc. Trained as an engineer, he occupied a high post in the Italian railways, and was for a long time active in the effort to induce the government of the day to adopt the principle of free trade, which he believed to be an essential condition of economic prosperity. This led to a conflict with the government so severe that he had to go into retirement. Before long, however, he was invited to occupy the chair of economics at the University of Lausanne, and from 1894 to 1923 he lived at Céligny 'shutting out the troubles of the world, cultivating and storing the finest wines and fruits, and enjoying the material and spiritual pleasures of life.' It is striking that one who has been called the chief theoretician of Italian Fascism should have been an aristocrat by birth, the son of a revolutionary father by upbringing, a disappointed politician in middle life, and a sybaritic Professor in old age.

How did Pareto go to work? In a few short chapters, very clearly written, Henderson (himself one of the greatest living biologists)

---

* *Pareto.* By Franz Borkenau.
   Pareto's General Sociology: A Physiologist's Interpretation. By Lawrence J. Henderson.
K

shows that he tried to apply to the social sciences, where the variable factors are the natures and interactions of human beings, the concepts of equilibrium which have been found so essential in the physical and biological sciences. First of all, however, Pareto's treatise is not 'normative'; that is to say, he is concerned with 'what men do, and not with what they ought to do.' He is interested in the concept of the social system. His social system contains individuals roughly analogous with the 'components' of the thermodynamical physico-chemical system of Willard Gibbs. It is heterogeneous, *i.e.*, in physico-chemical terms, it contains various 'phases,' for the individuals are of different families, trades, and professions, associated with different institutions and members of different economic and social classes. And as Gibbs considers temperature, pressure, and concentrations, so Pareto considers 'sentiments,' or, strictly speaking, the manifestations of sentiments in words and deeds; 'verbal elaborations,' and economic interests. The analogy with the Gibbs system drawn by Henderson is most illuminating, but neither he nor Borkenau seem to have sufficient acquaintance with the work of Marx and Engels. If they had studied this as carefully as that of Pareto, the suggestion could hardly have been made that Pareto was the first to elaborate the concept of the social system as an equilibrium mixture, alteration of which at one point duly affects all the other points.

But where the system of Pareto differs most profoundly from that of Marx seems to be that Pareto's is an 'idealistic' as opposed to a materialistic one. Pareto pays an immense amount of attention to the first two factors mentioned above; the sentiments and the verbal elaborations, which he calls respectively Residues and Derivations. He is therefore much more of a psychologist than Marx, for whom all ideological superstructure at least is secondary. Translated into psychological terms, Residues would be complexes, and Derivations would be rationalisations, but the translation would leave a good deal to be desired. Residues are well explained by Henderson as follows: for ceremonial purification some peoples have used blood, the ancients used water, and water is still used in Christian baptism to efface sin. In these phenomena there are manifested at least two sentiments, the sentiment of integrity of the individual, and the sentiment that actions favourable to this integrity can be performed. These are Residues. They may be thought of as the residuum left after all the variable features of the phenomena have been dissected away. But the phenomena also include explanations of these ritual processes. These are Derivations. An extremely large part of Pareto's book is devoted to analysing and classifying residues and derivations. He evidently regards them not as secondary effects of changes in the productive economic relationships of men, but as active causative agents in human mass actions.

The interest of this classification and analysis can hardly be disputed by any. But most of its details are disputable, as Borkenau demonstrates, and it is when we pass to other aspects of Pareto's work, such as his theory of élites and his treatment of utility, that the extreme disadvantages of his purely scientific approach make themselves felt. His theory of élites is completely vitiated by the unproved assumption that the class-stratification of modern European capitalism corresponds to some biological or genetic differences in the classes concerned. Borkenau's chapters on this subject are especially damning. Pareto assumes, moreover, as a basic point of his analysis, that class-domination *must* exist, since the special demands of a given society will lead to special treatment for those who possess the special abilities it most requires. This could not for a moment be accepted by those who advocate the communal ownership of the means of production. Class-domination is meaningless in the absence of property, through which alone hereditary classes can be perpetuated. Then secondly, his treatment of utility, though it involves scrupulous classification, is yet somewhat naive. The distinction is made between the utility *of* a collectivity (people, nation, state), and utility *for* a collectivity. Consider the population of a country. There will be a certain optimum population. But optimum for what? A great increase of population will increase the 'utility' *of* the country by leading to increased military and political power. For this the optimum would be high. A lesser increase in population, however, might lead to a maximum distribution of individual goods (utility *for* the country). Hence this optimum would be much lower. But is this more than a rather pedantic way of saying that an imperialistic foreign policy demands a large internal population as potential cannon-fodder? This we knew before. We had not failed to note the double activity of Mussolini and Hitler in discouraging birth control and demanding territorial expansion at one and the same time.

The effect of all this on one reader, at least, has been to confirm the profound conviction that in the world of theory there is a real dichotomy, an actual conflict ever proceeding, an unmistakable battlefield.

It is not always easy to ascertain on which side people are fighting. But now and then the smoke blows off and the lines of the battalions are clearly seen. Among the general staff of the Prince of the Powers of the Air Pareto stands beside Macchiavelli and Nietzsche. And over against them, among many who need not be named, we can see (strange though it may seem to those who read the letter rather than the spirit) Aquinas and Marx together. For he that despiseth Man, despiseth not Man, but God.

May 22nd, 1936

Existentialism*

JOHN WISDOM

Professor Kuhn agrees with the Existentialists when like many other 'teachers of humanity' they teach that it is necessary for man to die in order to live. He disagrees with them as to 'the nature of that reality which is to shatter the screens and shelters around us. In Existentialism, crisis is conceived as an encounter with "Nothingness," that is, the privation of meaning and reality, whereas, in truth, it seems to me that it is the incomprehensible fullness of meaning and reality, God alone, who is the rightful claimant to the role of the saving destroyer. The Existentialists take the road to Calvary, but arriving there they find the place empty except for two thieves dying on their crosses' (pp. x, xi). (It should here be recalled that there are Existentialists who call themselves Christians and Christians who call themselves Existentialists. But then if one were to put into the picture of an Existentialist only features found in every Existentialist the result would not be much like an Existentialist.)

In Chapter I, Professor Kuhn explains the Existentialists' use of 'exists.' 'We take an interest in the existence of the penny in our pocket or in the non-existence of the world. But, the Existentialist asks, are not these manifold and changing interests rooted in one basic and persistent interest—the interest which man takes in his own existence? This being so, we are justified in ascribing existence in a more specific sense to that being which in existing is infinitely concerned about his

* *Encounter with Nothingness.* An Essay on Existentialism. Helmut Kuhn.

existence. For it is true that the meaning though not the fact of the difference between existence and non-existence of things other than man is derived from, or at any rate elucidated by, man's passionate interest in his own existence or his equally passionate fear of annihilation' (p. 4). This explanation of a new meaning of 'exists' is, for me, still inadequate. What is it to be concerned about one's own existence? Is it merely to wish to live? No, see p. 61. Is it to wish to have a life that isn't 'meaningless'? And are we to say that a penny or a piano exists only in so far as it ministers to the meaning of life?

In Chapter II Professor Kuhn reviews the sources of Existentialism. Chapter III is on the experience of estrangement. Here Plato, Paul, Kant, Hegel, Kierkegaard, Kafka, Marx, Heidegger, Sartre, T. S. Eliot and others are set side by side and, in spite of the brevity of the treatment, we feel something of the desperateness of man's endeavour to find in what seems a waste land signs that it is not.

Professor Kuhn disagrees with those who regard Existentialism as an ephemeral fashion. 'The Existentialist claims to initiate us, through acquaintance with Nothingness, into the maturity of disillusionment. This claim faithfully expresses a thought latent in the deeds and events which compose our contemporary world' (p. xiv). But more—Existentialism 'reaffirms a universal truth about man. Man must purchase victory at the price of an ultimate defeat. But the grave question before us is whether Existentialism interprets this law of crisis correctly.

In Chapter IV, Subjective Truth, we get an impression of how Existentials use in a muddled way muddled metaphysics to give misery a more imposing appearance. But if the muddle is to be exposed the exposition of it must be itself less muddled. In Chapter V, Gravediggers at Work, Professor Kuhn says that the Existentialist deserves praise for repudiating the rationalist construction of man as a 'thinking thing' (*res cogitans*) and recalling to us that concrete whole which everyone of us is (p. 70), but urges that 'he mars his discovery by overlooking or rejecting three metaphysical (*sic*) concepts which alone could make it fruitful: the idea of contemplation, the idea of love and the idea of rational faith.' This chapter deserves the most serious attention. So do those that follow. Chapter VI is concerned with the passage through 'acute despair' necessary to the conquest of 'latent despair.' 'When the Existentialist (or, I would add, some incident of life) shows the abyss, we are startled. But at the bottom of our minds we may also feel that we knew all this before, that we had been standing at the brink of the abyss all our life and we dared not confess it' (p. xiv). It suddenly seems as if 'everything happens and nothing matters.' Out of this may come frantic action—for 'there is an active tedium just as there is a passive one' (p. 96), or inaction in which anguish has changed into a longing for death (p. xvi). Or again anguish may lead (Sartre, Bertrand Russell in *A Free Man's Worship*) to an attempt to feel at home in anguish and nothingness (p. 94). Or (Marcel), it may be said that *ennui* arises from an initial error and that 'I need only rise to those concrete experiences of participation through which the presence of my fellow man as a "thou" rather than a mere "he" is revealed to me, together with my own presence to myself, and finally to the presence of God... in order to... rejoin the inexhaustible plenitude of Being' (p. 95). The last chapters are called The Crisis of the Drama, Illumination through Anguish and Beyond Crisis. I cannot give even a summary here. On p. 158 it is argued that an Existentialist cannot consistently say that freedom does not involve irresponsibility and that the individual's freedom limits itself through his being with others. I do not follow this argument.

The metaphysics in this book, for example the discussion of objective truth (pp. 44 and 66), seems to me sketchy and slippery.

And the Existentialist's argument for despair outlined on p. xiii needs a much more critical examination. The Existentialist is, not unfairly I think, represented as asking, 'What do you will with unwavering devotion, so that everything else is willed and lived only for the sake of this first objective and greatest good?' (We are reminded of St Augustine's words, 'the chief good,—that which will leave us nothing further to seek in order to be blessed, if only we make all our actions refer to it ...' (*City of God*, Book viii. 8). The Existentialist is represented as answering with a string of negations 'not the promotion of what belongs in the field of my professional duties; not wife, children and friends: not wealth, learning or power; not higher living standards for all men; not ...'

Suppose it is true that no one of these things is sufficient to make life meaningful. It does not follow that life is not meaningful. Suppose further that if it is true that no one of these things is necessary to life's having a meaning. It does not follow that life hasn't a meaning nor even that it isn't these things which give it its meaning. After all no one of a horse's legs suffices to keep him standing up, and at the blacksmith's it is demonstrated that no leg is indispensable for his standing up, but of course this doesn't mean that no horse stands up nor that he stands up on anything but his own legs. To win a set at tennis is not *the summum bonum* but this doesn't prove that it is not *part* of what makes *a* life good. Maybe in Heaven they don't play tennis or make war. Maybe a world in which there is so much defeat and death is not worth the money. But if so it's not because it's nothing to the good to have what it takes to win when all seems lost—whether at Wimbledon or Stalingrad.

Saints and cynics alike too readily assume it agreed that birds, beasts, flowers and fast cars have nothing to do with the case or at any rate that they aren't good enough. It is true that even friends sometimes sadly disappoint one another, but ... However, there is no space to argue the matter here. Only, as Solomon remarked, a dish of herbs is under certain circumstances better than much grander food, though those circumstances are of infinite subtlety.

Nevertheless, this small book on the 'Encounter with Nothingness' seems to me good. It is sympathetic and serious and in it learning is used to bring together into illuminating conjunction the thoughts of great thinkers. I especially like its challenge to those who sometimes write as if cheerfulness *must* arise from intellectual inadequacy or dishonesty, stupidity or evasion. Anguish can be 'adulterated with longing for death' (p. xvi). When I read Existentialist writings I sometimes have an uncomfortable feeling that here in what I am reading is evasion. As Professor Kuhn says, Existentialists face what many human beings, for good or ill, don't face. But they do so only up to a point—after all one of the best ways of keeping concealed the most horrible is to emphasise the horror of the less horrible and to denigrate the good. Freud has a good deal to say about despair. But Existentialists and writers about Existentialists say very little about Freud. Why? There are no short cuts to honest optimism but nor are there to honest pessimism.

February 2nd, 1952

The Case of C. Wright Mills

E. R. LEACH

Those influential readers of *The Cambridge Review* who consider that the only proper place for sociology in this University is in an inaccessible attic labelled Part III of the Historical Tripos, will find plenty of support within the covers of this book, which sets out to catalogue all the sins of commission and omission to be encountered in contemporary American sociology.* The author has quite unambiguous views as to what sociology is about. 'All sociology worthy of the name is historical sociology ... it is ... an attempt to write the present as history.' With this premiss as base, the first hundred pages or so are devoted to knocking the paint off diverse reputations from rival sociological camps.

The Grand Theorists (e.g. Professor Talcott Parsons), contribute only platitudes wrapped up in impenetrable verbiage. Professor Mills does not deny that the analysis of concepts has a proper place in sociological studies, but this place should be small and the time devoted to it brief. Pursued on a Parsonian scale, the study of concepts is simply a device for avoiding the study of specific empirical problems. As they say in Spain, 'many can shuffle cards who can't play.'

The Abstracted Empiricists are those who equate sociology with the Gallup Poll type of public opinion survey. They collect 'data' by some procedure which combines the techniques of statistical sampling with the formal interview and these 'data' are then 'processed' with the aid of punched cards and a Hollerith machine to produce a synthetic picture of how a mass population might vote on this, that or the other issue. Where Parsons gives us theory but no facts, Stauffer, Lazersfeld *et al.* give us facts but no theory. Most research of this kind suffers from the limitations of what Professor Mills calls 'psychologism.' Since the unit of information is an individual selected at random, enquiry can concern itself only with the opinions and actions of individuals, never with the pattern of the relationships which link individuals together or keep them apart. Hence social phenomena come to be explained in terms of facts and theories about the make-up of individuals. The notion of social structure, which was fundamental

* *The Sociological Imagination.* By C. Wright Mills.

I. J. M. KEYNES: the Fellow of King's

2. G. E. MOORE: the Trinity philosopher; 'common sense' in a Cambridge of the 1920s

3. J. B. PRIESTLEY: Bournemouth, 1950s; time off for the ex-critic of the *Cambridge Review*

The divided legacy of Acton and Maitland; the generations of Cambridge history.

4 (*left*). HERBERT BUTTER-FIELD: the young critic

5 (*bottom left*). G. KITSON CLARK: the young scholar

6 (*bottom right*).
G. M. TREVELYAN: the inheritor

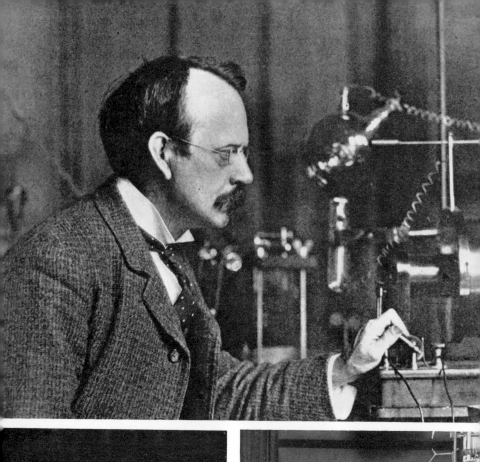

Cambridge science.

7 (*top left*). J. J. THOMSON: the Master in the Cavendish

8 (*bottom left*). JOSEPH NEED-HAM in the 1930s

9 (*bottom centre*). MAX PERUTZ: the codes of molecular biology

10 (*top right*). WILLIAM MORRIS: the artist and socialist in the 1880s

11 (*bottom right*). ROGER FRY: the critic and aesthete

The New Criticism.

12 (*left*). T. S. ELIOT in the 1920s
13 (*bottom left*). F. R. LEAVIS
14 (*bottom right*). WILLIAM EMPSON

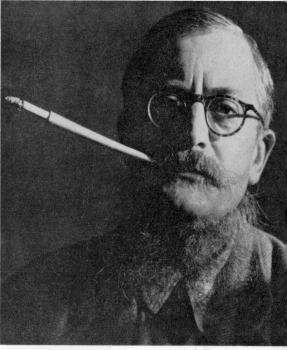

15 (*left*). JULIAN BELL: poet and critic; the 'typical Kingsman', killed in Spain, 1937

The post-war poets.

16 (*bottom left*). SYLVIA PLATH

17 (*bottom right*). THOM GUNN

18. BERTRAND RUSSELL: a Cambridge mind

in the sociological thinking of Marx, Weber and Durkheim, gets left out altogether.

The third target for Professor Mills' archery is labelled The New Illiberal Practicality, a phrase which seems to cover the whole socio-logical apparatus of the Welfare State as well as those research workers who concern themselves with 'the human relations in industry' or with 'human engineering.' In America (and in England, too) there has grown up during the post-war years a vast, wealthy, bureaucratic system of Institutes and Foundations concerned with the study of 'social problems.' A social problem is anything which deviates from currently accepted middle-class norms, so practical sociology is really no more than the political art of persuading the disgruntled that there is nothing to complain about. The practitioner of Illiberal Practicality takes for granted the moral values of the existing economic order and aims to create a world full of intelligent, rational, well-informed managers looking after happy, efficient workmen of good morale. Evidently the Brave New World of 1984 is not Professor Mills' idea of heaven and he is appalled that the insights gained from social studies should be prostituted in this way; but his comments lack bite. Here surely is a case for satire not for sorrow?

Professor Mills' caustic comments on his colleagues take us only half way through the book, the rest is mostly taken up with explaining why we should prefer our sociology in its classical guise as presented by Marx, Sombart, Weber, Comte, Spencer, Durkheim, Veblen ... Europeans almost to a man! But Professor Mills himself is still an American in a hurry and the jerky discontinuities of the book suggest that much of it must have been spoken into a tape recorder, in intervals between meals, flying the Atlantic. A clue to this will be found at p. 227 where it turns out that the text has been pasted up from various, originally unconnected, lectures, articles and broadcasts composed between 1953 and 1959. Professor Mills does a lot better with his sticks than with his carrots and those who would seek justification for con-temporary American sociology had best look elsewhere. They might do a lot worse than turn up Professor Mills' own volumes such as *White Collar* and *The Power Elite*.

October 10th, 1959

Max Weber: A Colossus in Precis

W. G. RUNCIMAN

Of social theorists since 'sociology' was coined, only Marx and perhaps Durkheim rival Weber in stature; and yet the English neglect of him, regrettable though it is, is perhaps more regrettable than curious. Weber's style is ponderous, his erudition suffocating, his quest for sociological patterns on the largest scale essentially suspect to the empiricist British mind. Worse still, he is often untranslatable: how are we to render even such apparently simple words as *Betrieb* and *Herrschaft*, let alone old enemies like *Gemeinschaft* or artifacts of Weber's own like *Alltagsgebilde*? And in addition, he has not been very well served by the haphazard sequence in which his works have become partly accessible in English. He is still best known for his thesis on the influence of the Protestant ethic, written as a tentative introduction to a broad comparative discussion of the interrelation between religion and society. Despite his own disclaimers, he has been consistently accused of the bald assertion that Capitalism was caused by Protestantism; and the general purpose and structure of his work have been too often misunderstood or merely ignored. Professor Bendix, of the University of California at Berkeley, has performed a valuable service in providing the first full-length study of Weber to be written in English.* His careful summary and discussion should adequately redress this disproportion of emphasis, and for those (like myself) who cannot claim thorough familiarity even with those of Weber's writings now available in English, Bendix provides a useful and perhaps even indispensable guide.

It must remain unlikely that anyone will again have the temerity let alone the competence, to attempt a comparative analysis of civilizations on the scale that Weber did. His monumental studies, lucidly charted by Professor Bendix, covered topics as diverse as Confucianism, the stock exchange and the social foundations of music. He was trained in history, economics, philosophy and law. His knowledge of languages included Russian and Hebrew. He had the respect and esteem of scholars as eminent and diverse as Mommsen, Simmel, Troeltsch,

* *Max Weber: an Intellectual Portrait* by Reinhard Bendix.

Toennies and Dilthey. Despite frequent ill-health, both physical and mental, the sheer volume of his writings is awe-inspiring. When he died of pneumonia in 1920 at the age of 56, his work was far from complete. Weber in some ways seems very much one of the old-style, stiff-necked, Teutonic polymaths who built up the legendary German scholarship of the late nineteenth century. But in his pessimistic detachment, his disenchantment with formal religion and his fear of the threat to freedom posed by bureaucracy and nationalism he seems very much more of the present. Perhaps it is this, as much as his formidable learning, which explains the welcome resurgence of interest in his writings. But in any event, whatever its causes, Weber deserves all the interest that he seems at long last to be attracting.

Professor Bendix first summarizes Weber's little-known early work on the agrarian problem and the stock exchange. He then traces out Weber's ideas on the relation of Protestant doctrine to the development of economic rationality, and from there leads in to an account of his comparative sociology of religion. The final section covers Weber's well-known typology of authority-structures, and deals separately with charismatic, traditional and legal *Herrschaft*. Bendix's aim is avowedly expository, and his deliberate emphasis is on Weber's substantive studies rather than his methods. However, it is difficult for an admirer of Professor Bendix's own comparative study of management ideologies not to wish that we could have been given a little more of Bendix even if this would mean a little less of Weber. There are in particular two topics to which I feel that this applies. The first is Weber's relevance to Marxism; the second is Weber's oddly ambivalent attitude to the use of statistical and quantitative methods.

As Bendix mentions but does not enlarge upon, Weber was persistently conscious of Marx's theories of history and society, and his own work is at many points a deliberate testing or modification of Marxian doctrine. The debate cannot, of course, be regarded as closed; but without wishing to assert categorically that Weber is right where Marx is wrong, it is strongly arguable that Weber's analysis of social stratification and of the relation between ideology and economic structure is more subtle, more acute and in practice more useful than that of Marx. Perhaps it is precisely because Weber's analysis was so subtle, his evidence so diverse and his conclusions so cautiously qualified that his ideas have been so much less influential than Marx's. But it is very often by contrast with Marx that Weber is most interesting and important, and it seems a pity that Professor Bendix should be unwilling to adjudicate at any length between them. Neither offers a complete and definitive account of the nature of the interrelation between the economic substructure of a society and its dominant ideas, but Weber goes a good deal more deeply into the problem than Marx did. As Norman Birnbaum has argued, ideas can in Weber's analysis enable the individual to *interpret* his economic or class situation and by this means give a direction to social change which does not directly derive from the substructure itself. Marx and Engels, on the other hand, are notoriously vague about the precise operations of the causal nexus which they in principle postulate; and there can be no question that they collected a good deal less relevant evidence than Weber did. On the general question of social stratification, the force of Weber's argument is once again not that Marx was wrong but that his analysis is insufficient to account for the evidence at hand; economic class is a crucial dimension of social structure, but it is not the only one. Bendix summarizes Weber's well-known distinction between classes and status-groups, but he seems to feel it unnecessary to emphasize how useful and important this distinction is. It would be nice to think that this was so; but unfortunately subsequent generations of sociologists (Marxist and non-Marxist alike) have persisted in remorselessly obfuscating an issue which with Weber's help need never have become so ambiguous. The use of Weber's distinctions need not commit us to his substantive theories, but it could make it possible to state any such theories of stratification in such a way as to mark off clearly questions of language from questions of fact. This had, alas, been so infrequently done (despite conventional lip-service to Weber) that a simple summary of his analysis is unlikely to bring its lesson home. I cannot help wishing that Professor Bendix, in giving us Weber's views on class and status, had taken the occasion to remind us more forcibly of their merits.

The other topic, Weber's views on quantification, is perhaps so relatively slight in relation to Weber's work as a whole that it would be unreasonable to ask that Professor Bendix should have touched on it in what is designed as an over-all survey of Weber's writings. But Weber's attitude is remarkable for two contradictory reasons: first, because he on one occasion did an extraordinarily good piece of quantified empirical research; and second, because he seems subsequently to have attached very little importance to it. In 1908 the *Verein für*

Sozialpolitik decided to start a series of empirical studies of industrial workers. Weber devoted a great deal of trouble and energy to the project and composed a monograph which, as well as giving general methodological discussion of the foundations of industrial psychology, contained an analysis of data collected from a textile factory which belonged to one of Weber's relations. Not only was the paper greatly admired at the time, but Paul Lazarsfeld, the outstanding methodologist of contemporary sociology, has recently spoken in extravagant terms of the 'brilliance' of the procedures Weber used. 'The monograph,' Lazarsfeld has said, 'anticipates in every respect the approach which today would be taken for an analysis of voting, radio listening, buying or any other action performed by large numbers of people under comparable circumstances.' Weber's analysis, indeed, is strikingly similar to Durkheim's much better-known analysis of suicide rates, although there seems to be no evidence that Weber was influenced by Durkheim. But he seems for some reason to have completely lost interest in the whole enquiry. He only once referred to it in his subsequent work (a cross-reference in a later edition of the *Protestant Ethic*) and at the 1911 meeting of the *Verein*, though he defended some of his statistical procedures against Bortkewitch (now best known to us for calculating the chances of a Prussian cavalryman being kicked to death by a horse), in general he poured cold water on the whole affair and declared that nothing very much had come of it. I do not know if it is known why Weber's attitude underwent this change, and it would be interesting if Professor Bendix could have thrown some light on it. It seems to make Weber's work even more impressive but at the same time more puzzling. He could almost certainly have produced empirical and statistical work as important as his historical studies—he expounded the use of the correlation coefficient when it was practically unknown in Germany; he developed the virtual logical equivalent of a mathematical learning model; he issued warnings of the dangers of *Begriffsrealismus* long before 'reification' or 'misplaced concreteness' had become household terms. But he chose not do do so, and apparently made no attempt to relate this one study to his ideas and terminology as a whole. Was it that he would have liked to and couldn't? Or did he really not think it worthwhile?

But all this is outside the chosen scope of Professor Bendix's study, which sets out only to give a careful and coherent exposition of Weber's more important writings. This it excellently does. There are inevitably a few small irritations (e.g. the French Revolution did not eliminate the monarchy in 1789 (p. 349), and 'mundane orientation' (p. 207) is surely pure jargon for 'worldliness'), but not many. If there is a general criticism, it is only to wonder whether there could not have been a little more interpretation for the amount of exposition. A summary of someone else's thought is always bound to read a little dull, and in this case the original author can seldom be called lively. But exposition rather than analysis or polemic is Professor Bendix's declared purpose, and no one will dispute with his contention of the need for it, or question his competence to carry it out.

Heinemann's have at the same time made available the Free Press edition of *The City*, the first translation into English of (in the 1956 Tübingen edition) pages 735 to 822 of *Wirtschaft und Gesellschaft*. The blurb would lead one to believe it was written yesterday, and the editorial preface (which is on the whole of a stupefying pedestrianism) tries to make it all unnecessarily relevant to contemporary America. But it is good to have another dribble of *Wirtschaft und Gesellschaft* made available in English, and even encourages the hope that one of these years we may at last have the whole thing. Until we do (and, indeed, thereafter), Professor Bendix has provided a most valuable guide to the work of the greatest sociologist of them all.

March 11th, 1961

Hannah Arendt on Revolution

JOHN DUNN

Miss Arendt has always been a teasing writer and *On Revolution*★ is far from being her most straightforward book. It is not that it is unenticing—as ever, she writes with intelligence and erudition, with a gift for the sharp phrase and the eloquent quotation which makes her work a pleasure to read. But for all the insight and brilliance, there is something thin and impoverished about the book. The taste for political etymology which has dogged her work from the first lends less and less light and at times degenerates into a sort of intellectual tic. The weight of the erudition continues to impress but there is little

★ *On Revolution*. By Hannah Arendt.

conviction in the lessons we are taught from the reflections of Jefferson and John Adams. Any continuity in the argument seems in retrospect more and more to have been subjective. At the beginning of the book it is not too clear what it is really about. At the end it is still not clear. It all seems vague and general and rather evasive.

But it would be unjust to consider such a work solely in an academic and unsympathetic perspective—as though all that needed to be said was that it belonged to an unattractive and self-indulgent intellectual style, an idiom in which rhetoric permanently infects the possibility of arriving at true statements. There may be a certain rashness but there is also a certain nobility in the scale of the task which Miss Arendt has taken upon herself. It is not an easy or a grateful task to attempt to disentangle the ambiguities of the heritage of 'revolution' to the contemporary world. That the values in terms of which most countries today conduct their politics derive from the achievements or the threats of revolutions is a simple historical fact. But how far this implies any more than a verbal coherence in their political experience seems more questionable. Miss Arendt is a moralist, even something of an aesthetician, of politics and the question never seems to have occurred to her in such a form. It is pre-eminently this failure which lends an air of slight artificiality to her whole enterprise.

Her inquiries begin with a dilemma which is as formal as it well could be and one which in its present form goes back at least to Burke —that revolutions promise freedom but deliver tyranny. The gap between what is dreamed of and what can be achieved makes it necessary to narrow the opportunities for recognizing what is happening and to restrict freedom of political expression. Leaders come to feel, perhaps correctly, that they can choose only between anarchy and autocracy. They do not appear to find the choice difficult. If the only value at stake was the authentically revolutionary value of freedom, there could be no such incoherence between the hopes and the reality —for freedom, for Miss Arendt, is the proper concern of politics and can only be realized in public action; freedom is what constitutes the political domain. But it is inevitably not the only value at stake in revolution—in all previous revolutions, except perhaps the American, the driving force of the revolution has been the pressure of physical need and its deepest aim has been to escape from such a dominance. It has been because so many revolutions have been in this way distorted by the physical that they have set so little store by the political value of freedom. Freedom can only be achieved by the creation, largely institutionally, of a public space within which men can act and which is insulated from the pressures of physical need. Such a space has always in the past been the preserve of an isolated élite exercising a formalized dominance over the rest of the community. The political values which represent one of the highest ideals of the human personality have thus been appropriated by one small section of the community and this process of appropriation has bled them of much of their significance. The key problem of politics is how to restore some real chance of access to these values to all members of a community as a part of the ordinary opportunities of their lives. It is a problem which in one perspective can be seen as purely institutional but which it is perhaps clearest to see as a problem of social psychology which could only conceivably be resolved under a restricted set of circumstances. Only in a community in which the blind anarchic threats of economic need can be contained can the world be made safe for politics and for its inseparable antithesis, privacy. Only in a community which self-consciously pursues the ideal of freedom, of what Miss Arendt calls with John Adams 'public happiness,' can the ideal be realized. The true heritage of revolution for us today lies in just this self-conscious pursuit. Most specifically it lies in the popular institutions which have emerged spontaneously in the course of revolutions, the Paris *Sections*, the *Soviets*, even the Hungarian *Räte*. These institutions embody a unique blend of spontaneity, creativity, and order and they offer to all the possibility of engaging in the political life. It is a measure of the failure of all previous revolutions, of how far their promise has been blighted that revolutionary leaders have sensed the emergence of these institutions as a threat and have set themselves to crush them. But, more importantly, it is a mark of the intrinsic connection between revolution and freedom that these have emerged repeatedly and unpremeditatedly in revolution after revolution.

To find Miss Arendt such a latter-day disciple of Rosa Luxemburg is both appealing and slightly surprising. Clearly any such frontal assault on the acceptability of all contemporary political systems is likely at best to be both interesting and inconclusive. What seems sad about this particular book is that it is so much more inconclusive than it is interesting. But what is sadder is that this inadequacy probably derives much less from anything jejune in what Miss Arendt, in some sense, 'has to say,' than from her notion of the proper form of book in which to say it. The work is often so clever and perceptive in detail that it is easy to believe that the flaccidity and generality of its categories is largely a literary failure, a defect in communication rather than in conception. In the mind of an author it is easy for sentences to mean something much more sharp-edged than they could do to any reader. Such a risk is inherent in the effort to communicate at all but Miss Arendt's style converts a risk into a near-certainty. And, when all allowances have been made, there remains a point at which defects in communication merge into defects in conception. In particular, there is a peculiar essentialist assumption about the nature of revolution which pervades the book and is both its *raison d'être* and its most unplausible feature.

The historical events to which we give the title 'revolutions' are extraordinarily complicated and various and there seems little reason to suppose that they have many features in common. Even if it were clear what it meant to say that the 'principle' of revolution was 'freedom,' it seems unlikely that such various social phenomena would all exhibit it. There are, it is true, a number of revolutions which do display a sort of homogeneity and they are on the whole those which have conferred on the word the sort of resonance which it has for us today. But it is scarcely an accident that their most dominating characteristic should be precisely that feature which Miss Arendt declares to be the antithesis of freedom—the pre-occupation with the satisfaction of elementary biological needs. Perhaps a more subtle empirical investigation of the course of a number of revolutions (and one which was less pre-occupied with the ethical reflections of the Founding Fathers of the American Republic) might have showed that the connection between the force of revolutionary aspirations and the enthusiasm for political participation was a simple one. The release of energy which could destroy a social system must derive from very powerful needs and these needs have usually been primitive. There seems often an intrinsic connection between the force of the drive towards freedom and that anarchic potential of the drive which leads to its suppression.

The political values which Miss Arendt seeks to extol, in so far as I understand them, seem attractive—but also somewhat elusive. It is not easy to conceive of communities which would embody them satisfactorily and it is not possible to point to any settled communities which have done so over a substantial period of time. They don't seem to be values which are very intimately connected with revolutions and

L

they don't much overlap with the most coherent feature of the experience of revolution in modern history. It is thus difficult to feel that the best way of reflecting upon such values is to reflect closely on 'Revolution'; and, even if it were, it is not easy to suppose that it would be as valuable to reflect at a level of great abstraction as it would be to conduct more sensitive and empirical historical investigations. As it is, the question of how far such values represent a dream of what life could be like and how far a sensible strategy for what life could be made remains as opaque as ever. The most convincing guess remains perhaps that they are something of a dream and that Miss Arendt, like the Third Earl of Shaftesbury (or even Plato?) is primarily an aesthetician of politics—to be valued as much for her ability to disclose the power of an almost irrelevant image as for any depth of empirical insight.

May 2nd, 1964

On Reading Marcuse

RAYMOND WILLIAMS

Marcuse has been called the philosopher of student revolt. It was interesting, when this description reached the newspapers, to see the hurried buying of back copies of his books. It seems to be always easier to meet concepts, in a university, than to meet people.

The themes which have been generally taken from Marcuse relate mainly to repression and to agency. On repression, he is one of several thinkers who have attempted an interaction, at times a fusion, of the concepts of Marx and of Freud. The lack of reference, in orthodox Marxism, to the intense personal problems of love and growth, left a gap which became unbearable in particular social groups, where an experience of social repression was not primarily in the economic process, and only secondarily in the political process, but mainly in the process of personal development within an apparently free but also apparently frustrating culture. This emphasis linked, in its turn, especially in North America but also, more doubtfully, in West European societies, with the political problem of agency, and especially revolutionary agency. If the (white) proletariat was incorporated, in late capitalist society, the task of agency, or at least of initial agency, could be held to pass to intellectuals and to students. Since these were the groups in which repression was experienced in its most apparently personal forms—in controls on what was called private experience, and in the pressures of money and of authority on unorthodox intellectual work—the emphases had an apparent unity: speaking to a particular condition, and offering immediate ways of revolt against it.

Marcuse's actual arguments, as opposed to the simple version which has been so widely passed from hand to mouth, are complex, qualified, intricate.* It happens that I think he is more wrong than right, in most of his general analysis. It happens also that I am neither (in any sense that helps) a Marxist or a Freudian, and one of my reasons has been the area of experience to which neither system speaks, in its orthodox forms: that area which in my view is neither personal, in a bourgeois sense, nor social, in the ordinary socialist sense. It seemed to me at first that the scrupulous applications of both Marxist and Freudian ideas might penetrate this area, which except in literature is largely unwritten. But I now believe that any instinct-theory, of a Freudian kind, is incompatible with the historical emphasis which is the most critical element in Marx, and with the emphasis on social learning which can also be taken from Marx and others. To put the revolutionary concepts of Marx and of Freud together is certainly explosive; but mainly, I think, at the level of rhetoric. There is a good example of what I take to be this failure in one of the most recent essays in *Negations*: on 'Aggressiveness in Advanced Industrial Society'. Marcuse first characterises what he calls, following bourgeois sociology, the 'affluent society', and then advances the thesis (also familiar elsewhere) that it is the 'normal' functioning of this society which produces certain characteristic individual stresses. The analysis becomes Marxist when it indicates the economic reasons, in minority capital power, which limit the satisfaction of certain constructive needs, and then Freudian in its description of the 'ubiquitous aggression prevalent in this society'. There are then several acute insights into forms of aggressive behaviour and of aggressive teaching and habituation: in militarism, in the destruction of privacy, in the competitive and violent language of some advertising, in the preference of the machine to the body, or the attempt to treat bodies like machines. These, especially when examples are given, connect and convince. But the central intellectual argument,

* *Negations.* By Herbert Marcuse.

the core of analysis, remains confused, and the limited success of the essay is its indication of symptoms—a rapid impressionism within the interaction of stated rather than examined concepts. The good heart, the consistent humanism, the naming of evident contemporary evils: these come through and recommend Marcuse to many of us, but at the very point, and in the very way, perhaps, that we are ourselves confused.

I respect Marcuse very much as a man. In these last years, especially, under severe pressures, he seems to me to have acted and spoken with an exemplary and quite uncommon dignity, intelligence and force. I find myself standing with him, or wishing to stand with him, in repeated political battles, and in the conflicts within the universities. But for me it is a case similar to that in which I find myself standing with Sartre: we see the world quite differently, at a level of primary experience quite as much as in developed intellectual work, yet the crises of imperialism and of late capitalism force us into necessary common (often defensive) positions.

But what I then find, as I read on into Marcuse, is a quite different interest: not the grafting of Freud into Marx, nor the grafting of both into an American sociology which, even in its most critical and even revolutionary forms, appears to me distorted by the very pressures and contradictions of its society, and which in one of its cardinal points—on the condition of the proletariat in advanced capitalist society—seems to me possibly wrong about West European societies of an apparently similar form. My interest, and it is deep, is in what can be loosely called the German rather than the American work, and this is in fact predominant in *Negations*. For historical reasons, we have been separated, in Britain, from a critical and philosophical tradition which, when we re-encounter it in Marcuse or in Lukács, is at once strange and fascinating: at once broader and more confident, more abstract and yet more profoundly involved than our own. I felt the size of this gap, and yet the interest and pleasure of a possible bridge across it, in one of Marcuse's essays from the thirties, reprinted in this volume, on 'The Affirmative Character of Culture'. The particular interest of the essay, for me, is that its analysis corresponded so closely with a central theme of *Culture and Society*, and that both were historical treatments, of very much the same problem, which were yet continents of countries apart in method and in language. It was a marvellous moment of intellectual liberation to read across that gap into a mind which in all but its most central area of concern and value was so wholly other and strange.

> Affirmative culture was the historical form in which were pre-
> served those human wants which surpassed the material repro-
> duction of existence.

This is exactly my own conclusion, of the essential origin and operation of the idea of culture, as it developed in England after the Industrial Revolution, at a time when we were very close, especially through Coleridge and Carlyle, to the German thought to which Marcuse's arguments relate. It is a sense of meeting, after a long separation. But then the essay has much more value than this. For, from the subse-quently different historical experience, Marcuse's exploration is into an experience I have not known directly: of the paradoxical use and rejection of culture by the specific authoritarianism of Fascism. His analysis is too intricate for summary, but it is, in my view, superb and permanent. Moreover, beyond its insights into the particular crisis of Fascism, it indicates in a very sharp and uncompromising way an issue which has been at the centre of my own concern since I returned to Cambridge: the social and political use of what appears to be the ideal or the beautiful content of what Marcuse calls 'affirmative culture'. That is, an idea of culture represented human values which the society repressed or could not realise. As such, it was critical. But the form of the separation became at a certain point (in England, perhaps, in the late nineteenth century, when the ethos of what we call traditional Cambridge was formed) a ratification, a system of values against social involvement and social change. The ideality of the culture—always to an important extent genuine—seemed to require preservation and pro-tection from a pushing, materialist social world. The institutions of preservation—the university and the museum, one has to say, not satirically—had a certain purity which was yet, because the separation of ideal and material life could only be abstract, a form of complicity, or at least of redirection of energy, stilling of doubt, reconciliation with what is true and lovely and past: an apparently spiritual emphasis, on cultural values, which prevented certain real and necessary crises and involvements. This was especially so in the use made of art and of literature; its outstanding examples, in Cambridge, have been the use made of the reconciling group in practical criticism, and the more openly ideological use of a late-nineteenth century idea of tragedy. When Marcuse argues that art, in this ethos, has the function of reconciling us to suffering, of softening the contrast between ideal and real because the art-work is beautiful and can be experienced as present, he is raising the central questions in contemporary literary studies. He argues, further, that those who point to the contrast are resented, not only because they disturb a particular settlement, but because they are seen, self-protectively, as the intruders who bring in political and material questions, where before there was only purity: a neat transference of disturbance from the actual social world, which it has been the function of the ethos to hold at a distance, to the individuals who indicate not only the function but also the world which has been there all the time. Reading this German essay from 1937, I felt Marcuse must have been here, especially during these last ten years. That is no particular reason for recommending the essay, but at least it indicates the possibility of reaching across what had seemed, in abstraction, quite separate intellectual traditions: in the fundamental experience of a certain kind of society, and of the function, in it, of certain kinds of institutions and ideas.

There are eight essays in *Negations*, and I have discussed only two, briefly. The reading and the argument will of course continue.

May 30th, 1969

4

The Natural Sciences

The Late Lord Kelvin

J. J. THOMSON

I have been asked by the Editor to write a few words on Lord Kelvin's influence on science in Cambridge. In addition to the influence which he exerted here as elsewhere by his marvellous discoveries and the instruments of precision which he invented, we at Cambridge enjoyed through his frequent visits the influence exerted by his personality. The days when Lord Kelvin came to the Cavendish Laboratory were red letter days for all its students; he would go from one experiment to another, full of enthusiasm, interest and encouragement, asking question after question, and often calling to Lady Kelvin to come and look at something which particularly interested him. His visits acted like a tonic, the interest which each student felt Lord Kelvin had taken in his work, increased his own interest in it, and spurred him on to further exertion.

It may help us to form some estimate of the magnitude of Lord Kelvin's contributions to Physics, if we remember (it seems almost incredible when we think of his vigour but a few months ago) that it is now nearly sixty-seven years since he published his first paper. Let us recall the state of physics at that time, heat was then regarded as a substance and indestructible, neither of the laws of thermodynamics had been discovered, the laws of magnetic induction, although discovered some time before by Faraday, were still unfamiliar, and the science of electricity, as we understand it now, hardly existed; a great part of the work which has transformed the physics of 1841 into the physics of to-day has been done by three Cambridge men, Stokes, Clerk-Maxwell and Lord Kelvin.

Lord Kelvin's first paper was on Fourier's theorem, a subject which always had a great fascination for him. I have heard that he once told his class at Glasgow that of all his investigations those which had given him the greatest pleasure were the ones based on Fourier's theorem. Within a few years of taking his degree he had published those papers on Heat and Electricity, which are certainly among the most important of his contributions to science, if indeed they are not the most important. The first paper on heat 'On an Absolute Thermometric Scale founded on Carnot's theory of the Motive Power of Heat, 1848,' carries us far back in the history of physics, for in it he assumes, following Carnot, that heat is indestructible, although he makes the remarkable proviso that this statement will not be true if certain results lately got by Mr Joule are confirmed. It is a curious point in the history of physics that we should probably have had to wait longer for the second law of thermodynamics if Carnot had held correct views as to the nature of heat. Carnot was led to the invention of his 'cycle' by the belief that heat was a substance and behaved like one, and it was Carnot's cycle which led first Clausius and, independently and but shortly afterwards, Lord Kelvin to the discovery of the second law of thermodynamics. None of Lord Kelvin's writings give, I think, a greater sense of his power than the paper 'On the Dynamical Theory of Heat,' in which he develops this law; he seems to wander through one branch of physics after another, trying on it as he goes the power of the new instrument and discovering important results at every step. Some idea of his activity and originality may be gathered from the fact that before he was thirty he had published more than sixty papers, most of them of the first importance.

One of the most direct influences he excited on Science at Cambridge, was by the publication, in 1867, of Thomson and Tait's *Natural Philosophy*; this was an entirely new departure in text books on Mathematical Physics, and was the forerunner of such books as Maxwell's *Electricity and Magnetism*, Lord Rayleigh's *Theory of Sound* and Lamb's *Hydrodynamics*. I can still remember the delight with which I first read it more than thirty years ago; in the books on Natural Philosophy before that time attention was chiefly directed to the mathematical scaffolding by which the results were attained, the results themselves were obscured by a cloud of symbols; in Thomson and Tait though there was certainly no shirking of any mathematical difficulties, it was on the result themselves that attention was chiefly directed, the dynamics never degenerated into differential equations, and in consequence the reader obtained vivid and clear ideas of the properties of matter at rest or in motion. We were told on the highest authority in the Senate House lately, that our students no longer read Thomson and Tait, but have returned to methods—easy but enervating —exclusively analytical. If this is so it is deplorable, for to quote the preface to the *Natural Philosophy*: 'Nothing can be more fatal to progress than a too confident reliance on mathematical symbols, for the student is only too apt to take the easier course and consider the formula and not the fact as the physical reality.' Many, but by no means all, of Lord Kelvin's papers and lectures have been collected and published in *Papers on Electrostatics and Magnetism, Collected Papers* (3 vols.), 'Popular Lectures and Addresses' (3 vols.), and the *Baltimore Lectures*, delivered in 1884, published in 1904. The last volume has a special interest quite apart from its scientific importance, for the earlier lectures are printed just as they were delivered, having been taken down in shorthand by Mr Hathaway, and they give a most vivid idea of Lord Kelvin's method of lecturing. To listen to a lecture by Lord Kelvin was about the most exhilarating form of instruction conceivable, it was full of human nature, and digressions of the most entertaining kind. These were apt to evaporate when the lecture was written out for formal publication, but fortunately they are preserved in the Baltimore lectures. Here are a few taken almost at random, speaking on the theory of waves, he says, 'The great struggle of 1815, not that fought out on the plains of Belgium, was, who was to rule the waves, Cauchy or Poisson.' — 'An anisotropic solid is not an isotropic solid.' — 'I said to Stokes — (I always consult my great authority Stokes when I get the chance).' — 'We have not the slightest reason to believe that ether is imponderable. — [Note, Nov. 17, 1899. I now see that we have the strongest possible reason to believe that ether is imponderable.]' — 'The brain wasting perversity of the insular inertia which still condemns British engineers to reckonings of miles and yards and feet and inches and grains and pounds and ounces and acres.' It is remarkable that though the lectures are on the wave theory of light, Lord Kelvin barely mentions in them the electromagnetic theory: his great contemporary von Helmholtz on the other hand based all his later optical investigations on Maxwell's theory. I think Lord Kelvin hoped to get at the nature of electricity through the study of light rather than that of light from the study of electricity, and that this perhaps led him to do less than justice to Maxwell's magnificent generalisation.

I have not space to do more than allude to the services rendered to science by his invention of instruments to measure electrical quantities of almost every kind; some years ago by far the greater part of all accurate electrical measurements in this country must have been made with his instruments; nor can we give even a list of Lord Kelvin's notable achievements in Physical Science; there are few indeed of the fundamental problems of Physics which have not been made clearer by his genius and with which his name will be connected as long as men study nature and seek to find out her laws.

January 16th, 1908

Thomson and the Cambridge School of Experimental Physics

W. C. D. WHETHAM (LORD DAMPIER)

The Publication of Professor J. J. Thomson's book on the *Conduction of Electricity through Gases*, marks a stage in the history of the Cambridge School of Physics which should be of interest to others than those who are directly concerned with that branch of knowledge. In these pages have been brought together for the first time the results of the many investigations of the electrical properties of gases, investigations which have been going on of recent years throughout the physical laboratories of the world. A large part of this work is directly due to Professor Thomson himself, and to those who have been inspired by his teaching and example. It is perhaps fortunate that the task of writing an appreciation of the volume, in which their researches are made readily accessible, should have fallen to one whose work has lain in other branches of physics, to one, that is to say, who can write of the subject with the detachment proper to a review.

Every physicist who wishes to keep abreast of the modern developments of his subject will, of necessity, make a careful study of the book before us. Its merits are great. From the experimental side it is comprehensive, and adequately detailed, and the theoretical treatment is from a master hand, a hand which has done more than any other to build up the subject under consideration. Its faults, too, are manifest. The arrangement fails in clearness and logical sequence, and the language is often somewhat obscure, largely owing to a want of system in punctuation. But the consideration of both merits and faults is beside the question. The book is necessary, and no one else could have written it.

To the general reader, the importance of the book lies in the account it gives of Professor Thomson's own momentous discovery of the ultra-atomic state of matter. Speculation from the time of Lucretius to that of Sir William Crookes has been busy with imaginings anent ultimate particles, which should be common to all different kinds of matter, and should compose these different kinds of matter by differences in their number or arrangement. Professor Thomson has not followed the facile and barren paths of speculation; he has first found the particles. He has detected them in the vacuum tubes, which for years have been familiar objects in the laboratory and popular lecture room; he has shown that they are much smaller than the chemical atom; he has proved them to be common to different kinds of matter.

Since the beginning of the nineteenth century, the chemical atom has been the ultimate unit in which our conception of matter has been expressed. The sixty, seventy or eighty different elements, progressively known at one time or another to the chemist, seemed to be essentially different in kind, though certain likenesses between them and periodic relations between their properties and masses vaguely pointed to a common origin. Now, after a hundred years of usefulness, the atom yields place to Professor Thomson's corpuscle, and the new phenomena of radio-activity are leading us to believe that one element can pass into another, thereby fulfilling in some measure the dreams of the mediaeval alchemist.

When an electric discharge is sent through a glass bulb, from which all but a small trace of air has been exhausted, a beautiful glow of light is seen, the appearance of which depends on the stage of exhaustion reached. In the last stages, green phosphorescent effects appear on the surface of the glass opposite the negative terminal, and, if an obstacle be interposed between the cathode, as that terminal is called, and the glass, a sharp shadow is formed. It is concluded therefore that rays, known as cathode rays, proceed from the cathode in straight lines. These rays are deflected by a magnet, and, as Professor Thomson found, by an electric force also. Such deflections indicate that the rays consist of moving particles charged with electricity. The magnitudes of the deflections will depend on three things, the mass of the particles, the charge they carry, and the velocity with which they move. Two relations between these three unknown quantities are given by the amounts of the magnetic and of the electric deflections, and a third determination, giving the charge alone, enables all three quantities to be calculated. The charge on the particles, or rather on particles similar to them, is determined by a method due to Mr. C. T. R. Wilson, who proved by a series of beautiful experiments that such particles could act as nuclei, round which little drops of water collect to form a fog in damp air. By an application of this method the charge on the particles has been shown to be the same as the charge on an atom when a current of electricity is flowing through a solution of common salt. By the deflections in a vacuum tube, the velocities of the cathode rays are found to vary round a value about one tenth the velocity of light, while the mass of each particle is calculated to be about the thousandth part of the known mass of the atom of hydrogen, a substance which has the lightest atom known to chemistry.

These results, first obtained in the Cavendish Laboratory, and since confirmed elsewhere, show that we have now isolated particles much smaller than the hitherto indissoluble chemical atoms. Further experiments are of equal interest. The mass of these corpuscles was found to be the same whatever the gas with which the tube was originally filled, and the same when different metals formed the terminal from which the rays proceeded. The nature of the corpuscles then is unchanged though they be produced in different ways. They seem to be common to different kinds of matter, and, Professor Thomson believes, form the common constituent from which different kinds of matter are constructed.

These corpuscles act as isolated units of negative electricity. The conception of a disembodied electric charge, called an electron, had previously been investigated from the mathematical side by Professor Larmor and others. If the electrons are the common constituents of all chemical atoms, matter must be looked on as essentially electrical in its nature. A rapidly moving body, which carries an electric charge, can be shown mathematically to behave as though its mass or inertia were increased; and, if we imagine the atom to consist of a system of electrons in rapid orbital or oscillatory motion, it becomes possible to explain the whole conception of mass in terms of moving electric charges. Striking evidence in favour of this view is given by the recent study of radio-activity, for, from radium and similar elements, rays like cathode rays are continually and spontaneously emitted. It is difficult to believe that the corpuscles in these rays acquire suddenly their enormous velocities, and we are again led to the idea that, in the atom itself, the corpuscles or electrons are always in rapid motion. An atom, then, must be regarded as a solar system in miniature, the electrons whirling round in their orbits as the planets swing round the sun.

The interest and importance of these researches from the philosophical, as well as from the physical side, is now clear. They profoundly modify our conceptions of matter. Many brave things have been written, and many capital letters expended, in the endeavour to show that Natural Science will some day be able to give a complete mechanical explanation of the Universe, and express all phenomena in terms of matter and motion. But here we see that mechanical ideas are no more fundamental than electrical ones. The function of science is merely to construct a consistent model of phenomena. Whether that model corresponds with the ultimate reality behind phenomena, whether indeed there be any ultimate reality, is a question for metaphysics, not for Natural Science. An imaginary model of the whole of Nature would be too complex for the mind to grasp. Hence the divisions of Science into sciences, in each of which we look on the model from one aspect only, neglecting for the time all others. Thus mechanics is, so to speak, one section cut through our model of phenomena, a section which, for historical and other reasons, has been cut further and more clearly than any other yet known to us. But as Mach said long ago in his great work on the *Principles of Mechanics*, 'the science of Mechanics does not comprise the foundations, no, nor even a part of the world, but only an aspect of it.'

November 26th, 1903

Rutherford and Radioactivity

F. W. ASTON

It is difficult to overrate the importance of this volume, being as it is a practically complete compendium of our present knowledge of the phenomena of Radioactivity by the foremost of all its investigators, and, probably, the standard text-book on this very important domain of Physics and Chemistry for some years to come.* Since the second edition of 'Radioactivity' in 1905 the subject has widened its scope so enormously that so far from the present volume being a third edition of that work, it is rather the first edition of one

---

* *Radioactive Substances and their Radiations.* By E. Rutherford, D.Sc., Ph.D., LL.D., F.R.S.

commanding a larger although more special field, and though the change of title is not advantageous in itself, the author has good reason for it.

The most striking change in the subject is probably the recent great improvements in experimental methods which have now reached a delicacy quite undreamt of at the time of the discovery of Radium and the author's clear descriptions of the very definite and astonishing phenomena brought to light by their employment by highly trained investigators make reading of the most fascinating description. Thus by two entirely different methods, that of scintillation used by Rutherford, Geiger and Regener, and of cloud formation by C. T. R. Wilson; the ionisation due to the discharge of a single α particle from a radioactive substance can be detected with absolute certainty and measured with considerable exactness. By a simple, system of counting, based on the first method, it has been shown that 'the number of α particles expelled per second from one gram of radium itself is $3 \cdot 4 \times 10^{10}$; our most reliable value of ε the fundamental unit of electrification has been obtained by the same means. After exhaustive and delightfully clear accounts of α, β and γ rays and the methods of studying them, the author goes on to the work on the radioactive gases or emanations of which the most important, that from radium, has been recently examined with great care in regard to its physical constants. Its atomic weight determined by Ramsay and Gray by direct weighting on a quartz microbalance agrees astonishingly well with the theoretical one predicted by Rutherford some time before. Some of the most important pages in the book are devoted to the author's theory of 'successive transformations' which is developed at some length. By its means the thirty odd radioactive elements already known are marshalled into groups as they are derived from the parent substances Uranium, Radium, Actinium and Thorium, the processes attending the change of one element to the next following in its group being clearly indicated.

These elements must form an amazing spectacle to the arm-chair scientist. Some discharge α rays, some β rays, some both, in their death throes, while yet others have a peaceful and rayless end. Their periods vary from the venerable one of ten thousand million years ascribed to Thorium down to that of Actinium A which has recently been determined at one four-hundredth of a second; while a still more remarkable individual, Thorium C, manages to discharge β, γ, and the swiftest of α rays yet observed, during its brief existence of a million-millionth of a second.

To the practical physicist these extraordinary numbers, although none the less stuff to wonder at, are the inevitable results of consistent observations by many investigators correlated with the strictest mathematical reasoning and representing facts as definitely to be accepted by our reason, although as inconceivable to our imagination, as the sun's distance from α Centauri.

May 1st, 1913

Lord Rutherford: An Obituary

J. J. THOMSON

When I was asked by the editor of the *Cambridge Review* to write an obituary notice of Lord Rutherford, I felt obliged to decline as I had already agreed to write one for *Nature*, and the two would necessarily have much in common. The editor of *Nature* at the suggestion of the editor of the *Review* very courteously agreed to allow the one I had written for *Nature* to be reprinted in the *Review*. I should like to preface it with a few words on Rutherford's relation to Trinity College.

As soon as he was elected to the Cavendish Professorship Trinity College offered him a Fellowship which to our great gratification he accepted. He dined regularly in Hall on Sunday evenings and frequently brought distinguished and interesting men of science from other countries as his guests. His personality made him from the first a leading figure in our Society, as indeed it would in any other. It is difficult to imagine any one less like the traditional idea of a College Don than he was. To sit next to him in Hall was most invigorating, he was so full of vitality and his conversation so breezy and unconventional that one felt as much refreshed as if one had been for a brisk walk on a bracing day. He was never commonplace, there was nearly always a great deal to be said for his point of view, and he said it very forcibly. I think he enjoyed vigorous discussion. I have heard him say that he liked a good 'scrap' now and then. I never knew him in better form than he was the last time he dined in Hall only ten days before

M

his death. I happened to sit next to him and he seemed in almost exuberant good health and high spirits.

He has left behind him memories which will long be cherished by his friends, and his great discoveries will for ever be one of the glories of his college.

I have been asked by the Editor to give a brief account of my personal recollections of the late Lord Rutherford. I met him first in October, 1895, when a regulation had just come into force by which graduates of other universities were admitted to Cambridge as 'research students,' and after two years residence were eligible for the B.A. degree. Rutherford was the first student to apply: he was succeeded in an hour or so by J. S. Townsend, who has since become Wykeham professor of physics at Oxford, so that the first two research students become professor of physics at Cambridge and Oxford respectively. Rutherford, when in New Zealand, had invented a magnetic detector of wireless waves, and his first work in the Cavendish Laboratory was to try to improve its sensitiveness. He showed, even at this early stage, that he possessed exceptional 'driving' power and ability as an organizer. To test his detector, it was necessary to take observations simultaneously at two places, and the transport of the instrument required organization. He surmounted these difficulties by getting assistance from his friends, and at one time held the record for long distance wireless in England, having observed at the Laboratory signals which came from the Observatory about two miles away. He had not worked for more than a very few weeks before I became convinced that he was a student of quite exceptional ability.

Whilst Rutherford was engaged with this research, Röntgen rays were discovered, and we had found at the Laboratory that when these passed through a gas they made it conduct electricity even with the smallest electric forces. For ten years experiments on the passage of electricity through gases had been going on in the Laboratory; these were excessively difficult as the only ways of getting the electricity to pass through the gas were to use large electric forces and so get sparks, or make the gas so hot that you got flames. Both these were exceedingly capricious in their behaviour. The Röntgen rays gave a very simple and reliable means of making the gas conduct electricity even under the smallest forces, put researches on gases on quite a different footing, and promised to add greatly to our knowledge of the subject. Rutherford devised very ingenious methods for measuring various fundamental quantities connected with this subject, and obtained very valuable results which helped to make the subject metrical, whereas before it had been only descriptive.

Yet another fundamental discovery was made while Rutherford was working in the Laboratory, that of radioactivity, which in one form or another occupied his attention for more than twenty years. Henri Becquerel found in 1896 that salts of uranium gave out radiation which, like Röntgen rays, could penetrate opaque bodies and affect a photographic plate. The radiation was not all of one type: one part of it was very easily absorbed; another part could penetrate much greater distances and was defected by magnetic force in the same direction as a negatively electrified body, and a third, present only in small quantities, seemed even more penetrating than the second. In 1918 Rutherford made a careful study of these types of radiation, which he called α, β, γ, a notation which is now universally used; he did not find any irregularities, and commenced a study of the radiation from thorium. He had not completed this when he was elected to the professorship of physics in Montreal in succession to H. L. Callendar, who was also a Trinity man and who had worked in the Cavendish Laboratory with remarkable success.

Rutherford had not been long enough in Cambridge to entitle him to be able to sit for a fellowship when he was elected to the professorship and left Cambridge for Montreal. When he got there, he resumed the experiments on the thorium radiation. These, until the clue was found, were terribly perplexing; what seemed a trivial thing such as a puff of air would produce a great difference in the radiation, while large changes in temperature produced no effect. The thorium seemed to infect bodies placed near it and make them radioactive; they recover after a time if the thorium is taken away. These anomalies, though troublesome, were really a blessing in disguise, for in his attempt to account for them, Rutherford arrived at the view about the processes going on in radioactive substances which is now universally accepted. His view was that the thorium, besides giving out radiations, gives out a radioactive gas which he called an emanation. This may be wafted about, or settle on solids and make them appear to be radioactive. The emanation is not permanent, but after a few hours changes into non-radioactive substance.

Rutherford's scientific activity was never greater than when he was at Montreal. In the years between coming to Cambridge and leaving

Montreal to be professor of physics at the University of Manchester, he had published between forty and fifty papers; a few of these were joint papers, but the great majority were about researches of his own which had led to results of first-rate importance and which could not have been obtained by anyone who was not an experimentalist of the very first order. In those days laboratories had no funds to buy instruments as sensitive as those which are now available, and to detect small effects required exceptional skill, patience and self-criticism.

After Rutherford went to Manchester I did not see much of him until 1915, when Mr Arthur Balfour, as he was then, created the Board of Invention and Research for the co-ordination and encouragement of scientific effort in connexion with the Great War. Lord Fisher was the president of the Board, and I was a member of the Central Committee. The most pressing need at the moment was some means of detecting submarines. We got Rutherford to draw up a report on the methods which had been used or suggested for this purpose. He reported strongly in favour of a particular method, and we were fortunate enough to secure the services of Prof W. H. (now Sir William) Bragg as director of a research for this purpose, and provided him with a laboratory and staff. Rutherford also visited the United States to find out what they were doing in this matter and to tell them what we were doing. His help was continually being asked on a great variety of questions and there was no one whose opinion carried greater weight.

The Cavendish Laboratory has made great progress under his direction; the Mond Laboratory for magnetic research and the High-Tension Laboratory have been created. When he came, the supply of instruments for research was too scanty; it is now in this respect one of the best equipped physical laboratories in existence. Lord Rutherford's activities were very wide-spread; he was professor of natural philosophy at the Royal Institution, and also held with conspicuous success the very responsible post of chairman of the Advisory Council of the Department of Scientific and Industrial Research. That he could discharge so many duties was due to his powers of organization and that his claim to know a good man when he saw him was amply justified by results. With this faculty he could delegate some of his work to others without injury to the efficiency of the Laboratory, and get time to spare for his other activities. His death just on the eve of his having in the High-Tension Laboratory means of research far more powerful than those with which he had already obtained results of profound importance is, I think, one of the greatest tragedies in the history of science.

November 5th, 1937

Mon Anxiété Devant Le Problème des Quanta

LOUIS DE BROGLIE

I was nineteen years old when I first became conscious of a vocation for theoretical physics. I had passed the first part of the Baccalauréat in latin-with-sciences, and the second part in both mathematics and philosophy; I then read history at the Sorbonne, for this was a subject which attracted me and which has never ceased to interest me, and I took my degree at the age of eighteen. After this, I began to study law, but it was at this point that my reading, of the works of Henri Poincaré in particular, brought me back to the sciences.

I therefore began to read for a scientific degree, although it was from this moment that my own preference began to crystallize. My brother Maurice, a young scholar still, had been entrusted with the task of editing the proceedings of the first Solvay Congress which had been held in Brussels in October, 1911. The object of this Congress had been to study the quantum theory, and the greatest scholars of the period in the field of mathematical physics had participated: Max Planck, Einstein, Henri Poincaré, Lorentz, to name but a few. Shortly afterwards, my brother showed me the preliminary versions of the proceedings he was editing. I read these difficult papers eagerly, and I discovered the importance of this new quantum theory which Planck had advanced by a stroke of genius in 1900, and which Einstein had extended in a new form in 1905 in his theory of light quanta. The deeper meaning of this major revolution in theoretical physics was clear to me: the notions of waves and corpuscles, which had hitherto been employed in different contexts by theoretical physicists—waves for representing light and radiation in general, corpuscles in connection with matter and its structure—should in fact *both* appear in every case. How could such a synthesis be achieved, granted that the mysterious

'Planck's constant' which today, more than half a century later, has still not yielded its secret, would play some role without the slightest doubt? A number of remarks had already caught my attention: in the middle of the nineteenth century, Hamilton and later Jacobi had noticed a curious analogy between the laws of mechanics governing the motion of corpuscles, and the laws of wave theory, which determine the propagation of radiation. This analogy was generally regarded as a purely formal one, but my youthful imagination began to wonder whether this analogy had not some deep physical meaning, whether it might not lead us to the synthesis of the concepts of wave and corpuscle which seemed to me a necessary consequence of the mysterious Quanta of theoretical physics. Once I had passed my Licence ès Sciences, I promised to devote myself to this problem.

In that year of 1913, however, I was only a humble adolescent, whose future was still in the lap of the Gods. In October, I left to perform my military service with the Radiotélégraphistes of the 8ème Régiment du Génie. Then the 1914–18 war broke out, so that for six years, my plans for studying quanta, waves and particles were almost wholly abandoned, and I devoted my time to the techniques of Radio-tele-graphy. These techniques were at the time undergoing a rapid and conclusive revolution, however. Still somewhat embryonic in 1914, a complete transformation was to take place during the next few years; with the introduction of the triode valve, the radio-telephone soon appeared, and later, radio as we know it today. As I was present at the birth of these new modes of communication, I have never lost interest in their subsequent development, and during the last twenty years, I have been particularly interested by the growth of the new techniques of radar, very high frequencies and transistors.

The first world war over, I returned to the laboratory of my brother, who was at the time particularly concerned with X-rays and the photo-electric effect; on returning to the preoccupations of my youth, there-fore, I found myself once again face to face with this problem of waves and corpuscles, which pervades every aspect of very high frequency radiation. For a long time, I pondered over this problem, and after various preliminary efforts, I managed to establish a precise correlation between the motion of a corpuscle and the propagation of a wave, first in a number of notes published during the autumn of 1923, and later in more detail in my doctoral thesis, of November, 1924. In the theory, Planck's constant appeared, and I was able to show that many things which had hitherto been a mystery—the existence of stationary states in atoms, for example—become comprehensible through this correlation. The ideas which I proposed very rapidly met with a success for which I had not dared to hope. In 1926 they were analysed mathematically by Schrödinger, in 1927 they were confirmed experimentally when the remarkable phenomenon of electron diffraction was discovered, and they are at the very root of what is now known as wave mechanics, and the origin of an immense amount of other work.

While this medley of ideas progressively developed at an ever increasing speed, I myself remained somewhat perplexed. When the ideas at the basis of wave mechanics had not yet been thought of, I had not doubted for an instant that they must eventually lead to a clear synthetic picture of the relationship between waves and corpuscles, leaving the essential parts of the classical notions of these entities intact. Whereas eminent foreign scholars such as Bohr, Born and Heisenberg were following a quite different line of thought which was leading them to propose an interpretation of the wave-corpuscle duality totally different from the one I was seeking, I was developing an idea which had been inspired—more or less consciously—by the profound remarks of Einstein on this subject. In 1926-27, I developed this interpretation of wave mechanics, styling it 'the theory of the double solution.' Without going into too much detail, I can say that the theory suggests that every corpuscle—element of matter or light photon—constitutes a kind of singularity at the heart of a wave of finite extent, into which it is incorporated and which guides its motion since it forms an integral part of the wave. The picture obtained from this theory seemed satisfactory to me, for it gave a clear and exact representation of the union of waves and corpuscles in physics on the atomic scale. The role of the wave which is usually considered in wave mechanics still remained to be interpreted, however; this wave is homogeneous and contains no singularity at which a particle could be localized. I thought that I could overcome this by showing that the continuous wave of wave mechanics is a fictitious wave, which gives a statistical description of the various possible positions of the corpuscle; I thought that this was an exact interpretation, but that like all statistical descriptions, it was incomplete in that it allowed the individual to escape through describing only averages. I felt, therefore, that to each of the usual kinds of solution of the wave equations of wave mechanics, which give only a statistical description, there must correspond another solution, possessing a singularity and characterizing the true union of wave and corpuscle in the most fundamental physical reality. Hence the name which I had given my efforts, 'the theory of the double solution.'

The picture which I had advanced lacked a complete mathematical justification, however; it lacked, too, as I have realized during the last few years, certain vital features without which it could hardly be tenable. At the fifth Solvay Congress, which met in Brussels in October, 1927, the purely probabilistic interpretation of wave mechanics proposed by Bohr, Born and Heisenberg carried the day, despite the objections raised by Einstein and Schrödinger; as a result of this, and because of the difficulty of casting my ideas into a really satisfactory form, I was led to halt my efforts, and seek elsewhere.

Why was I so discouraged, and why did I cease to pursue the aim which had hitherto always drawn me on: the desire for a precise image of the microphysical world, for a genuine synthesis which would make the coexistence of waves and corpuscles clearly comprehensible? Obviously one of the foremost reasons was that the task that I had undertaken entailed solving some exceedingly difficult problems, as I realized perfectly, and that I felt myself overwhelmed, whereas the opposing theory had all the appearance of a very elegant and very rigorous mathematical edifice, reposing on relatively simple foundations, and every day, experiment showed that it could predict or explain important phenomena. A further reason for my renunciation of my theory, more curious from the psychological point of view, perhaps, was the following: in 1928, at the very moment at which I realized how difficult my efforts to follow up my interpretation would be, I took up a University teaching post; a professor, entrusted with teaching physical theories in the Faculty of Sciences at Paris, I found myself confronted with a task wholly new to me, a task which I performed during thirty-four years. Lecturing, however, obliges one to present the subject in question in a coherent fashion, and in the case of theoretical physics, with mathematical exactitude; at University level, the students must be kept in touch with the most recent advances, and with the most valuable new results. Intuitions which have not yet acquired their definitive form, and newly-hatched theories cannot be accepted, therefore. It is for these reasons that one can say that to some extent at least, teaching alienates research.

At the age of thirty-six, therefore, I was a professor, giving lectures and beginning to train my own pupils. I began this career under the most brilliant auspices, for I had spent barely a year in my new post when the Swedish Academy of Sciences awarded me the Nobel Prize for Physics. This lofty reward demonstrated how much importance was attached in scientific circles to the ideas that I had introduced on the union of waves and corpuscles, and which had been confirmed so strikingly by the major achievements of wave mechanics, and by the recent fundamental discovery of the phenomenon of electron diffraction in crystals.

This is not the place to summarize my activities as a professor during more than thirty years, the lectures I gave on the principles, developments and applications of wave mechanics, the work I performed myself in an attempt to improve some of the theories or to introduce new ideas into them, and the lectures and addresses in which I have tried to broadcast new aspects of quantum physics. The only point I wish to make here is that until 1950, I never returned to the projects for a new interpretation which I had once attempted, and then abandoned, and that I contented myself with the purely probabilistic interpretation of Bohr, Born and Heisenberg which the majority of physicists had adopted. In 1950, however, and almost, I might say, to my own astonishment, I found myself wondering whether this interpretation of wave mechanics and quantum physics was truly satisfactory, and whether one ought not to return in some way to the ideas that had guided me in my youth, if a real explanation of the relationship between wave and corpuscle were to be found. I should now like to say a few words about this new turn of events in my thinking.

To make its origin comprehensible, I should first of all have to explain exactly what this purely probabilistic interpretation of quantum physics adopted by the majority of physicists is. This is not easy, however, for this interpretation has been presented in rather different ways by various authors, and by its very nature, it is rather vague and appears somewhat startling to the uninitiated mind. I can only give a very brief account of it here, therefore. This interpretation is based upon certain new ideas which seem both important and exact. Thus it seems certain, for example, that every measuring procedure, the object of which is to provide us with information about the microphysical world, in general modifies the previously existing situation to an extent which cannot be neglected; hence it may be impossible to measure, simultaneously and with precision, certain quantities which characterize corpuscles, such as their position and their state of motion. It is this impossibility that is expressed by Heisenberg's celebrated 'Uncertainty Relations'; there is no doubt as to their correctness, although the way in which they are at present interpreted is, I feel, arguable. Setting out from these exact statements, the theories which are held at the present time depend upon a number of postulates often adopted without critical discussion, and which are perhaps questionable, and after passing through progressively more abstract forms, they have somewhat paradoxically finished by removing all physical reality from both waves and corpuscles. The wave is now no more than a mathematical expression which enables one to evaluate probabilities, while the corpuscle—which is generally spread out 'in a virtual state' over an extended region of space—seems to exist no longer except when it manifests itself by fugitive detectable localized appearances. To characterize this notion which is difficult to express precisely, Bohr once found a word which seemed a godsend: he said that wave and corpuscle are 'complementary' aspects of reality, that is, they are incompatible pictures, but they are both necessary if all the observed phenomena are to be represented. If the word 'complementary' is employed solely to convey that phenomena sometimes display corpuscular behaviour and sometimes behave like waves, which is undeniable, then its use is perfectly legitimate; but in no sense whatsoever does it provide a genuine explanation of the duality of waves and corpuscles. We might compare this complementarity with the 'vertu dormitive' of opium, which Molière derided: it is perfectly legitimate to explain the soporific properties of opium by attributing to the latter a 'vertu dormitive', but we must resist any temptation to find an explanation of its properties in these words. Attempts have been made to base all sorts of philosophical considerations on Bohr's complementarity and on doubtful extensions of the uncertainty relations; they are, to say the least, perilous. It is often tempting to construct general philosophical theories on the facts of science which are always subject to revision.

Thus, some twelve years ago, I began once again to wonder whether the interpretation of wave mechanics which is at present accepted was really definitive, and whether the true and fundamental nature of the coexistence of waves and corpuscles were not obscured by the undeniable successes and apparent rigour of this interpretation. It is not, of course, a question of doubting the statistical truth of the elegant and exact formalisms with which the theoreticians of contemporary quantum physics juggle, but rather, of asking oneself whether these formalisms really go to the bottom of the problem and whether the interpretation that is offered really possesses a definitive character. As I have followed the hypotheses which form the foundations of the present interpretations while they were being established, I have been able to criticize them carefully; furthermore, I have been able to find a number of weak points, some paradoxical consequences, and to single out some postulates which do not perhaps correspond to physical reality even though they were naturally suggested by the mathematical formalism. I was thus led to reconsider the ideas which I had developed some thirty years earlier; furthermore, I could now introduce a number of modifications and additions which today I feel to be indispensable. During the last ten years, progress has been made in this re-interpretation of wave mechanics, and new horizons of the very greatest interest have opened to my gaze.* I have been considerably assisted in this task by a number of young research workers, who have been bold enough to follow this path; I use the work 'bold' advisedly, for it requires courage to try to swim upstream against the dominant current of ideas, and to oppose the opinions of eminent and influential scholars. Personally, I have devoted only a rather limited effort to this arduous task. At my age, and in my situation, one is burdened with obligations of various kinds, and it becomes almost impossible to find the necessary time and strength steadily to pursue difficult studies of one's own.

Today, therefore, I find myself in a rather odd situation. Forty years ago, I was one of the initiators of wave mechanics and contemporary quantum physics. Not without some surprise, I have witnessed the extremely rapid success of my ideas, their striking experimental verification, and the extraordinary extent to which they have been developed in widely different domains. Even so, however, I am not satisfied. In the springtime of my life, the problems of quanta and of the co-existence of waves and corpuscles in the microphysical world obsessed me—I made major, if incomplete, efforts to find the solution to them. Today, in the autumn of my existence, the same problem still preoccupies me, for despite all the victories gained and all the route that has been covered, I do not believe that the enigma has really been solved. Perhaps the future—a future that I shall doubtless not be present

* See the bibliography.

to see—will settle the question; future generations will decide whether my present point of view reflects the folly of an elderly man who remains attached to the ideas of his youth, or whether, on the contrary, it represents the foresight of a scholar who has spent a lifetime pondering the most fundamental of the problems of contemporary physics.

October 17th, 1964

BIBLIOGRAPHY

Etude critique des bases de l'interprétation actuelle de la Mécanique ondulatoire. Gauthier-Villars, Paris, 1963; English translation, Elsevier, Amsterdam, 1964.
  La thermodynamique de la particule isolée. Gauthier-Villars, Paris, 1964.
  'Photons et ondes électromagnétiques,' *Note aux Comptes Rendus de l'Académie des Sciences de Paris*, Vol. 258, p. 6345.

The Biology of Fate

JOSEPH NEEDHAM

The walls of Cambridge combination-rooms must often have heard disputes in the sixteenth century in which the words 'predestination' and 'free-will' constantly recurred. Whether they recognise any approximation to the same problem in the words 'heredity' and 'environment' which they now re-echo, may well be questioned. It is at any rate certain that the conception of fate, after its long journey from Greek tragedy downwards, has, like all other conceptions connected with living organisms, been taken into the laboratories of biology and given a thorough examination. The attitude of the biologist to these fundamental problems is now rightly regarded as being important for those who have to administer the practical affairs of human life, and the conclusions of biology about them therefore require exposition in terms which the practical economist or politician can appreciate.

Professor Jennings, of the Johns Hopkins University in Maryland, has had a remarkable success in the account of the present position in genetics and experimental embryology, which is the subject of this review.* His first five chapters summarise the biological foundations

* *The Biological Basis of Human Nature.* By H. S. Jennings.

for the matters which he deals with later, and here his description of the living cell, the nucleus, the chromosomes, and the particulate units therein which are concerned with heredity and which are known as genes, is as concise as possible and as accurate as the necessarily small space will permit. From this any intelligent person can get some idea of how the chromosomes are passed on in the germ-cells from one generation to another, how the genes contained in them are continually shuffled into new combinations, and how sex-linked inheritance, for instance, differs from inheritance according to Mendelian ratios. Elementary principles such as the carrying by normal individuals of recessive defective genes, the production of offspring without personal defects by parents both of which are defective, the dependence of the effects of inbreeding on the nature of the stocks started from, all are well and carefully described. A certain amount of historical treatment freshens this part of the book, as when, in describing the development of modern genetics, Professor Jennings points out that it was the X-chromosome, that which is specially concerned with sex-determination, which gave the clue for all later research and showed how the gene-mechanism might operate. We know now that 'the laws of inheritance are the rules of distribution of the parts of the chromosomes.'

Professor Jennings' description of the fundamental features of embryonic development is equally good. He dicusses such matters as the interaction of genes and cytoplasm, the difference between 'mosaic-eggs' and 'regulation-eggs,' the production of two or more organisms by suitable treatment of one egg, and the work of the organisers in self-differentiation. Read in conjunction with Professor J. S. Huxley's[1] simply-written paper on the development of the frog, it should be sufficient to give anyone whose work lies in other than scientific fields a clear idea of the elements of what is now known about the early stages of animals.

By a series of transitional chapters Professor Jennings leads on from this survey of facts to their application in specifically human problems. His book can be recommended as a highly salutary exercise to all those (unfortunately numerous) persons who talk about heredity and environment without giving attention either to what the words really mean or to the experimental evidence which exists regarding their operation. Thus it is quite clear that the same gene-combination may

[1] J. S. Huxley: 'The Tadpole: a study in developmental physiology' in *Essays in Popular Science*.

produce very different results according to the internal and external environment which its products meet with as the egg develops. The genes in the fertilised egg do not irrevocably decide what sort of a creature is going to be the finished product; all they do is to provide a limited set of potentialities, any one of which will be actualised according to the environment which the developing organism meets with. The mere fact, as Professor Jennings says, that a defect is hereditary, does not mean that it must occur; it only will occur if the favourable conditions are present in development. This applies, of course, to mental characteristics just as much as physical ones, for both are undoubtedly subject to the rules of inheritance. On the question of the extent to which human mentality is a product of inheritance or of environment, Professor Jennings takes up a very sane and reasonable position, holding that both factors play a part of about equal importance. He completely dissents, of course, from the extreme environmental position of Professor J. B. Watson and other behaviourists, who claim that by subjection to adequately diverse environments, diverse training, diverse instruction, etc., a normal human being can be made to take any place in the social organism. This claim is easily seen to conceal a fallacy, for by limiting it to 'normal' individuals, Watson excludes by definition all genetic classes that have not capabilities of adjustment sufficient to justify his assertion.

Fallacies, indeed, are as common as flints in Breckland in the usual discussions of heredity. Professor Jennings has done well to marshal them into a kind of classification, with the following results. There is (1) the fallacy of non-experimental judgments, due to the temptation of judging propositions in genetics on the basis of one's general impressions of the rest of the universe. (2) The fallacy of attributing to one cause what is really due to many causes. Having found 'it', the investigator assumes without further consideration that other alternative causes are put out of court, whereas in fact negative conclusions cannot be proved by means of positive observations. A common form of these fallacies in biology is (3) the view that the characteristics of organisms are divisible into two distinct classes; one due to heredity, the other due to environment. Characteristics do not arise as units directed by representative particles, but through the co-operation of many genes, and through their interaction with other things, including the environmental conditions. Cruder is (4) the fallacy that heredity is some mysterious force tending to make children resemble their parents, the notion that 'like produces like.' It is true that statistically considered, heredity results on the whole in a certain degree of correlation between parent and progeny, but this is a matter of averages and not of individual similarities. 'These fallacies,' says Professor Jennings, 'interbreed, producing offspring that loom large in biological discussions.' Thus we get (5) the fallacy that showing a characteristic to be hereditary proves that it is not alterable by the environment, and vice versa. It would be much nearer the truth to say that any characteristic which can be affected by the environment can also be affected by a change of genes, and vice versa. Directly following upon this is the fallacy (6) that since all human characters are hereditary, heredity is all-important and environment negligible, in human affairs; and conversely, that since a great many very significant human characters are environmental, therefore environment is all-important and heredity negligible.

When we come to the sphere of practicable applications and what is known as Eugenics, we find a number of fallacies which are just as serious. From fallacy (4) above, it is often concluded (7) that to prevent the breeding of hereditary defectives will largely or entirely get rid of such defectives in later generations, and conversely, that the superior individuals which we have with us now must have come from superior parents, and that these things will continue to happen. Uncritical eugenists have a simple proposal—cut out the defective parents and you will not have the defective offspring. 'Any society,' says Professor Jennings, 'that succeeds in carrying out this plan, is of course in for a great disappointment.' For unfortunately the great majority of the defective genes which cause the troubles we want to get rid of are contained in normal people who carry them within their germ-cells in a manner analogous to those persons who harbour the bacilli of typhoid fever without ever suffering from it themselves. Thus it is known that about 0.3% of the world's population is actually suffering from feeblemindedness, but no less than 10.0% of the population is composed of normal individuals carrying the defective genes. Dr R. A. Fisher's calculations* showed that about 11% of the feebleminded of any generation come from the mating of the feebleminded of the previous generation, while 89% of them come from matings among the carrier group. The converse case of genius is equally interesting. Prof. Raymond Pearl, in an interesting paper, gave the results of an

* R. A. Fisher, 'The elimination of mental defect,' *Journal of Heredity*, 1927, 18, 529.

examination into the recorded parentage of men of genius, choosing as their definition, the possession of two whole columns in the *Encyclopaedia Britannica*. The most frequent result was some such description as 'dissolute and wandering lute-player,' and it was obvious that in most cases carriers of the genes of genius had been responsible for the great men.

Our final fallacy (8) is that biology requires an aristocratic constitution of society. Each grade of society, it is said, reproduces itself. Criminals produce criminals, public school men produce public school men, intellectuals produce intellectuals. The children of the Platonic Guardians become Guardians too. Whereas the fact is that from the higher many lower are produced, from the lower many higher, and from the great mediocre mass are produced more of the higher than the higher produces itself, more of the lower than the lower produces itself. A democracy that can produce experts is the form of society called for by the facts of biology.

Professor Jennings does not, of course, decry the value of sterilisation of defective stocks, for every gain, however small, is desirable, but he makes it clear that in the present situation environmental measures are likely to have a much bigger and more immediate effect than sterilisation. There is, in fact, a striking paradox inherent in the often-repeated cry that humanity should be bred just as prize stock is bred. For ordinary family mating is designed to cover up (by avoidance of inbreeding, etc.) precisely those defective genes which the breeder, if he were allowed free play with human affairs, would bring out into the light in order to reject. The most pressing need at the present time is for some method (chemical or otherwise) which would enable us to detect the presence of defective genes in apparently normal people, and until we have this insight into the make-up of our friends, practical eugenics has not very much to do.

The book concludes with some chapters devoted to questions such as marriage and the family, problems of race mixture, and the method of evolution. Particularly interesting is the chapter entitled 'Biology and Selves,' where the question (which should be considered by theologians and psychologists) is raised as to whether the gene-combination plus the environment is sufficient to account for the phenomena of personality, the capacity of the conscious organism to say 'I.' But it will be already clear from this review that Professor Jennings has produced a book which should be of much value to anyone who is concerned to form opinions on the government of human society. In the councils of this government biology must play a part, the value of which is clearly to be found in Professor Jennings' examination of the ministers of human fate.

October 17th, 1930

The Brain and its Place in Nature

FRED HOYLE

The relationship between science and society is a recurring theme in Professor Young's book,* and this is very fit and proper, since the relation of science to society is of decisive importance in the history of mankind. We tend to think of science as belonging only to the last few centuries, but a primitive sort of science must have been practised from very early times; the development of agriculture may be taken as an outstanding example of its application. Nevertheless an important distinction can be made between recent science and early science. It is probable that the concepts of early science were in a large degree common to all members of the human race—for example, primitive notions of space and time; whereas the concepts of modern science are peculiar to a small minority.

Now, even on the face of it, there is something strange in the way the views of this minority have come to affect the activities of the majority. For instance, how comes it that, while only a tiny proportion of humanity has a clear idea of what electromagnetism is about, yet the science of electromagnetism lies at the base of the whole organisation of modern industry? An observer from another planet might possibly seek to answer such a question by saying that scientists must be politically powerful persons, who have in some way managed to seize the instruments of government, thereby enabling their ideas to be impressed on the rest of the community. Our visitor would no doubt be surprised to learn that, so far from this being the case, scientists scarcely possess even vestiges of political influence. Nor can it be said that scientists are effective propagandists; whenever a scientist feels impelled to discuss some sociological implication of science the rest

* *Doubt and Certainty in Science.* By J. Z. Young.

N

of the body politic seems determined to act, not on any advice that may be offered, but in the direct contrary. The scientist is told that he 'oversimplifies social problems' (as if all problems in science were simple!), that he has taken no account of 'imponderables,' that science is 'one-eyed,' etc.

The apparent paradox outlined above may be summarised in a direct question: As no immediate degree of effectiveness can be attached to the sociological pronouncements of the scientists, how does science come to exert such a profound influence on society? Some might answer, through the material gadgets that science produces:—steam engines, dynamos, radio, telephones, aircraft, and so on. This I think is part of the answer, and an important part, but there is a complementary side that must not be overlooked. Gadgets of this sort would be a negligible social factor if they simply remained as toys in the scientist's laboratory. What lends importance to them is a slow absorption of certain associated beliefs into the general community. Electromagnetism has widespread application to-day only partly because of the discoveries of such men as Faraday and Maxwell. Their discoveries would in themselves have remained socially unimportant if nearly everyone of us had not become infused with a new set of beliefs; that dynamos and radios are desirable things to have, that blind trust can be placed in what the scientist says about electromagnetism (the distrust we noted above, of scientists in non-technical matters, arises because the self-esteem of the rest of the body politic apparently demands some such reaction in order to offset its helplessness in technical matters), and so forth. We may therefore conclude that a scientific discovery or theory only attains real social force when the community at large has come to accept a corresponding set of new beliefs.

All this relates closely to Professor Young's book. For Professor Young believes that discoveries at present being made in the mathematico-biophysical field will, when the associated beliefs have had sufficient time to percolate through into the public consciousness, result in a far greater impact on society than science has ever had before. These discoveries concern the question of how our 'minds' work. To understand Professor Young's general point of view we may note that so far the effect of science on society has been largely confined to notions arising out of our enquiry into the nature of the physical world. Powerful as have been the ideas thrown up by this enquiry, it seems likely that a satisfactory theory of 'what makes us tick' would lead to profound modifications in our civilisation. Indeed, it seems possible that society may be able to gain a real understanding of itself, and may thereby be able to eliminate the general seizures that we find so painful.

Is this anything more than an appeal to psychology, it may be asked. It is certainly more than an appeal to what in the past has often been described as psychology. The psychology of the first half of the twentieth century (in so far as it has affected popular beliefs) is an empirical, qualitative study (interlarded sometimes, one may suspect, with a fair measure of charlatanism), whereas what Professor Young has in mind—or should I say in brain—is a much more quantitative approach to the subject. The psychology of the past may be compared with the physics of the Middle Ages; the new developments have not yet reached the age of Newton, but it is hoped that we are nearing that of Galileo.

By way of contrast with the above remarks, I should now like to take up a more personal view. Recent work on the problems of brain activity has been of a perhaps surprisingly mathematical character, and for this reason I have been much interested in the developments in this field. It was not until I read Professor Young's book, however, that I became aware of the sociological importance of this work. Thus on page 8 we already have the essence of Professor Young's plan:

'The method that I am going to suggest as a working basis is to organize *all* our talk about human powers and capacities around knowledge of what the brain does. When the philosopher studies the way in which people think, let him consider what activity this represents in the brain: for certainly there is some. When the theologian studies the fact that human beings tend to organize their activity around statements about gods, let him consider the activity that this involves in the brain. When the educationist and psychologist follow the ways in which the child grows to his mature powers and later perhaps goes astray, let them consider the processes of the development and decay of the activities of the brain.'

At first I thought that some of the claims for this working basis were being rather overdone:

'As we learn more of brain processes it should be possible to increase very much the amount of information that can be conveyed in this way (by writing and by speaking). Our methods of teaching to read and to use chemical and mathematical symbolism are at present quite empirical and are clearly of only limited effectiveness. As we come to know more in detail what we are doing we should be able to make the content of our written language very much fuller, and more quickly and widely learned. The possibilities of improved co-operation produced in this way may be very great. There is no obvious reason why a large proportion of the population should not read pages of mathematical symbols as readily as they now read print. By this means we could come to explain all the complexities of life more fully to each other, and therefore become correspondingly better at co-operation.'

I found passages such as this so arresting that I put aside this review until I had had time to ponder on the matter, and as a result I have come to think that Professor Young may be putting his case rather mildly: for, now in agreement with him, I can scarcely see any limit to what may eventually be achieved through this new branch of knowledge. It may well be that mankind to-day is on the verge of developments of greater import than any that have yet occurred during its long history.

To refer, finally, to the make-up of the book, it should be noted that there is more here than a reprint of Professor Young's Reith Lectures; much new material has been added as comments on the lectures themselves. The ideas discussed above are but a selection: I have considered only those issues that happen to be of special interest to me personally —it goes without saying that there is much else to excite the reader's attention. Scientists and non-scientists alike will find the makings of a revolution in thought in this remarkable book. For myself I would like to see it become compulsory reading for all persons suffering from strong emotional convictions.

December 1st, 1951

The Structure of Large Molecules

MAX PERUTZ

The life of the cell depends on the interplay of various kinds of very large molecules. For instance, nucleic acids are the carriers of heredity, proteins act as enzymes which catalyse chemical reactions, lipoids are used as electrical condensers, and polymerised sugars provide stores of energy. These different types of compounds form molecules containing thousands of atoms tightly bonded together. Their complexity increases as we pass from the smallest enzymes of molecular weight of about 10,000 to the plant viruses which have molecular weights of millions; these viruses are self-reproducing and might almost rank as organisms rather than molecules.

At present little is understood of the detailed mechanism of living processes, partly because we do not know the structure of the large molecules involved in them. If only we knew exactly how the atoms are arranged in space then we could fit together the jigsaw puzzle of their molecular patterns and understand the active interplay between them. Most of our knowledge about large biological molecules comes from the researches of chemists, but in the last few years X-ray crystallographers have made several decisive contributions. Some of these have come from a Research Unit in the Cavendish Laboratory which receives its main support from the Medical Research Council.

In the past, X-ray crystallography has revealed the atomic structure of minerals and metals, and of all the main types of organic compounds. Its most recent and striking success has been the unravelling of the constitution of Vitamin B_{12}, a molecule of baffling complexity with the brutto formula $C_{63}H_{90}N_{14}O_{14}P$ Co. This was done by Mrs D. C. Hodgkin and her colleagues at Oxford in collaboration with Sir Alexander Todd's laboratory at Cambridge. Vitamin B_{12} contains 183 atoms, whereas even the simplest protein contains several thousands. How then can we hope to jump the gap and apply X-ray methods to molecules more complex, by orders of magnitude, than anything that has been attempted before?

Part of the answer lies in the repetitive nature of most biological molecules. Some of them are helical chains in which similar units repeat at regular intervals. Others are compact, roundish bodies, but they also are known to consist of chain molecules doubling back on themselves and bonded together in space. In each case X-ray analysis can reveal the configuration of the repeating unit, or, more often, it can test whether a structure proposed for that unit is compatible with the experimental observations.

The major part of the Research Unit's work is devoted to two molecules of outstanding biological importance: the haemoglobins of blood and muscle. The former combines with oxygen in the lungs and carries it to the tissue; the latter (which is called myoglobin) takes the oxygen over from the blood and keeps it available in the muscle, ready for use by the enzyme system which burns glycogen and turns its energy into muscular work and heat. The oxygen in haemoglobin actually attaches itself to the iron atom contained in a red pigment called haem, and haem itself is bound to the protein part of the haemoglobin molecule in a manner not yet understood. Nor is it known why iron forms a compound with oxygen when it is part of haemoglobin, whereas iron or haem by themselves do not.

Haemoglobin and myoglobin can both be crystallised and give beautiful X-ray diffraction patterns, but the interpretation of these is a problem of formidable complexity. The difficulty is that the diffraction pattern of a crystal gives us only half the information needed to solve its structure: it tells us the amplitudes but not the phases of the diffracted rays. In classical X-ray analysis a start is often made by guessing the approximate structure; with luck, this is accurate enough to calculate the phases of some of the diffracted rays: with their help and with the measured amplitudes more is found out about the structure, and this knowledge in turn leads to the determination of more phases. In this way the structure is gradually refined until the positions of all the atoms are determined. In crystalline proteins this method breaks down, because we have no certain knowledge of what even the approximate structure is likely to be.

A method of very great promise, well established in X-ray analysis but new for proteins, has recently been discovered, by which the phase problem may nevertheless be solved. Its physical principle is this. Two kinds of crystals of the protein are prepared which are identical in all respects except one. In the first kind of crystal a heavy metal atom is attached to the protein molecule in a position which is filled by a light atom in the second kind. Although the number of electrons in this heavy atom is insignificant compared to the total number present in the protein, it nevertheless alters the diffraction pattern in a measurable way. This is because the electrons in the heavy atom are concentrated at a point, whereas the other electrons are so spread out that most of their scattering contributions are obliterated by interference. The changes in the diffraction pattern allow one to determine the positions taken up by the heavy atoms and, once these are known, to calculate the phase of the diffracted rays.

By this method the first detailed pictures of protein molecules ever to be seen have now been worked out. They are pictures of the density distribution in haemoglobin and myoglobin seen in projection on a plane. In themselves they tell us little as yet about the structure of these molecules. Their importance lies in establishing the principle that the structure of proteins can now be solved by X-ray analysis despite the complexity of the problem.

The next step in the research will be to try and get additional pictures of the molecules, projected on other planes, in order to obtain stereoscopic views. Finally their structure should be determined in three dimensions by calculating the density distribution along a series of closely spaced parallel sections. This last step should reveal all the main principles of their molecular structure and provide the explanation for some of the chemical and biological properties mentioned above.

Another piece of research in the Unit which has already received some publicity concerns the structure of (deoxyribo-) nucleic acid, the material responsible for the transmission of hereditary information from one generation to the next. This acid is a double helix of two intertwined chains; the hereditary code itself consists in the sequence in which four alternative chemical units are arranged along the length of each chain. The arrangement of the units in the two chains is such that the sequence in one chain determines that of its partner. It is this last feature which is so exciting, because it suggests a possible method by which the structure might duplicate itself. It is conceivable that the two chains of the double helix may separate, and that each chain may then act as a template for the formation of a new chain of complementary structure. In this way two 'daughter' pairs of intertwined chains could be formed, each 'daughter' pair carrying the same hereditary code as the original pair from which it was formed.

Other work going on in the Unit concerns the structure of plant viruses, which are compounds of nucleic acid and protein; and the structure of collagen, a fibrous protein which forms the dominant component of skin, bone, tendon and connective tissue. Research on the chemistry of haemoglobin and myoglobin is also being carried out. Finally, an X-ray tube with a rotating anode has been developed which is probably the most powerful one ever built for crystallographic research.

In conclusion the names of some of the research workers in the Unit should be mentioned. The work on haemoglobin has been developed by Dr M. F. Perutz in association, until recently, with Sir Lawrence Bragg. The discoveries on myoglobin are due to Dr J. C. Kendrew and his collaborators, and the structure of nucleic acid was solved by Drs J. D. Watson and F. H. C. Crick. Collagen is being worked on by Drs A. Rich and Crick, and plant viruses by Dr Watson. The chemical work is in charge of Dr V. M. Ingram, and the rotating anode tube has been designed by Mr D. A. G. Broad.

November 19th, 1955

The Two Towers

JOHN ZIMAN

At Cavendish coffee the other day we were designing the ideal Palace of the Sciences. Each department is to adjoin its intellectual neighbours; between Physics and Chemistry we place Physical Chemistry and Metallurgy; Geology is to be flanked on the one side by Mineralogy, on the other by Botany and Zoology; Biochemistry must lead through Physiology to Medicine, and so on. The metaphorical borderline subject must occupy an actual room between the regions governed by greater neighbours. Thus we should encourage contact between workers in cognate fields, and scientific knowledge would grow even more lustily.

Unfortunately, the New Museum site, even with its skyscraping towers, could not hold our grand design, which has already been compromised by moving Chemistry to Lensfield Road. It must remain an entertaining intellectual problem, to fit them all together, in two or three dimensions, compactly, and without violating natural affinities. Yet, fifty years ago this was no problem at all. Chemists, Physicists, Biologists (A) and Biologists (B) could each have had a separate building, as tight as a medieval castle, for all the commerce there might be between them. Each was a 'discipline,' and although you might use, say, chemical analysis in the design of an experiment in physics, that did not permit you to assume the chemical way of thought without a long apprenticeship.

But from those centres, those clearings in the forest, the frontiersmen set out, and blazed new trails, so that now their territories join to make a complex, multiply-connected map of knowledge. In imagination we can travel from the seashore of quantum theory, through the rocky ranges of atomic physics, over the bridge of the valence bond, into the green prairies of organic chemistry. All the way the path is more or less charted, more or less clear to see; our job nowadays is only to broaden the trails and mop-up the islands of ignorance that have been left between. So our new Palace is just Whitehall, or the Pentagon or the Kremlin, replacing the old castles by a single, co-ordinated, centralized administration.

Permit me to enlarge a little further upon this metaphor. Over there, at Sidgwick Avenue, on the far bank of the Cam, they are building just another such Palace—for the Arts and Social Sciences. It, too, has an interesting topology, with History laying claim to the whole site, Philosophy as a Fifth Column in every Department, Law sturdily repelling all advances, and Theology half remembering that it once ruled a great Empire. I commend this problem to Dr Plommer, for a modern Pantheon where Politics, Philosophy and Economics may be worshipped simultaneously.

Yet, on both sides of the Cam there are still men and institutions who refuse to accept their interdependence and claim autonomy. Moreover, there is almost universal agreement that the two Palaces themselves are separate and apart, like Kremlin and Pentagon in the World of Scholarship. They represent, it is said, two cultures, two ways of thought, two sorts of minds. They are principles of Yin and Yang, they are Liberals and Conservatives, and we are polarized towards one or the other, from birth. You have either an 'Arts' mind, or a 'Science' mind, just as you are either male or female.

It seems to me to be of the utmost importance to analyse and refute this doctrine, which has invaded our educational system, and lives there like a hermit crab, protected, by hard shells of expediency and institutional snobbery, from serious intellectual investigation. It does us as much harm as the folly of 'permissive education,' for which we mock our American friends, and it is just as silly. It is time we thought seriously about whether there is any essential disjunction between the two great realms of scholarship, and whether we are wise to maintain that they are, if not oil and water that will not mix, then, say, oil and vinegar, to be shaken together to make a dressing for a salad but by nature fundamentally unlike.

Now, of course, if you start an argument on a question like this you will soon find yourself saying, 'It all depends what you mean by "Different".' So let me say that I am not denying that there are some differences between the logical techniques used in, say, Theoretical Chemistry, and those used by, for example, a student of the Dead Sea Scrolls. The subject-matters are different, and the means of investigation must be chosen appropriately. We can draw our divisions broad or narrow, and categorize scholars and scholarship as we please. The metaphorical map of science itself provides us with suitable coordinates for a classification scheme; a man is as precisely placed if we say that he is an Experimental Physicist working on the properties of Liquid Helium 3, as if we were to give the street and town in which he lives. And we can rightly say, that it is a long way from Electron Microscopy to Economic Statistics, just as it is from Samarkand to Bangkok. But my thesis is that there is no impassable barrier between them, no clear and obvious natural boundary, such as between Europe and America. The frontiers are artificial, arbitrary, and only such as have been erected by historical accident. Moreover, both Samarkand and Bangkok are cities, where men must live in much the same way; so, Electron Microscopy and Economic Statistics are disciplines requiring similar powers of the human intellect, even though clothed in very different garments.

This thesis is obviously very large and pretentious; all that I can attempt here is to illustrate it from one book and one man. The man is Michael Polanyi whose seventieth birthday is commemorated in a book*—a volume of Essays written by his friends. Michael Polanyi is, in himself, a living witness to the unity of the world of learning, for he has contributed significantly in Chemistry, in Physics, in Philosophy, and in Sociology. The essays in this book have been written by as wide a range of scholars as ever came together to honour a friend. But it is not merely because he is a Hungarian scientist who has lived many years in England that he has friends in all sorts of intellectual circles; journalist Koestler, historian Wedgwood, sociologist Shils, economist Devons, philosopher MacKinnon, biologist Calvin, chemist Eyring and even that grey eminence of modern Theoretical Physics, Eugene Wigner—all these, and others equally distinguished, have written essays which, though not directly related to each other, are all relevant to the man, and to his intellectual theme.

* *The Logic of Personal Knowledge:* Essays presented to Michael Polanyi on his seventieth birthday.

It is not unknown, of course, for a man to be expert in several different fields of scholarship. Read the Profiles and the Obituaries. What do we take as better proof of a transcendent intellect than the revelation that although our hero is really the world authority on Greek drama he has 'almost professional standing' as a classifier of snails; or 'surprising as it may seem in a professor of Metallographic Quantization, his real love, known only to his intimate friends, was the translation of the works of Jane Austen into Middle Pushtu'? But these revelations are only intended to shock us a little, and the tone reminds one of Dr Johnson's comment on a Woman Preacher: 'It is like a dog's walking on his hinder legs. It is not done well; but you are surprised to find it done at all.' In other words these are just reflections of the two-culture dogma; for a man to have interests on both sides of Cam is, if not indecent, then so unnatural as to be noteworthy. In many cases there is an element of schizophrenia in the man himself, so that he keeps his 'Work' and his 'Hobby' strictly separate, fearful that, like Wife and Mistress, they might tear each other apart if they ever met.

But Polanyi's work is all of a piece. His interests in Sociology and Philosophy have grown out of his scientific research. He has seen that an economic problem is capable of the same sort of mathematical analysis as one would use in Statistical Mechanics. Or he has set forth the important analogy between scientific freedom and political liberty. Or, in greatest depth, he has attempted to analyse science itself, as he knows it from his own experience, and to set forth its philosophical basis. His work on the Arts side has not been a mere hobby, nor has it been a series of 'excursions' across the frontier, informed only by an arrogant belief that 'Science' can conquer all problems, if only Scientists took them in hand. It has been serious, it has been painstaking, and it has shown clearly that the ground between the two great palaces is worth exploration.

His philosophical argument itself, which he sets out elsewhere in detail in a large book, *Personal Knowledge*, is an attempt at a reconciliation between the two cultures. It is too great a theme to summarize justly in a few sentences, but one may characterize it as humanist and anti-positivist. That is, he sees science as a human activity, and scientific knowledge to be coloured and limited by the tinge and limits of human minds. He would have nothing to do with any sort of super-logical automation, called 'scientific method' or 'inductive reasoning' which would guarantee the delivery of new truths as quickly as one turned the crank handle. The solution of a scientific problem always requires an intuitive jump beyond the logical premises and is always provisional. In other words, scientific problems and scientific knowledge are much more like ordinary problems and ordinary knowledge than the conventional philosophy of science would allow us. The same doubts and uncertainties that assail the historian about the objectivity of his ideas are implicit in the work of every scholar, right through to quantum field theory; they are the price (or the glory) of being a conscious responsible being, able to choose between right and wrong.

The differences between the scholarly disciplines are then only differences in the degree of organization of their subject matter. Physics seems logically clear because it deals with the smallest, least organized systems. The steps upwards to chemical molecules to cells, to larger organisms, to conscious beings, to human societies, each involve more complexity and more difficulty, so that the logical structure of the scholarly arguments seems to change. But these are matters of emphasis, rather than of essential nature; in the end we are always appealing to the mind of a man, convincing him of the truth of our propositions. Of course, the existence of his hierarchy of organized systems (and perhaps Polanyi's insistence that one cannot directly cerebrate the properties of a higher-order entity, such as a cell, from all one's knowledge of the properties of its lower-order elements, such as molecules) does suggest proper boundaries between the disciplines, so that we need never fear that all history will be reduced to Physics. But this does not justify the belief that the boundary separating the Arts from the Sciences, with Economics, Sociology, Anthropology and History on one side, and Psychology and Physiology on the other, is more difficult to cross than the boundaries between dead and living, between cell and multi-cell, between animal and human, all of which are normally encompassed within the 'Natural Sciences'. There is a case for seven cultures, or eight cultures, or ten cultures (it depends on how you count them), but nothing to show that these must divide precisely where the Cam now flows through.

Unfortunately, most of the essays in *The Logic of Personal Knowledge* do not relate directly to Polanyi's philosophical ideas. Too many are merely bits of current work in some specialized field, and their role is more as evidence of the breadth of his personal influence than as extensions of his own intellectual themes. On these it is impossible to comment. But the central essay in the volume, 'Max Weber and Michael Polanyi' by Raymond Aron, shows the value of this attitude to science when one comes to think about Sociology. Here is the bridge subject itself. The extraordinary prejudice that so long opposed the introduction of Sociology into the ancient British Universities had little to do with the false supposition that it was an abominable American invention. It was much more like a demarcation dispute between the Amalgamated Association of History Mongers ('Human nature has so many fascinating facets') and the Psychological and Allied Trades Confederation ('Just watch that rat; amazing'). Neither side could properly occupy the disputed territory, so it was preferable to leave it a no-man's land. A treaty is needed between them, in which the scientists will recognize that historians and other humanists are often extremely shrewd at drawing valid conclusions from very complex and intractable material, whilst the historians must admit that some aspects of human behaviour are more amenable to statistical analysis than to qualitative description and intuitive appraisal. Such a treaty was long ago established between the Physical and Biological Sciences (where, as pointed out by Marjorie Grene in another essay in this collection, the study of Animal Behaviour already takes one beyond the ordinary limits of impersonal cold observation). Whatever may be the ultimate status of Polanyi's ideas as a complete philosophy of science, they provide the ideological foundation for an academic Concordat, to settle the place of Sociology as an independent discipline.

It is my view that Sociology also has another role in this reunification of the 'Cultures.' The philosophy of *Personal Knowledge* is constructed about *man* as he is, with all his mental limitations and powers of intuition. It could have gone further in this direction by discussing *men* as they are, and seen science and scholarship in their social setting. Bertrand de Jouvenel's essay, 'The Republic of Science' in *The Logic of Personal Knowledge*, is an extension of some of Polanyi's ideas on the social organization of science with the aim of applying them to the general problems of political organization. These arguments can be inverted, so that one can see science itself as a social product, like a cathedral, or a joint stock company, or a steel works, created and working through the co-operation of numerous individuals, itself more than is conceivable as the work of one man alone. That is to say, scientific knowledge is social knowledge, transcending the personal knowledge of each one of us, just as an animal is more than the sum of its cells. By studying the logical and sociological implications of this proposition I believe we may come to see Science, and the traditional Humanities and even the Fine Arts, Literature, and Religion, as essentially similar systems, from all of which we academics can draw valid and useful propositions, and to all of which it should be our aim to contribute.

October 21st, 1961

5

Art and Artists

Art Under the Plutocracy

WILLIAM MORRIS

In spite of improvement on the surface, the art of to-day is in an unsatisfactory condition; popular or co-operative art only exists as foolish survival or galvanised imitation, while the more intellectual or individual art is injured by the isolation of the artists who of necessity work in protest against the general spirit of the age: as to the general surroundings of life they are yearly growing worse and more repulsive, so that all natural beauty is threatened with destruction by the restlessness and hurry of our present civilization: in short, whereas once it was the rule that all that man made was more or less beautiful, now, on the contrary, all that man makes is ugly unless by conscious effort for special beauty. This is admitted tacitly by most people of refinement, but they usually shut their eyes to it and try not to think of it, because they suppose that civilization naturally and necessarily tends towards the degradation of our external surroundings. They are driven to this opinion because they suppose that the present system of economy, founded on what is called free contract, *i.e.*, unlimited competition, is final and unalterable, but I, being a Socialist, deny this, and assert that competition is bestial and association human. This gives me an assured hope that the causes which have poisoned art may be dealt with and changed: those causes are referable to one thing, the making of wares for a profit only: it is this which has destroyed the pleasure in labour, which is the soul of art.

In the Middle ages, when there was little competition outside the gilds, and inside the gilds no division of labour, this pleasure was always present in handicrafts, and the craftsman was an artist or free workman. In those days the unit of labour was one fully instructed workman. When at the end of the Middle ages competitive commerce took hold of civilization, the system of the workshop with division of labour supplanted the craft system, and the unit of labour became a group of men: this system still exists in small manufactures side by side with the system of machines and big factories, but is speedily being crushed out by it. When the last system is complete the skilled workman will no longer exist, but his place will be taken by expert overlookers, and machines tended by unintelligent labour.

This system is destructive to art or the beauty of life if carried out to the utmost; it is founded on the theory that the only essential end of manufacturing is making a profit. This doctrine is what has disappointed the natural hope that machines would lighten the labour of man, which as J. S. Mill admits they have not done. This profit-making system has not only destroyed art, but has made mere anarchy of all society and produced horrors in our civilisation which everyone admits. What is the remedy? Most men of advanced or radical opinions conceive it possible to mend and patch the system in such a way that there shall be a large rich middle-class, a large well-to-do middle-class, and a large artisan middle-class, all contented and at peace with each other; they would turn all the world bourgeois, big and little bourgeois. Let them do it if they can, but they cannot; nay, they have tried it and are no nearer to it than they were at the time of the repeal of the corn laws. For the competitive system is really war, continuous and implacable, so that under it there must always remain a large class of *sans-culottes*, which will draw the main part of the proletariat to it, and so for ever mar the bourgeois ideal; a class of victims is necessary to the existence of the present system of commercial war. The real remedy is discontent with our present anarchy and the evolution of an intelligent and powerful proletariat from it which by the antagonism of classes will destroy all class distinctions. This revolution the middle-classes must either help or hinder, crush it, or be crushed by it; the middle-class conscience itself will forbid them to crush it; so they must either help it or be crushed by it. Some, indeed, may have the base slaveholders' hope that the people in England may be too degraded to have any hope of such things; but if there is little hope there is plenty of despair, and despair means the threat of anarchical instead of reconstructive revolution.

I appeal to you, therefore, to educate that discontent while there is yet time, and to join any attempt which is being made to organise the reconstructive instincts in the working classes; and not to let over-refinement or dread of the roughness or coarseness of the revolutionary party and its methods stand in your way. Union is the only weapon of oppressed people; organised brotherhood is the only answer to plutocratic anarchy; through that alone we can put aside the threat of fresh anarchy and bring real peace to the world.   December 5th, 1883

George Moore and Modern Art

ROGER FRY

With the name of Mr. George Moore,* most people will in-stinctively associate all that is most *outrecuidant* and young-mannish in art criticism and literature. The man that imported French realism into England would be the natural answer to anyone who showed such ignorance of topical affairs as to enquire who Mr. G. Moore might be. And yet, strange to say, he describes himself as at heart '*un vieux classique*' and the definition is not bad. The exponent of Whistler, Manet and Degas, the irreconcileable enemy of the Academy, he looks at modern painting with eyes that have grown accustomed to the old masters and selects for his admiration those modern painters whom he conceives to have imbibed the great artistic traditions of the past. His whole temper of mind is conservative, retrospective, anti-democratic; he distrusts revolutions in art; he distrusts new schools with new scientific systems. It is a somewhat pessimistic creed; art reached its apogee more than two thousand years ago, and along with other pleasant and romantic graces of barbarism is disappearing inevitably before the triumph of scientific civilisation, and widespread education. It is the opposite of the generous enthusiasm of Walt Whitman and J. A. Symonds, who looked for a new art based on the new sense of brotherhood, the new interest in humanity which democracy was to foster.

Art, according to Mr. Moore, is a delicate wild-flower, which is destroyed by official manuring and withers in the hot-house of an organised institution. Above all it is an individual passion, a desire which possesses a few human beings and for which they will sacrifice everything. It is irrational, whimsical, unrelated to all other human activities. How far is such a view due to the necessary reaction from Mr. Ruskin's attempt to make art acceptable to Puritanism by admiring a picture in proportion to the artist's adherence to the ten command-ments? Surely to some extent it is so, and surely an inquisitive and carefully pigeon-holed modern mind will not be content to leave so amazing a phenomenon as the artistic impulse uncatalogued. But then Mr. Moore does not sympathise with the modern mind, least of all its

* *Modern Painting.* By George Moore.

patronage of art. His cry to the Bourgeoisie is, let art alone, leave it to go its own entirely incomprehensible and useless ways, and do not make it 'grind moral corn in Philistine mills.' Free trade in art—that is the motto on his banner—and for that purpose he demands the destruction of the Royal Academy and the diversion to scientific purposes of all grants made by the State in aid of artistic education. It sounds a modest request on the part of artists—'please stop spending money on us,' and yet what chance is there of its being granted?

Perhaps to the uninitiated it may seem a contradiction that Mr. Moore, the Champion of the New English Art Club and the sworn enemy of the Academy should declare himself 'un vieux classique.' Is it not against the old cut and dried academic traditions that the exponents of impressionism fight, are they not preaching a new artistic gospel and must they not begin by destroying the law and the prophets? But that is not at all Mr. Moore's view for while on the one hand he regards Degas, although he has adopted new methods of technique to satisfy new demands on art, as the lineal descendant of Holbein, tracing his descent through Ingres, on the other hand he regards the academy as having no artistic tradition, no predisposition, no bias except towards that which is pleasing to the stockbroker and therefore fetches a high price. 'It is impossible,' he says, 'to suppose that Mr. Orchardson and Mr. Watts do not know that Mr. Leader's landscapes are like tea trays, that Mr. Dicksee's figures are like bon-bon boxes, and that Mr. Herkomer's portraits are like German cigars. But apparently the R.A.'s are merely concerned to follow the market and they elect the men whose pictures sell best in the City.' It is certainly hard to find any other explanation of the astonishing facts which each exhibition of the Academy reveal, and if we are inclined to resent the bitterness of Mr. Moore's tone and the virulence of his sarcasm we shall be forced to sympathize with him when we reflect that to all the arguments advanced on behalf of nearly the whole artistic talent of England against the present management of the Academy it has never vouchsafed a single answer—except by its acts to render more clear its position as a private commercial enterprise with the advantages of a government monopoly.

All this is put very clearly and fearlessly by Mr. Moore, nor are his attacks confined to official Philistinism—the dealer and the press that acts as the dealer's dupe are not spared and his essay on Religiosity in

Art is perhaps the most brilliant piece of satire in the whole book.
Throughout Mr. Moore shows sound common sense combined with
a love of painting for its own sake, which are most refreshing qualities
in an art critic. The enormous difficulty of giving any conception in
words of the undefinable, unanalysable qualities of a work of art, just
those qualities of technique wherein its greatness lies, has led most
critics from Lessing down to Ruskin to talk about principles, psychology, ethics, anything in the world but the essential and untranslateable
meaning of the picture. But Mr. Moore succeeds at times in conveying
almost a visual impression; he gives one a conception of the prevailing
colour harmonies which the artist affects, of the delicacy or strength
of his methods of handling; and by comparison of various artists'
methods of treating similar subjects he seeks not to establish a list
arranged in order of merit but to convey the peculiar and individual
excellences and limitations of the master under discussion. And this is
done in most readable English that hardly ever becomes ecstatic and
incoherent, hardly ever unnecessarily technical or pedantic. It is not
truly a very careful or faultless style that he employs—it is rough and
casual, full of neologisms and phrases from the studios of Paris, but
after all to present the more serious talk of the studios weeded of its
extravagance and exaggeration is not a bad way of showing the intelligent outsider the artist's view of art, and that is the difficult task Mr.
Moore undertakes.

We think that at times his love of classical traditions leads him to be
somewhat unfair to revolutionary schools—his appreciation of Monet
for instance is very much qualified by dislike; now Monet's claim to
recognition must rest on his discovery of a whole aspect of nature to
which the human eye had been quite blind and if he has never reduced
it to complete artistic expression, never found exactly the most beautiful way of saying what it was that he saw, his must still remain as one
of the great names of modern art by virtue of his naturalism if not of
his art, in the limited sense. Art always wavers between the poles of
nature and past art, and every great artistic advance is preceded by an
advance in the knowledge of the appearance of nature—by a scientific
discovery in fact. In the same way while Mr. Moore laughs, and we
think, fairly at the absurdities of the scientific doctrinaires who practise
the 'division of the tones' he fails to mention that the method of optical
mixture of colours is undoubtedly capable of giving more brilliant
effects of light and colour than the mixture on the palette ever does,

and that therefore it becomes a right and legitimate technique for the expression of certain effects of sunlight.

Mr. Moore attributes the failure of the art of the Nineteenth Century as compared with other periods of great artistic activity to the deadly influence of the subject in art, and he considers Greuze to have been the offending Adam through whom all Artists fell; but surely this is hardly borne out by the facts. The great pictures of this Century are as free or freer from the diseased interest in dramatic painting as those of the Florentines—freer we should say. There is less of a subject, as Mr. Moore understands it, in Ingres Source, in all Whistler's work, in all of Degas (at least if we except l'Absinthe) than in the work of Raphael or Mantegna. Raphael's frescoes undoubtedly have dramatic interest, his Sistine Madonna has a theological interest; they are fine pictures as well, but no one can deny that there is much in them, due moreover to the conscious intention of the artist, that Mr. Moore would reject as of purely literary interest. But be that as it may it is well that the artist's view of art should be asserted forcibly to a public that craves for sentiment, and that Mr. Moore has accomplished.

June 22nd, 1893

Mr Murry and the
Question of Style

J. B. PRIESTLEY

At Oxford, last summer, Mr J. Middleton Murry delivered a course of six lectures on Style.* These lectures are now published by the Oxford University Press, under the title of *The Problem of Style*. To any genuine critic, the subject of style, like the ladies whom the poets celebrate, is at once inspiring and treacherous; it braces him to do his best, hints at magnificent conquest, and then too often lures him to disaster. Mr Murry, however, has not been tempted to disaster; at the worst, he has only turned to pursue some Will-o'-the-Wisps. On the other hand, he has certainly felt the inspiration, for he has not only surpassed his own previous critical performances, but has given us one of the books of the year, one that is a delight to the ordinary

* *The Problem of Style.* By J. Middleton Murry.

reader and a treasure-house of suggestion to any fellow critic. The famous quip at the 'ouvrage sur le style où il n'y a point de style' cannot be pressed into service against Mr Murry, for his book is very well done indeed. It has aroused opposition already, and it will arouse much more, I trust, in the future; but this is—and will be—all to its credit, for, like any piece of fresh genuine criticism, it does not deal in smooth commonplaces but overhauls the stock of critical ideas; and opposition, reasoned opposition and not that which is born of the dislike of anything new, is no little testimony to its value. It is sure to be widely read, but every student of letters should take it up again and again.

Nevertheless, though I shall act as advertising agent for Mr Murry's new book for some time to come, I do not think that it has brought us any nearer to a solution of the time-old problem. Indeed, I incline to think that it has only left us more confused than ever. Do not mistake my meaning. When Mr Murry is talking about what he chooses to call Style, he gives us some very fine criticism indeed; but he leaves the problem of Style very much as he found it. He begins by disengaging three distinct meanings of the term Style: Style as personal idiosyncrasy; Style as technique of exposition; Style as the highest achievement of literature. Then, after dealing shortly with one and two, throughout the rest of the book he concentrates upon division number three, Style as the highest achievement, etc. He does it very well, too, as I have said. But of his three divisions, it seems to me that the third has the least claim to monopolise the term Style; and a man who uses it in this sense does more violence to language than the people who still cling to the other two meanings. When a man who has just put between his lips one of Havana's noblest products, cries out 'Now, this is a *cigar!*' his enthusiastic tone tells us exactly what he means, namely, that it is an extraordinarily good cigar. But such a one does not refuse from that time onwards the name cigar to anything costing less than eight shillings; he has the sense to keep the general term and to add to it various attributes. It is better to talk of good cigars, bad cigars, indifferent, poisonous, ravishing, miraculous cigars, than simply to speak of cigars and things that look like cigars but are not. But this last is just what Mr Murry tends to do with Style.

The fact is, Mr Murry of late has reacted very strongly against that preoccupation with literature as an art which has been so fashionable these last thirty years. True, we have had too much of it; but still literature is an art, and it is the writer's acquaintance with his chosen medium, expression in words, rather than his greater sensibility and the like, that marks him off from other men. It is this reaction that has made Mr Murry look at literature from what appears to me, in any discussion of style, the wrong angle. He is chiefly interested in the relation between an author's mind and his book, whereas I, for one, would say that the writer on style would occupy himself more profitably with the relation between books and the minds of their readers. A writer's books are public property; his head is not. I do not like a style because I suspect that its creator has felt certain requisite emotions, or that it is the result of an approved process; I like it because it produces in me a certain pleasurable effect, and, if I am a critic, experience leads me to suspect that this is due to the presence of certain qualities in the style itself, and I shall therefore make it my business to determine what these qualities are. Even if I were a good critic, I should probably fail, but I should in all likelihood go some way towards success and send readers back to the text with a greater appetite for literary pleasure. For this reason, it seems to me that so far the discussion of Style has been carried on with most profit by those bold critics, probably despised by Mr Murry, who have come out into the open with some discussion of the technical elements of Style. Like Stevenson with his initial consonants and what-not or Professor Saintsbury with his elaborate notation of prose-rhythm, such critics have always been inclined to emphasize one quality at the expense of all the rest; but still, they have usually carried us some way forward, sent us back to our books with an added zest, made us more in love than ever with fine literature and more able to point the way to others less fortunate. I am not absurd enough to want to lay down for a critic of Mr Murry's calibre the method he should employ in criticism, and I would not willingly lose a word of his present treatise, but I can at least express my own regret that, given such a theme, he did not see fit to adopt what seems to me the more profitable method of treating it. There is so much still to be said on this subject of Style, and we have so few critics at once so enthusiastic, sensitive and patient as Mr Murry to do the work, that my regret is only kept within bounds by the hope of my seeing, in the near future, a further volume by the same hand on the same subject.

I have the feeling that lack of time and shortage of space have made me unjust to Mr Murry, inasmuch as I have probably not fairly presented his really valuable ideas. But then my own ideas have suffered likewise, and Mr Murry has at least the consolation of knowing that his are set forth pleasantly and at length in a volume that no man who is interested in the subject will be foolish enough to miss.

May 5th, 1922

Forster and the Novel*

I. A. RICHARDS

To be provocative, if it is *thought* that is provoked, is merely a duty or a decency in a critic. What can be accepted with undisturbed placidity is probably not worth much when received. The provocations of Mr Forster's Clark Lectures, now published in book form, are not mitigated by the charming, unobtrusive, almost feline modesty with which they are given. The soft blow to our cherished preconception comes with such coy disarming grace that for a while we feel doubly disabled. The reply only occurs to us in some connection so far removed that it hardly seems a reply at all. For example, Mr Forster's defamation of 'the story.' 'It runs like a backbone—or may I say a tape-worm, for its beginning and end are arbitrary … It can only have one merit: that of making the audience want to know what happens next … It is the lowest and simplest of literary organisms.' Only much later when we sense something missing in Mr Forster's handling of 'pattern' do we see where his unkindness to 'the story' has landed him. For the story, the mere narrative of the succession of events, can, as the Book of Job witnesses, be given a pattern and then it obtains both a wide and a delicate power upon us. Our interest, our desire to hear further, may be noble as well as ignoble; and if Mr Forster were to say that its nobility always derives from its superstructure, from the other aspects, he could be faced with the dilemma: —either a story is inseparable from the character of the events which make it up, or it is something not worth mentioning even as an object for witty abuse.

Or consider Mr Forster's dealings with what he calls 'prophecy.' It is 'an accent in the novelist's voice … His theme is the universe, or

* *Aspects of the Novel.* By E. M. Forster.

something universal, but he is not necessarily going to "say" anything about the universe; he proposes to sing.' This quality is illustrated by four writers, Dostoevsky, Melville, D. H. Lawrence and Emily Brontë; Mr Forster can find no others. The claims of Hardy and Conrad are set aside. 'Hardy's novels are surveys; they do not give out sounds' a judgment that applies perhaps to any one of Hardy's novels taken as a whole but not to the separate pulses that make them up, though it must be admitted that their sounds have a desolate ring. So too with Conrad, 'He has seen too much to see beyond cause and effect.' To have a philosophy—even a poetic and emotional philosophy like Hardy's and Conrad's—leads to reflections on life and things. A prophet does not 'reflect.' But Dostoevsky and Melville also reflected, and we have to separate their reflections from their 'prophecy'. Mr Forster himself in an admirable passage makes this separation for D. H. Lawrence. What then does his distinction between 'prophecy' and what is not 'prophecy' come down to? I cannot help thinking that it is a question, not of the depth of implications, the way in which characters or scenes 'reach back'; but of the very thing Mr Forster sets as the limit of his subject, the prophet's message. That prophecy 'gives us the sensation of a song or a sound' will not do as a criterion itself. Too many other writers, in addition to Mr Forster's chosen, give it, and his own four 'sing' in such different ways. If degree of significance be the test, Tolstoy, Arnold Bennett (though this is a thing too often difficult to believe), George Moore, as at the end of *Esther Waters* and in at least one place in *The Brook Kerith*, James Joyce in patches, Flaubert, Voltaire and at least as many more would have to join Mr Forster's quartet. The implications are as infinite, though it is true that these authors only become 'prophets' at rare moments and 'prophecy' is not what we think of as the constant quality of their work. If Mr Forster excludes them I believe it is because the 'messages', the implications conveyed, are less congenial, not because the work is essentially of a different order.

Mr Forster's strength as a critic is the more shown the nearer he comes to the actual text of his authors. His amazing knack of collocation wins him his best points at once. To set Samuel Richardson beside Henry James, Dickens beside Wells, and Sterne beside Virginia Woolf was a stroke of genius, and later on George Eliot and Dostoevsky in his hands generate a mutual blaze of illumination. He grows less certain and less satisfying when he stands back from his novelists to toy with definitions, to contrast the life of time with the life of value, to indulge fantasies about people in life and people in books. At such passages a reader in a controversial mood may become irritable, he may find himself scoring points which seem hardly worth making. For the theoretical apparatus of *Aspects of the Novel* was never intended for this kind of discussion. And while trying to hunt a little further some of the hares Mr Forster has started, with even a doubt whether they are hares at all and not rather the herrings of fantasy, we run the risk of forgetting that these were simply some of the pleasantest lectures ever given in Cambridge. And in again deploring (it is the theme of all his work) Man's inability to be at the same time impressive and truthful, Mr Forster has brought the real difficulty of all this kind of criticism to light. The job of unpicking the hard unnecessary knots in our received ideas cannot be made into a graceful performance. Choosing to delight our minds rather than to disentangle them he has not made us any the less his debtors.

March 2nd, 1928

Wyndham Lewis and the Zeitgeist*

I. A. RICHARDS

It is customary to lament that our age lacks prophets. Scientific fortune-tellers we have, in plenty, and a sufficiency of scolds, but who is there with any awakening power or anything to say if we should awaken? Who will supply the redeeming perception, or even denounce our age for us in any but the most reassuring and familiar pulpit manner? Spengler's ineffectual drone is already dying in the distance, and D. H. Lawrence in Mexico now stridulates in vain. Only Mr Wyndham Lewis, a visual specialist with the combined curiosity and audacity of the born diagnostician, seems possibly to possess the talismanic virtue. Besides an eye of peculiar penetration he has the sinewy strength. To judge this you have only to watch him bundling Spengler off the scene; lifting the whole top off *Ulysses* to show us the chassis; sweeping away with his little broom down there in the sandy desert

* *Time and Western Man.* By Wyndham Lewis.

of the theory of perception; or putting up his fences round revolutionary millionaire-Bohemia. But his great joy is fighting—both the
shadow kind and the real thing. Bergson here is his prey; the Bergson
he describes as 'of course, the perfect philosophic ruffian, of the darkest
and most forbidding description, (who) pulls every emotional lever
on which he can lay his hands.' Whitehead, on the other hand, 'is, I
believe, an *honest* sentimentalist of the "radical" English schoolmaster
type.' (p. 174). It is clear, even from this specimen scrap, that Wyndham Lewis needs to learn nothing from Bergson about emotional
appeals, he even seems to have a thing or two to teach anyone in the
less boasted arts of controversy. If the one is a ruffian the other is some
sort of Palladin-Apache. It is hard to know which to admire more
—his high ideals or the cunning efficiency of his methods.

But, when the dust kicked up by all this has settled, what has
happened? I believe a very great deal results for hardy readers. And
even those not tough enough to follow Mr Wyndham Lewis everywhere in his arduous manoeuvres will at least get exercise, and shocks
more likely to be healthful than hurtful.

Time and Western Man (Mr Lewis is always to be congratulated on
his titles) is part of a crusade. Its object is to recover and defend the
commonsense view of the world. Literally the *view* of the world, for
Mr Lewis is interested primarily in visual perceptions. Bergson, the
Relativist philosophers (Whitehead, Russell, Broad, Alexander), the
Behaviourists, the Italian idealists with their equivocations about history,
Spengler's romance about Culture, Freud, and though he does not
give this its due prominence—the neurological account of perception,
have co-operated, he thinks, to make the commonsense assumptions
about how we perceive the world shaky. According to commonsense, here are we, fairly stable distinct selves; over against us are the
trees and tables, things quite separate from us, an alien external world
that we have gradually learnt to perceive. These things, like ourselves,
are fairly stable, they persist, they are solid, they have laws of their own.
Now this commonsense view, according to Mr Lewis, is also the
inevitable and necessary view of the plastic or graphic artist. And if
the doctrines he is combating gain acceptance, this way of seeing things
will, he thinks, be interfered with. 'These philosophers are busy dis-
integrating for us our public material paradise, and propose to give us
in exchange the dark and feverish confusion of their "mental" truth.'
(p. 186). In place of 'real' trees and tables we shall have complexes of

sensations or constructions of sensa, a shifting, instable, time-saturated phantasmagoria of abstracted semblances; 'a highly complex disintegrated world, of private "times" and specific, amputated, "spaces"; of serial-groups and "events" (in conformity with the dominance of the time factor) in place of "Things".' (p. 432). It is not only the doctrine of these schools that is abhorrent to Mr Lewis. He is afraid of its possible effects upon our actual perceptions. He agrees that the ordinary 'thing' is to some degree a mental product. 'The material world that the human intellect has created is still there, of course: but, as it is a creation of our minds, it will no doubt be found that we can even physically disintegrate it. Already for the time-initiate it is getting a fluid, or flabby, texture and appearance.' (p. 186). If it went, the task of re-creating it would he insists, be gigantic.

This, I believe, is the root of Mr Lewis' detestation of contemporary 'Time views,' a collection of doctrines which he lumps together because they seem to him to threaten in various ways his plastic world; or because they discourage contemplation in favour of action; or because they make man out more a slave and less a master of circumstances than he need feel himself to be. He manages in the midst of his main offensives a number of minor wars, more or less connected with the central issue. The 'uplift' endeavours of Alexander, Whitehead's patronage of the Romantic poets, mental tests in the hands of Yerkes and Yoakum, the 'religion of science' as the apostle of the gland-theory promulgates it, to name but a few, provoke some of his finest passages of sardonic commentary. Few writers can ever have had a better eye for the ludicrous in intellectual contingencies. In fact he appears to enjoy himself prodigiously through almost the whole of the discussion; in view of its subject matter, an astounding triumph of gusto.

Upon the main point, the central argument, a doubt may be raised, which some time I hope Mr Lewis will discuss. Whatever the world picture presented by science (or by the philosophic mediators or vulgarisers of science,) an intelligence that remains master of itself can always choose for its particular purposes (the purposes of the plastic artist for example) whatever other world picture seems most desirable. As Mr Lewis himself says, (p. 250) 'probably science and art should be kept rigidly apart, in our present situation; and with our greatly enhanced resources.' Those of us who do keep their opinions (as curious intellectuals) about the fundamental problems of science and philosophy apart from their emotional or impulsive make-up (their moral order, their outlook, their attitudes as poetry and the arts engage and control them), escape the dangers Mr Lewis so cogently points to. A psychologist *can* (1) be *qua* psychologist an uncompromising behaviourist and (2) be unreservedly a responsive reader of Dante. That is to say, *qua* psychologist he denies the existence of the soul or the self, and stands prepared to translate all statements about the 'spiritual' into terms of visceral reaction systems and yet *qua* imaginative individual he fully undergoes all transformations of feeling and attitude that the poet compels. And this without any splitting up of the personality into two distinct selves and merely through the proper separation of science or art as separate activities of the one self. If this can be done, and in fact those who deny its possibility are wasting their energies, for it is done, the danger Mr Lewis points to only threatens people (they are, we must admit, the immense, overwhelming, majority) whose feelings, mode of perception, and capacity for response are welded (by accident or education) to their opinions about the world picture. For these there is a problem and a danger, but would it not perhaps be a better policy for Mr Lewis, who wields the sharpest, heaviest cleaver of any living critic, to cut art and poetry loose from science (and philosophy) rather than to expend his invaluable energies in attacking semi-scientific doctrines that are probably too mixed and confused, too much themselves half amateur science and half amateur poetry to be susceptible of refutation?

About the ways that political and other influences may distort philosophy or science Mr Lewis writes with great sense and discernment. He manages not to overstate his case. But inevitably he has to discuss these doctrines more in relation to their social effects than in relation to the theoretical problems they have arisen to meet. This sometimes gives an air of irrelevance and unfairness to his most telling jibes. But it is no slight witness to his intelligence that throughout this long discussion of the most entangled productions of contemporary philosophy he so rarely gives us the impression of being himself the amateur critic from outside. There are few other external critics, or writers whose main interest is not professional philosophy, capable of such a feat. And as a writer he makes all the professional philosophers sound jejune. Let me quote some phrases of his theophrastian 'character' of the Revolutionary Simpleton, a product, he considers, of time philosophy on the plane of vulgarisation.

'This personage is, in one word, romantic—that is the essential diagnostic for his malady. He is sick for things he has never experienced, or which he is incapable of experiencing—as the schoolboy, or the curate or spinster of stage tradition is sick for highly-flavoured, "wicked" or blood-curdling exploits and adventures. The revolutionary simpleton is a death snob; though generally the most inoffensive and often engaging of people himself—the sort of man who would hurt a fly, and say *boo*! very truculently, to a goose; mammock a butterfly; or, with motor gloves and a fencing casque, swing a small cat by the tail.'

This is an energy and exuberance that has not been seen in English criticism for a long while. Even though his strategy be not quite so good as his tactics, he is almost the only living critic who has sense of the current intellectual landscape as a whole, and the only writer who can combine this general's eye with the enthusiasm of the adventurous recruit.

March 9th, 1928

The Idealism of Julien Benda*

T. S. ELIOT

M. Julien Benda is a critic who does not write often or too much. His *Belphégor*, which some of us recognised as an almost final statement of the attitude of contemporary society to art and the artist, was published in 1918 or 1919. *La Trahison des Clercs* is the first book of the same type that M. Benda has written since *Belphégor*; it represents some years of meditation and study; we expected a book of the same importance. We are not disappointed. And just as *Belphégor*, although based upon an examination of French society alone, applied to the relation of society to the arts in all Europe and America, so is *La Trahison des Clercs* of general application. It is indeed more general; for M. Benda now draws his illustrations from England, Germany, Italy and America, as well as from France. In these illustrations I do

* *La Trahison des Clercs.* By Julien Benda.

not think that he has been altogether fair; and as he has cited William James and Kipling, we are entitled to cross-examine him on his examination.

M. Benda's thesis may be divided into two parts, upon which we may find that we give separate verdicts. The first part is a general criticism of the political passions of the present time. The second part is a scrutiny of the culpability of certain noted men of letters, and implies a rule of life which M. Benda would lay down for men of letters of our time. In the first general diagnosis, I am inclined to yield complete assent; in the second part, he does not seem to me to have carried his analysis of individuals far enough; and the ideal that he holds up to contemporary men of letters seems to me to be infected with romance. But he puts a problem which confronts every man of letters; the same problem which Mr Wyndham Lewis has solved for himself in his own way by writing his recent books; the problem of the scope and direction which the activities of the artist and the man of letters should take to-day.

With the first part of M. Benda's thesis I cannot deal in this short space. No one can disagree with his statement of the 'modern con-summation of political passions'; his classification of passions of race (*e.g.* the Nordic theory and the Latin theory), passions of nation (*e.g. fascism*) and passions of class (*e.g.* communism). I say that no one can disagree with the statement, which is made with all M. Benda's usual lucidity and concision; but the analysis could be carried much further than M. Benda carries it. A new Rémy de Gourmont could 'dissociate' these ideas of Nationalism, of Class, of Race into their local com-ponents; and there is also the Religious Idea (not discussed by M. Benda) to be dissociated (with special reference to an actual contro-versy in England) into components such as conviction, piety, prejudice and politics. Each of these subjects would take a chapter by itself. Let us merely accept M. Benda's general statement of the 'perfection' of these passions in the modern world—in universality, in coherence, in homogeneity, in precision, in continuity and in condensation; and proceed to the question: what is the role of the man of letters; does he to-day involve himself in these passions, and if so why; and what is his proper function?

M. Benda brings a grave accusation against the modern 'man of letters,' whom he calls the 'clerc.' The accusation is retrospective, for it applies to most of the 19th century. The 'clerc,' instead of sticking to his business of pure thought or pure art, has descended into politics in the widest and sometimes the lowest sense. M. Benda's instances are mostly contemporary and mostly French. For the sake of completeness, no doubt, he has added a few foreigners, such as D'Annunzio, Kipling and William James. Between these three 'clercs' I can see nothing in common. D'Annunzio is a brilliant prose artist of pseudo-decadence, who took up with Italian nationalism as a new excitement; Kipling (it seems to me) writes of the Empire because he was born in India instead of Sussex (and, as Mr. Dobree has said, part of his interesting peculiarity is that he makes the deck of a P. & O. liner seem as much British soil as Sussex or Shropshire); James is included merely because he voiced a rather silly enthusiasm for the American war with Spain. M. Benda is more exact with his own compatriots. Two of those whom he accuses are Barrès and Péguy. But one asks the question: has he carried his analysis far enough? I dislike both of these writers as much as M. Benda does. But the question is: are these writers dangerous because they have concerned themselves with practical and political matters, or rather because their attitude, both in art, speculative thought and practical thought, was wrong?

It is not necessary to enter upon an exposition of the work of Barrès or of Péguy, although to those who already know something of these popular authors my remarks will be more immediately intelligible. My point is that M. Benda has carved his chicken without taking any notice of the joints, and most of the bones are cut in the middle. I should like to give a summary and tentative account of the way in which the 'man of letters,' by which we mean either the artist in language, or the critic of the artist in language, is involved in practical matters of the day.

There is one obvious distinction: that between the 'man of letters' who, having secured a solid reputation for literary ability—say as a novelist—exploits his reputation for the purpose of exerting influence over human beings in other ways. Manifestly, popular journalism encourages writers to such divagations. The Dean of St. Paul's is an example; having acquired a deserved distinction as an authority on Neo-Platonism, he expresses his opinions upon art, literature and society with an air of authority which no doubt convinces the general public. I do not for a moment suggest that either the prelate mentioned, or any other popular writer, is influenced by the prices paid; for I believe that the love of power and the love of notoriety are much

P

more insistent motives. Nor do I wish you to think that every notable author who writes in this way is unjustified; I would even say that the Dean of St Paul's sometimes writes in newspapers about subjects on which he is fully qualified to write, and that he sometimes writes sound sense. It may also happen that a successful writer may be keenly interested in some alien subject, may feel a vocation to write about it, and then he can hardly be blamed for using his reputation to get his writings published and read. I should probably do the same thing myself. I do not agree, for instance, with the political views of Mr Arnold Bennett, but I am sure that Mr Bennett himself agrees with them and believes that they should be propagated; and if I were as important as Mr Bennett I should probably write political articles myself. If one really cares about certain things, and if one's reputation in other ways is such as to gain one a hearing on any subject, one can hardly be blamed for talking. It is a matter between the celebrity and God, whether the former is sufficiently interested and informed to write in that way; it is a matter between the celebrity and the public intelligence, whether he should be heard.

The abuses of this sort of influence are encouraged, as M. Benda says, by popular journals. But there is a distinction which I think M. Benda fails to make. He tends to assume that writers like Barrès and Péguy are good artists in prose, but pernicious when they appeal to popular passions in practical affairs. On the latter point with regard to these two authors, I agree. But I should ask the question: do not the same vices, which make these authors dangerous guides, vitiate their work as literary artists? I do not want to enter upon an analysis which would presuppose a knowledge of the work of Barrès and Péguy. I only offer as my opinion, the view that not only the practical judgment but the theoretic judgment of these two writers is poisoned by an excess of sensibility over thought. I have myself found them both quite futile. But where M. Benda merely seems to say that such writers are dangerous because they have tackled politics, and applied to affairs a sensibility appropriate only to literature, I should say that their sensibility is wrong altogether. The Nationalism of Barrès, the Socialism and the Catholicism of Péguy, and I should add the Catholicism of Léon Bloy (who begat Maritain, who begat the emotional and popular vulgarised neo-Thomism of our time) seem to me due to a romantic excess of feeling over thought. But to say that all Nationalism, or all Socialism, or all Catholicism, or all Thomism is romantic, is a very different matter. We must on the one hand analyse the Idea, and on the other hand analyse the particular author under consideration.

There are therefore two questions which must be pondered separately and together: first, what are the causes of the inclination of men of letters—including poets, novelists and even painters (there is as yet no instance of a musician)—to occupy themselves with social theories? And second, to distinguish the artists or men of letters who excel in their proper sphere but fail in their public occupation, from those who exhibit the *same* faults in their art as in their public activity, and finally from those who (if there are such) excel and are right in both.

I think that one can admit that ours is an unsettled age. No one is sure to what 'class' of society he belongs: at no time has 'class' been more uncertain, and yet at no time has the consciousness of 'class' been greater. Everyone is now conscious of class, but no one is sure what class is; every one is conscious of nationality and race (our very passports impress that upon us) but no one is sure who or which or what is what or which race; or whether race is divided north and south or east and west or horizontally; or whether any of us is any thing but a mongrel; and we suspect that the more we know about race the more clearly we shall see that we are all merely mongrels. We are conscious of these questions as a man with indigestion is conscious of his stomach. It might almost be said that everybody is conscious of every question and no one knows any answers. This has been called an age of specialisation, but it is very much the age of the amateur. Not long ago I attended, with some curiosity, a 'religious convention'; I heard a popular novelist and a popular actor talk nonsense for half an hour each, and then I left. There is, in fact, very little respect for authority: by which I mean respect for the man who has special knowledge of some subject of which oneself is ignorant.

The causes are of course many; and I merely mention these things in order to point out that the meddling of men of letters in practical affairs, to which M. Benda objects, is only one phenomenon of a general confusion. The publicist who writes about everything on earth responds to the demand of a public which has a mild and transient interest in everything on earth. All this is perfectly commonplace, and I only mention it in order to point out that it is, in practice, extremely difficult to draw a line between the mere vulgariser of knowledge, of the American type, and the 'intellectual' of wide interests. It is furthermore fallacious to group all the intellectuals who may be accused of doing somebody else's business, or of pandering to popular political passions, into one category; as an examination of M. Benda's instances will show.

'To-day,' says M. Benda (p. 57), 'it is enough to mention the Mommsens, the Treitschkes, the Ostwalds, the Brunetières, the Barrès, the Lemaitres, the Péguys, the Maurras, the D'Annunzios and the Kiplings, to agree that the intellectuals (clercs) exercise political passions with all the characteristics of passion: tendency towards action, craving for immediate results, indifference to everything but the end in view, contempt for argument, violence, hatreds and obsessions (idée fixe).' This classification seems to me rather summary. To take the historians first. It is quite true that certain German historians, and still more certain German philosophers of history, have exhibited a bias in favour of national passions. It is also true of several other historians, not all contemporary with ourselves. Sometimes, when an historian has exactly the same bias as ourselves, we have the optical illusion of no bias at all; to many people Gibbon or Mr Lytton Strachey seem to possess the virtue of detachment, instead of the virtue of a pleasant bias. The judgment of any historian must depend both on the degree of his prejudice and (I am afraid) upon our moral judgment of the prejudice itself. And the historians, I submit, are in a class by themselves.

Far different is the case of writers like Péguy and Barrès. If anyone has done more harm than Barrès, it is Péguy. What these two authors have in common is a gift for language, and a sensibility for the emotional values of words, completely unrestrained by either logic or common sense. Like Hugo and Swinburne, they had no gift whatever for thinking; but unlike those poets, they disguised their lyricism in a form which looks to many people like a form of thought. But the question about such writers as these is not whether they have abused their gifts by applying them to the wrong uses, but whether they had any right to exist at all. The faults of the political outbursts of Péguy and Barrès are the faults apparent in all of their work; and if they are pernicious in politics, they are still more pernicious in literature. These two writers, again, are in quite a different category from Kipling. To make this difference quite clear would require a separate essay on Kipling, so I can only say this much: there is no doubt a bit of political jingoism in Kipling, but it does not affect his best work. The Imperialism which is in all of Kipling's work, and in the best of it, is not a

political passion at all; it has no practical aim, but is merely the statement of a fact; and there is all the difference in the world between the
vision of an Empire which exists, and the incitement to passion for an
Empire in the future. On this point, M. Benda is perhaps no more
unintelligent than any other continental writer.

Another author of our time, whom M. Benda does not mention,
is equally to the point, and cannot be classified with any of the preceding. It is Mr Wells. Wells is nearer to Barrès and Péguy than to
Kipling, but must be distinguished from them very sharply. For
whereas, to my thinking, there is a hopeless confusion in Barrès and
Péguy which was bound to vitiate everything they wrote, Wells has
positive, self-contained gifts for one or two types of imaginative fiction
which are peculiarly his own. His imagination is that of the Common
Man raised to the highest power. But being that of the Common Man,
and of the Common Man of our time, it does not know where to stop.
Hence there is a sharp division. Mr Wells has all of the Common
Man's respect for facts and information, and his imagination depends
upon facts. When he uses the facts for imaginative purposes he is
superb; when he uses his imagination to expound facts he is deplorable.
He has the Common Man's habit of assuming that if you have enough
facts, you can dispense with reasoning, for the reason is supposed to
be in the facts instead of in the human mind; he is the reverse of Mr
Belloc, who supposes that if you have reason behind you, you can do
what you like with the facts. The expected happens: when Belloc deals
with facts, he fits them into his reason: when Wells deals with facts,
he hampers his magnificent imagination, and becomes the quite
unconscious victim of the parish prejudices. What a pity that Belloc
supposes himself to be an historian, and that Wells supposes himself
to be a biologist!

Another case which M. Benda does not mention, very different from
that of Wells, is that of Shaw. Shaw has this in common with Péguy,
that some of his faults must be referred to his masters—though it be
as reprehensible to choose a bad master as to be a bad master. Péguy
owes much to the philosophy of Bergson, which he translated into his
own muddy rhetoric; the philosophy of Bergson after all is at least
a philosophy; but what can be said for a disciple of the amateur cranki-
ness of Samuel Butler? I cannot go thoroughly into the case of Shaw,
but would only point out that here is the case of a kind of *trahison*
not discussed by M. Benda; Shaw the master of a lucid and witty

dialogue prose hardly equalled since Congreve, and of a certain power of observation, squandering these gifts in the service of wornout home-made theories, as in the lamentable *Methuselah*.

Here then, in England alone, we have at least four instances of *clercs* who might incur M. Benda's displeasure: Kipling, Inge, Wells and Shaw, and no two of them in the same category, or doing the same thing for the same reasons. I do not say that there are not the same social circumstances behind them all to account for them all, but merely that you cannot pass the same judgment on any two of them as individuals. In France there is perhaps more uniformity, but great differences appear there too. The great weakness of Benda's argument is that you cannot pass directly from the criticism of an age to the criticism of the individuals who represent that age. It breaks down further when you recognise that for practical purposes there is not much difference between a *clerc* who excites popular passions himself, and a *clerc* who does so by his influence upon others. Bergson, one would say, fulfilled Benda's requirements for the pure philosopher; for apart from one pardonable outburst in 1914 when, as I remember, he identified France with Life, and Germany with Machinery, he has written nothing but pure philosophy. Yet half of the most excitable authors of our time, in France at least, have been Bergsonians. Péguy himself is a conspicuous example; and Péguy is also the remarkable example of a writer who managed to influence many people, largely because he had so confused a mind that there was room for everything in it somehow. He was a nationalist, a Dreyfusist, a republican who went into rhapsodies over Napoleon's tomb, a socialist and a catholic of a rather doubtful sort. The influence of Bergson again, as well as that of Péguy and the ecstatic Léon Bloy, is strong upon the leader of the Catholic rationalists, M. Jacques Maritain. I have a warm personal admiration for M. Maritain, though it is as much for his saintly character as for his intelligence; but I have never seen a more romantic classicist, or a thomist whose methods of thought were less like those of Aquinas. His occasional intemperance of language, and his occasional sentiment, hardly qualify him for the philosophical crown which M. Benda is waiting to bestow on someone.

And on the other hand it is doubtful whether M. Benda himself deserves it. He holds up to the artist, to the critic, to the philosopher, an ideal of detachment from passions of class, race, nation and party, which, even though he does not clearly distinguish *passion* from *interest*, looks very admirable. But it implies a complete severance of the speculative from the practical which is itself impossible, and leads, in M. Benda's implications, to an isolation which may be itself a romantic excess. I must avoid entering upon any question which would require a definition of those terrible terms romanticism and classicism; but that is unnecessary, for we are concerned only with what is *called* romanticism. It is apparent, I mean, that when anyone nowadays attacks anything on the ground that it is romanticism, he is always himself in danger of falling into an opposite extreme which is also and equally romantic. M. Benda attacks Maurras and the 'neo-classicists,' for instance, on the ground that their neo-classicism is itself a phase of romanticism. I think he is right, though the charge does not seem to me to be nearly so deadly as he seems to suppose. What he does not see is that his own brand of classicism is just as romantic as any one else's. It is to be observed of the nineteenth century that a reaction against romantic individualism, liberalism, humanitarianism, sometimes leads to a romantic exaltation of herd instinct, or race (we have heard quite enough about the Nordic race and of the Latin mind and Latin civilisation) or tradition and the soil, etc., whilst on the other hand the reaction against romantic collectivism (including all forms of communism, fascism, etc.) may just as well lead straight to a romantic individualism. M. Benda, I suspect, is an admirer of Spinoza: and I am not altogether sure that Spinoza's isolation was not rather a misfortune to be pitied, than a quality to be admired.

The only moral to be drawn, therefore, is that you cannot lay down any hard and fast rule of what interests the *clerc*, the intellectual, should or should not have. All you can have is a standard of intellect, reason and critical ability which is applicable to the whole of a writer's work. If there is a right relation of emotion to thought in practical affairs, so there is in speculation and art too. A good poem, for instance, is not an outburst of pure feeling, but is the result of a more than common power of controlling and manipulating feeling; the faults which made D'Annunzio, for instance, rather a deplorable politician made him a second-rate artist. The surest way, perhaps, of judging the work of an author who ventures into a new field, whether it be that of political controversy or some other, is to trace if we can the growth of his interests and their relations among each other. A man may be led, by the connections of things themselves, far from his starting point, just as Ste. Beuve, as literary critic, was led to study the

whole of social life. Where there is no vital connexion, the man may
be a brilliant virtuoso, but is probably nothing more. Even within one
sphere of business, as in a novel or a play, the vital connexion may be
absent; and if it is absent the novel or poem or play will not endure.

June 6th, 1928

Pascal: the Great Layman*

T. S. ELIOT

Every student of Pascal in this country must be acquainted with
Dr. Stewart's earlier book, *The Holiness of Pascal*. The title of this
second small book does not reveal its meaning so clearly; but it is
as well that we should be provoked to read the book in order to find
out what the secret is. It is, for the purpose of this book, Pascal's style.
French critics have analysed and criticised this famous style, but an
explanation of it for English readers can best be given by an English
critic, and no one is better qualified, first, by his knowledge of theology
and erudition in French literature, and, second—what is equally important—by a lifelong devotion to Pascal, than is Dr. Stewart.

The book consists of three chapters: Pascal in Debate, Pascal as
Moralist, and Pascal as Poet. The second chapter is not so directly
concerned with style as the first and third. We admit, that with Pascal
if with anyone, it is impossible to appreciate so ardent a style without
some understanding of what he was ardent about; my only criticism
of this second chapter—which is perhaps merely a complaint that the
book is so brief—is that one would like to see Pascal as moralist set in
his proper place in that great French tradition of moralists—a tradition
so definite in France as to produce its own *genre*—which begins with
Montaigne, which proceeds to La Bruyère and Vauvenargues, which
comprehends minor figures like Chamfort and Rivarol, and which is
even at the back of a book most agreeably read in a French translation,
Goethe's *Conversations with Eckermann*. It is true that Dr. Stewart says
significantly, in describing the composition of a particular *pensée* in
his third chapter, that Pascal 'has his Montaigne in hand or in his head,'

* *The Secret of Pascal*. By H. F. Stewart.

but one would have liked to find a more general statement of the relationship of the two writers.

In the first chapter, Dr. Stewart is, of course, concerned with the *Provinciales*. Whether Pascal was *quite* fair to his antagonists (who certainly were not fair to him), whether he did not sometimes pounce with glee upon the works of the more unlucky exponents of the principles of their order, whether he was not sometimes carried to excess by delight in the exercise of his own prowess, are questions about which I have doubts, but which I have not the learning to resolve: Dr. Stewart, certainly, is convinced of Pascal's rightness. At one point, however, it seems to me that he reprimands Pascal without justification. Pascal has said of the Jesuits: 'they have such a good opinion of themselves that they think it useful and almost necessary for the welfare of religion that their credit should spread until all consciences pass into their keeping.' If the Jesuits in question thought this, they may have been mistaken, but I fail to see that Pascal's accusation is, as Dr. Stewart takes it to be, an 'accusation of personal ambition.' Whether Pascal accused them of personal ambition or not, he does not appear to be doing so in this passage. But in the matter of style, certainly, Dr. Stewart does, in the second chapter, make a very important point in favour of Pascal against the Jesuits. He points out that

in the first half of the seventeenth century a wave of bad taste swept over France, tainting every branch of intellectual activity; and the Society of Jesus, which might have taken as its second motto *humani nihil a me alienum puto*, did not escape the infection.

The wave of bad taste was not, of course, limited in its motion to France. It rises in Marinism in Italy, sweeps over Catholic Europe, and finally washes the shores of England with the excesses of Benlowes and Cleveland. According to Mario Praz, who has probably read more of the unreadable verse of the 17th century, including much in Latin, than anyone else, the Jesuits did take a hand in this literary movement with more zeal than inspiration. Dr. Stewart's suggestion that Pascal, while combating the casuistry of the Jesuits, was also combating the bad literary taste with which they had associated themselves, strikes me as a valuable one.

But if the secret of Pascal is style, we have still to find the secret of the secret; and this is to be found primarily, as Dr. Stewart makes clear at the beginning, in a passion for exact definition of terms. His adversaries—his scientific adversaries first—failed in this *seriousness* about language. As a preparation for the *Provinciales*, Dr. Stewart says truly, Pascal 'knew little or no theology; but he knew an equivocal term when he saw it.' This remark is one that every reader of Pascal should keep in mind. He is not a professional theologian; he is not to be read as a theologian: he is the great layman, the man of the world (*honnête homme*) as well as scientist, whose worldly wisdom rises and consummates itself in spiritual wisdom, and whose spiritual wisdom is very firmly set on a knowledge of the world. His wisdom, like that of many great writers, is more in his writing than in his life; he who, in his *pensées*, saw the necessary balance of reason and feeling, was, Dr. Stewart reminds us, 'extravagant in his thoughts and acts.' It was the extravagance of an intensely passionate man; and his rational powers only pushed his austerity of life and personal relationships to their extreme.

In the third chapter, Dr. Stewart analyses particular *pensées*, examines Pascal's method of composition, the improvements he made in re-writing, and discusses the reasons for his superiority as a writer to Nicole and Arnauld. The comparison of his style, by parallel columns, with that of Descartes, is very illuminating. This chapter especially renders a service to English readers more helpful to them than anything of the sort that could be done for them by a French scholar in his own language.

I cannot help hoping that Dr. Stewart will consider rendering one further service to posterity by producing another edition of *The Holiness of Pascal* and *The Secret of Pascal* welded into one book. For Pascal is not simply the writer of a volume of controversial letters and the fragments of an Apology any more than he is merely the physicist. He is primarily the man, and his influence, which those who have experienced it never escape from, is that of an immensely powerful personality. Therefore the different aspects cannot altogether satis-factorily be contemplated separately: and we should like to study them in the one volume which Dr. Stewart might give us.

November 29th, 1941

T. S. Eliot: a Reply to the Condescending

F. R. LEAVIS

Under the title 'For Mr T. S. Eliot,' there appeared in a recent number of the *New Statesman* a review of Mr Eliot's last book.*

'Mr Eliot's great reputation among the young,' pronounced the reviewer, 'is due to two facts: that, of those men who practise and criticise the more recent fashions in literature, he has some acquaintance with the past—an acquaintance that strikes with awe the young men whose reading begins with the Edwardians; that he holds very distinct and reasonably dogmatic opinions, and evidently writes from his mind rather than from his "dark inwards" or "the red pavilion of his heart." '

One recognised the note. It tends to recur when the consciously adult, especially in the academic world, speak and write of Mr Eliot. One remembered the distinguished scholar who, reviewing not long ago some work of Mr Eliot's, spent a good deal of his column pointing out how much better it had been done by another distinguished scholar, a friend of the reviewer, but nevertheless conceded that Mr Eliot, though 'not a critic of the first trenchancy' was not wholly without critical gifts. Those of us who are aware of our debt to Mr Eliot have learnt not to be too provoked by this kind of condescension. It offsets the snobism attendant, inevitably, upon the vogue that Mr Eliot enjoys, and suffers from. But the challenge quoted above does seem to give one who still counts himself among the young, and who discusses literature a good deal with others of the young, a fair opportunity to acknowledge the debt and to define its nature.

First of all, we recognize in Mr Eliot a poet of profound originality, and of especial significance to all who are concerned for the future of English poetry. To describe him as 'practising the more recent fashions' is misleading, and betrays ignorance and prejudice. It suggests that he is one of a herd of 'modernist' poetasters. But there is no other poetry in the least like Mr Eliot's: he is an originator, and if he has his mimics, he could be confused with them only by the malicious or the incompetent. Nor is it his fault if he is included in the Sitwellian 'we.' 'Pro-

* [R. Ellis Roberts], *New Statesman*, December 29th, 1928.

found originality' were considered words. Mr Eliot says in *The Sacred Wood* that the historical sense is 'nearly indispensable to anyone who would continue to be a poet beyond his twenty-fifth year; and the historical sense involves a perception, not only of the pastness of the past, but of its presence; the historical sense compels a man to write not merely with his own generation in his bones, but with a feeling that the whole of the literature of Europe from Homer and within it the whole of the literature of his own country has a simultaneous existence and composes a simultaneous order. This historical sense, which is a sense of the timeless as well as of the temporal and of the timeless and of the temporal together, is what makes a writer traditional. And it is at the same time what makes a writer most acutely conscious of his place in time, of his contemporaneity.' Mr Eliot is now well beyond his twenty-fifth year, and his latest poetry has a new vitality. *Salutation*, which appeared in the *Criterion* for January, last year, and *Perch'io non spero*, which appeared in the last 'Printemps' number of *Commerce*, have a power and a beauty that might, one would think, compel recognition even from an anthologist. The poet bears out the critic. His poetry is more conscious of the past than any other that is being written in English to-day. This most modern of the moderns is more truly traditional than the 'traditionalists'—and he is a poet.

'By losing tradition,' he says in *The Sacred Wood*, 'we lose our hold on the present.' It is because of his hold on the present that he has his great reputation among the young. Poetry tends recurrently to confine itself by conventions of 'the poetic' which bar the poet from his most valuable material, the material that is most significant to sensitive and adequate minds in his own day; or else sensitive and adequate minds are barred out of poetry. Something of this kind has clearly been wrong with poetry in this century, and efforts at readjustment, those, for instance, of Mr Masefield, Mr Binyon, and Mr Squire, have commonly served only to call attention to its plight. Mr Eliot is so important because, with a mind of very rare sensitiveness and adequacy, he has, for himself, solved the problem, and so done more than solve the problem for himself. His influence will not be measured by the number of his imitators, but will manifest itself in indirect and subtle ways of which there can be no full account. In any case, the academic mind charting English poetry a century hence will not be tempted to condescend to Mr Eliot.

His influence has made itself so profoundly and so widely felt in so short a time because he is a critic as well as a poet, and his poetry and his criticism reinforce each other. One would hardly guess from the description of him as 'criticising the more recent fashions in literature' that his criticism had been almost wholly confined to writers of the past. If Dryden and Donne are in fashion Mr Eliot may have had something to do with their being so; it is he alone who has made them more than fashions. 'The important critic,' he says in *The Sacred Wood*, 'is the person who is absorbed in the present problems of art, and who wishes to bring the forces of the past to bear upon the solution of these problems.' We who are aware of our debt to Mr Eliot find his criticism so important because it has pursued this aim with such indubitable success. The present writer, having undertaken to lecture on contemporary poetry, looked through several years of the likely journals, and found that the helpful review or critique almost always showed the influence of *Homage to John Dryden*.

Mr Eliot's acquaintance with the past, then, has impressed us so much because it has illuminated for us both the past and the present. We find commonly that the erudition of the constituted authorities does neither. His acquaintance with the past is profound enough to have reshaped the current effective idea of the English tradition. If no serious critic or poet now supposes that English poetry in the future must, or can, develop along the line running from the Romantics through Tennyson, this is mainly due to Mr Eliot. But for him we certainly should not have had this clear awareness; and for this debt alone—it is a very great, though incalculable debt—the histories of English literature will give him an important place.

All this might suggest that Mr Eliot's criticism is pervaded by the propagandist spirit. It is not so. 'English criticism,' he has remarked, 'is inclined to argue or persuade rather than to state'; but his own is the last against which such a charge could be brought. It is so entirely controlled by the will to 'see the object as in itself it really is' that some people reading it, and missing the non-critical that they expect to find in criticism, think (or so they report) that it contains nothing at all. It makes some of us feel that we never read criticism before. At any rate Mr Eliot represents for us the essentially critical, and when, intimidated by the insinuation of priggishness, we are told that criticism is 'any kind of writing about books,' we are stiffened by the thought of him as by a vicarious conscience. Those of us who are giving a good part of our lives to the study of literature are especially grateful to him.

For no one has set forth for us our justifying ideas so clearly and cogently, and no critic has served them in his practice with such austere integrity.

The critic, he concludes, in an essay on the function of criticism, must have 'a very highly developed sense of fact.' This suggests well enough where, in his account of criticism, the stress falls. The critic must cultivate this sense of fact in regions where there are no facts that can be handed round or brought into the laboratory. He must aim, in so far as he is a critic, to establish the work of art as a fact, an object existing outside of, and apart from, himself. Actually, of course, this cannot be done, and there is no one demonstrably right judgment. But a critic is a critic only in so far as he is controlled by these ideals. And their inaccessibility leads, not to arbitrariness, but to askesis, not to assertiveness, but to docility. He seeks help, confirmation, and check from as many qualified minds as possible. 'For the kinds of critical work we have admitted,' writes Mr Eliot, 'there is the possibility of co-operative activity, with the further possibility of arriving at something outside of ourselves, which may provisionally be called truth.' All this may be both old and obvious to the adult, but we who admire Mr Eliot had never before had it made obvious to us; and we are grateful to him for the clearness and force with which he has set forth the idea of criticism, and for the athletic rigour with which he has verified his principle in his practice.

We have learnt from Mr Eliot what is meant by 'an interest in art and life as problems which exist and can be handled apart from their relations to the critic's private temperament.' And it seems to us the only kind of interest that can justify a prolonged study of literature. But there will always be people who find Mr Middleton Murry's kind of interest more exciting (though we ourselves acknowledge a debt to Mr Murry for stimulus, derived mainly from his early work). It is not, however, only those who prefer prophecy, exaltations, and the ardours of the private soul who find Mr Eliot's criticism unrepaying. There are others, sober enough, who are baffled and repelled by the very purity of its devotion to literature, by its very rigour. For Mr Eliot never forgets that poetry is made of words. His approach is commonly by way of technique, and his dealings with 'content' are always rigorously controlled and disciplined. He is not (to adapt some words of his own) one of those who, in writing about Hamlet, forget that their first business is to study a work of art. So those who are accustomed to think of Hamlet as a man with a life antecedent to, and outside of, the play, a subject for psycho-analysis, feel that Mr Eliot induces cerebral corrugations to no end. 'To the member of the Browning Study Circle,' he says, 'the discussion of poets about poetry may seem arid, technical and limited. It is merely that the practitioners have clarified and reduced to a state of fact all the feelings that the member can only enjoy in the most nebulous form; the dry technique implies, for those who have mastered it, all that the member thrills to; only that has been made into something precise, tractable, under control. That, at all events, is one reason for the value of the practitioner's criticism—he is dealing with his facts, and he can help us to do the same.'

Although Mr Eliot never forgets to see poetry as a texture of words, he is as much concerned with what lies behind as other critics, and more effectively. 'Their words', he says, comparing Shakespeare, Donne, Webster and Tourneur with Jonson, 'have often a network of tentacular roots reaching down to the deepest terrors and desires. Jonson's most certainly have not ...' This suggests fairly well the manner of Mr Eliot's approach to the more inward critical problems, and the kind of control he maintains. And with this continence he is, we find, as fertile in generalizations, explicit and implied, as any critic we know. 'Eriger en lois ses impressions personnelles, c'est le grand effort d'un homme s'il est sincère': it is not for nothing that he set this sentence from Rémy de Gourmont at the head of the first essay in *The Sacred Wood*. For instances of his generalising one may adduce his elucidation of impersonality, of the relation between the work of art and the personality of the artist, and the account which he gives in *Homage to John Dryden* of the relation between thought and emotion in poetry. Such things as these we find in the essential structure of our thinking about art. They seem to us to be among those ideas which, says Mr Eliot, 'stand forth luminous with an independent life of their own, so true that one forgets the author in the statement.'

And among such ideas, for some of us, is Mr Eliot's conception of order. The more we brood over the critic's problem of making his judgment something more than an assertion of personal like or dislike the more inevitable we find the conception of European literature as an organic whole, and within it, English literature as an organic whole, an order—an order in which each new thing must find a place, though the existing order is modified all through by the addition. Here we come to the wider implications of Mr Eliot's 'classicism,' and about these there is, naturally, less certain agreement than about statements of principle that arise immediately out of considerations of technique. And, of course, the 'classicism' involves things outside of literature.

These other things are to the fore in Mr Eliot's last book. The 'very distinct and reasonably dogmatic opinions' that he holds concerning these things, whether we agree with them or not, seem to us to give *For Lancelot Andrewes* the 'coherent force' that we have always found in Mr Eliot's work. The reviewer's judgment to the contrary* seems to us so perverse as to call for something other than ordinary critical incompetence to explain it. In any case, to liken Mr Eliot's 'dogmatic opinions' to Dr Saintsbury's 'predilections' will not do. Dr Saintsbury's high Toryism appears mainly as accidental to his writings on literature. And whoever found in the expressions of it anything more than traits of a personality, racy and assertive, a Character? Mr Eliot's 'predilec- tions' are central to all his work; they are its structure and articulation, its organization, and if we leave them out we leave out everything. This is not to intend any disrespect to Dr Saintsbury: we know the debt that we owe to scholarship. But the mention of his name serves to bring out the peculiar nature of the debt we owe to Mr Eliot. It is because of Mr Eliot that such erudition as Dr Saintsbury's does not merely overwhelm us, and make us feel that life is not long enough to take literature seriously. For if Mr Eliot has told us that erudition is 'useless unless it enables us to see literature all round, to detach it from ourselves, to reach a state of pure contemplation,' he has also given us inspiriting, if chastening, examples of erudition being used to such end. It is he who has heartened us and shown us the way to a study of literature that may hope to produce something other than mere accumulation.

In his latest utterances, now that he has passed on 'to the problem of the relation of poetry to the spiritual and social life of its time and of other times,' we may not always follow him, in either sense of the word. But we await eagerly the promised statements of his position. And we believe that, whatever this may be, it is compatible with the completest intellectual integrity. Meanwhile we are much impressed

* '... a collection of essays on miscellaneous subjects to which the author has not succeeded in giving that coherent force which is the quality of a very determined character – the kind of force, for instance, which Dr Saintsbury, whose predilections are very much what Mr Eliot asserts his own to be, gives to all his writings.'

by his way of stating the problem—the problem of preserving civilization. At any rate, we feel that we must consider very seriously his view of civilization as depending upon a strenuously achieved and traditional normality, a trained and arduous common sense, a kind of athletic poise that cannot be maintained without a laborious and critical docility to traditional wisdom.

Even were the problems that Mr Eliot is concerned with less urgent to us he would be notable for the spare and sinewy scrupulousness of his writing. It is this that has enabled him to exert so much influence with a bulk of published work that would fill no more than a middling-sized book. 'When there is so much to be known,' he says, 'when there are so many fields of knowledge in which the same words are used with different meanings, when everyone knows a little about a great many things, it becomes increasingly difficult for anyone to know whether he knows what he is talking about or not.' There could be no more effective awakener of the intellectual conscience than Mr Eliot: he has made it less easy to shirk.

February 8th, 1929

Cambridge Poetry*

F. R. LEAVIS

It is at the best without eagerness that I open anthologies of modern verse: they are commonly so depressing. And I have learnt to shun above all University anthologies. It is not merely their poverty of talent, or of poetic achievement that depresses me. I know that the immaturity is inevitable, and that it would be extravagant to expect to find any considerable proportion of original poets among the contributors. What is so depressing is that the immaturity is of so utterly unpromising a kind, and that all these apprentices, who are interested enough in poetry to be at considerable pains to write some, show themselves to be imitating models, and working under influences, that must frustrate any gifts they may have. The conventions, the techniques, and the preconceptions of 'the poetic,' coming down from the last

* *Cambridge Poetry 1929.*

Q

century are manifested in these anthologies as none the less blighting for a growing looseness and debility.

It is time now to say that *Cambridge Poetry*, 1929, is not in the least depressing: on the contrary, I find it cheering, as I have found no other anthology of modern verse. For, whatever its faults and weaknesses, they are not of the old hope-destroying kind: it betokens a decisive throwing-off of the fatal conventions and preconceptions. Georgianism, which was never alive, is now well on the way to being forgotten. Squirearchy, which once held paralysing sway, is dead. For it is not mere rebellion, mere 'modernist' intransigence, that *Cambridge Poetry*, 1929, exhibits: Sitwellism counts for very little in it, and E. E. Cummings is not there. (See, for contrast, *Oxford Poetry*, 1928, which favours also the most debile of 'traditional' verse). It is the nature and direction of the 'modernising' that makes the Cambridge book so encouraging.

Certain dominant influences will be apparent on a casual reading. And it might be asked whether immature studies 'after' Mr T. S. Eliot and Gerard Manley Hopkins are any less unpromising than uninspired echoes of Swinburne, *A Shropshire Lad*, Rupert Brooke and Mr Squire. To a general question of this kind I think the answer should be 'Yes.' For the 'traditionalist' conventions and habits are to-day incompatible with the expression in poetry of the interests and urgencies of adult sensitive minds; whereas the habits and techniques of Hopkins and of Mr Eliot are congenial: starting from these a sensitive and intelligent modern (such as future poetry must come from—if there is to be poetry in the future) might develop a manner adequate to his individuality.

But this is no place to dwell on general questions. Let us examine the particular ways in which Mr Eliot's influence (for Mr Eliot's, of course, predominates) is present in *Cambridge Poetry*, 1929. It is present as frank and simple imitation of a given poem or mannerism of Mr Eliot's in *The World is Weary of the Past*, by Christopher Saltmarshe, and in other poems that need not be specified. These are not among the most interesting. It is very obviously, and more elaborately, present in *Dying Gladiator*, by John Davenport, a poem that many readers will find very attractive. It is plain that Mr Davenport has read the whole of Mr Eliot's published verse with close attention: echoes of Mr Eliot in all his manners assert themselves everywhere. So many are at once so obvious that there is no need to exemplify. *The Boston*

Evening Transcript, The Waste Land, Fragment of an Agon, Portrait of a Lady, The Love Song of J. Alfred Prufrock, Whispers of Immortality — they are all there. And let the reader compare the third section (starting where Edith Sitwell stops) with *October Casuistry*, by J. Bronowski. The likeness is no accident; and Mr Bronowski's poem is clearly parasitic upon *A Song for Simeon*, *The Journey of the Magi*, and *Salutation*. But although Mr Davenport has carefully imitated some of Mr Eliot's habits of movement, he has found Mr Eliot's essential rhythm beyond him. Hence an amusing discrepancy between the explicit burden of *Dying Gladiator* and its tone and movement. It is no use Mr Davenport's telling us that Time

has lopped

> from their fierce mouths the brazen trumpets' tongues,
> so that this dull world dances to no tune;

or that the poet walks

> . . . . fearful, sadly, dumb;
> Cruelly cold and barren in this dark
> and fecund month that heaves and swells with life,
> standing against an anaesthetic sky,

(like a patient etherized upon a table?): we cannot believe him. The gusto with which he elaborates his disillusion is too infectious. For Mr Davenport is a young Romantic, of a kind not new in literary history, venting his fine energy in embroideries upon themes from Mr Eliot. His opening passage, with its vague suggestiveness (so unlike anything of Mr Eliot's), is a romantic manifesto. His habit of mind betrays itself in his quite unironical (and probably quite unconscious) recourse to Keats—

> through the dark verdure of my fading thought,

and to Swinburne—

> in the dim hollows of the dark earth's womb.
> (With sadder than the Niobean womb,
> And in the hollow of her breasts a tomb.)

And when the end approaches,

> Annihilation, like a courtesan,
> solicits earnestly my waning strength

very appropriately in the Grand Style. Whether Mr Davenport will
be able to do anything by himself is impossible to guess from this
poem. But it is very much more interesting to read than a Georgian
exercise, and at least took skill and intelligence to put together.

When we come to William Empson we find something that we
must take very seriously. There is nothing parasitic about his work.
But although he does not borrow from Mr Eliot, it is clear that he
knows Mr Eliot's criticism, or, at any rate, has profited by the ideas
that Mr Eliot has put into currency. For it is Mr Eliot who has indicated the right place of the Seventeenth Century in the English tradition, and suggested that the modern poet would do well to study the
metaphysicals:

> Twixt devil and deep sea, man hacks his caves;
> Birth, death; one, many; what is true, and seems;
> Earth's vast hot iron, cold space's empty waves.
>
> King spider, walks the velvet roof of streams;
> Must bird and fish, must God and beast avoid;
> Dance, like nine angels, on pin-point extremes.

It is plain that Mr Empson knows his Donne. But I hasten to disavow
the suggestion that he is derivative. He is an original poet who has
studied the right poets (the right ones for him) in the right way. His
poems have a tough intellectual content (his interest in ideas and the
sciences, and his way of using his erudition, remind us of Donne—
safely), and they evince an intense preoccupation with technique. These
characteristics result sometimes in what seems to me an unprofitable
obscurity, in faults like those common in the Metaphysicals. (Some
things in *Letter*, for instance, remind me of 'Our eyes upon one double
string'). But Mr Empson commands respect. Three of his poems, *To
An Old Lady*, *Villanelle*, and *Arachne*, raise no doubt at all in me: there
is a compelling drive behind them. I look forward to seeing more of
Mr Empson's work.

Mr Empson more than justifies his allotment of six poems. The only
other contributor with as many is Timothy White, and here my critical
judgment is at odds with that of the editors. Mr White diligently
modernises: it is plain that he admires Mr Eliot, Gerard Manley Hopkins, and (to a lesser degree) Miss Sitwell. But surely, in *Interim* it is a
familiar piece from *Poems of To-day* that he modernises, and in *The*

Deaf Mutes a piece of Georgian country sentiment. None of his work seems to me more subtle. And a favourite mannerism of his, exhibited most elaborately in *Happy Paris*, looks to me like a stunt. Mr White is, in any case, still very immature.

Concerning Richard Eberhart, again, my judgment does not jump with that of the editors. It is plain to me that he ought to have had at least as much room as anyone. He not only merits more generous representation; he is peculiarly handicapped by not having it. For he is so original, so strongly individual, that we need a good deal of his work in order to learn, and become familiar with, his idiom, his characteristic rhythms, and his habits of imagery. Half of the contributors could have been spared to make room for more of him—and more of Mr Empson. But, on his showing here, Mr Eberhart is indubitably a poet. The general considerations I have thrown out have no obvious bearing on him. There is no sign that he went to Mr Eliot or Hopkins or Donne for help to find himself. He clearly admires Yeats, and other Irish poets, and Blake. But he is no disciple. His three poems, with all their strong personal quality, exhibit considerable variety of manner, and it would be interesting to know their dates. It is time that he published a body of his work together.

Cambridge Poetry, 1929, then, presents two poets, Mr Eberhart and Mr Empson, and some verse of no great intrinsic value that is interesting and encouraging because it shows that the Georgian fashions have passed, and that the attempt to carry on along the line running from the Romantics through Tennyson has been abandoned by the generation from which any new poets must come. It does, indeed, contain some accomplished pieces of the kind that we have become familiar with in earlier anthologies, pieces that are, as it were, collective ghosts of the great masters. And there are other poems that would receive comment if there were room for critical equity. (Mr Wilson's translation from Gongora, for instance, rouses a desire for more). I should like, too, to make some conjectures about the influence of the Union copy of Kreymborg's *Less Lonely*. But I must end with a general commendation: *Cambridge Poetry*, 1929, is worth buying, which is more than can be said of its predecessors, or of the recent volumes of *Oxford Poetry*.

March 1st, 1929

On D. H. Lawrence*

F. R. LEAVIS

I have repented a great deal my undertaking to write on D. H. Lawrence: it was rash. There have been many warnings. Eminent critics have shown by example how difficult and perilous it is. To make Lawrence an occasion for asserting one's superiority over Bouvard and Pécuchet, Babbitt and Sir William Joynson-Hicks is easy, but it is hard to be critical without getting oneself confused with Mr J. C. Squire. And although one does not mind being called 'highbrow,' it is painful to remember that someone whom one respects has been provoked to endorse the term with his authority. It is a delicate business. Mr Eliot, for instance, in the *Nation*, replied to a challenging letter of Mr Forster's by asking some very pertinent critical questions, and Mr Forster, to our surprise,—Mr Forster, of all people—dismissed them with an angry retort.

I start by assuming that 'genius' is the right word for D. H. Lawrence, though Mr Eliot did this, and it did not save him. Perhaps the ascription has been too long a commonplace. 'In the early days,' says Lawrence, in an *Autobiographical Sketch* printed in *Assorted Articles*, 'they were always telling me I had got genius, as if to console me for not having their own incomparable advantages.' So I had better say at once what I mean by ascribing genius to Lawrence. I have in mind the same kind of thing as when I say that Blake obviously had genius. Lawrence had it as obviously. He had the same gift of knowing what he was interested in, the same power of distinguishing his own feelings and emotions from conventional sentiment, the same 'terrifying honesty.' The parallel might be worked out in considerable detail, starting from the book of squibs that is the occasion for this article. They remind one of the similar verse in which Blake sought relief, and they also are interesting mainly because of their author, though they show again and again an amusing and effective idiosyncrasy, as, for instance, in the lines on the *London Mercury*, or here:

> Oh what a pity, oh! don't you agree
> that figs aren't found in the land of the free!

* *Nettles*. By D. H. Lawrence.

Fig-trees don't grow in my native land;
there's never a fig-leaf near at hand

when you want one; so I did without;
and that is what the row's about.

Virginal, pure policemen came
and hid their faces for very shame,

while they carried the shameless things away
to gaol, to be hid from the light of day.

And Mr Mead, that old, old lily
said: 'Gross! coarse! hideous!' — and I, like a silly

thought he meant the faces of the police-court officials,
and how right he was, and I signed my initials

to confirm what he said; but alas, he meant
my pictures, so on the proceedings went.

The content of these lines reminds us of the community between
Blake's and Lawrence's preoccupations: they may both be said to have
been concerned with the vindication of impulse and spontaneity against
'reason' and convention. The difference between them is the more
interesting in that it is more than the difference between individuals.
In the background of Blake are Rousseau and the French Revolution.
In the background of Lawrence are the social transformations of the
Nineteenth Century, Darwin, the War, and an age of psycho-analysis
and anthropology. So his search for the inner reality, for the hidden
springs of life, took Lawrence a good deal further:

He turned away. Either the heart would break, or cease to care.
Whatever the mystery which has brought forth the universe, it is
a non-human mystery, it has its own great ends, man is not the
criterion. Best leave it all to the vast, creative non-human
mystery... The eternal creative mystery could dispose of man, and
replace him with a finer created being. Just as the horse has taken
the place of the mastodon.

It was very consoling to Birkin, to think this... The fountain-head was incorruptible and unsearchable. It had no limits. It could bring forth miracles, create utter new races and new species in its own hour, new forms of consciousness, new forms of body, new units of being. To be man was as nothing to the possibilities of the creative mystery. To have one's pulse beating direct from the mystery, this was perfection, unutterable satisfaction. Human or inhuman mattered nothing.

Blake, if he could have thought this, would not have found it consoling. Birkin, of course, though one of Lawrence's obvious self-dramatizations, is not to be taken as completely representative, but it is fair to make this passage an opportunity for noting that Lawrence's pre-occupation with the primitive fosters in him a certain inhumanity: the context gives the judgment the appropriate force.

His originality asserts itself in his earliest books. In *Sons and Lovers*, his third novel, he is mature, in the sense of being completely himself. It is a beautiful and poignant book, showing a sincerity in the record of emotional life, such as is possible only to genius. There we find the complexities of personal relations—the tangled attractions and repulsions, self-abasements and tyrannies, of love in particular—exposed with the fanatical seriousness characteristic of Lawrence. According to Mr Middleton Murry (in the current *New Adelphi*) it was quickly discovered 'that in *Sons and Lovers* Lawrence had independently arrived at the main conclusions of the psycho-analysts, and the English followers of Freud came to see him.' Besides this psychological subtlety the book (like *The White Peacock* and all the early work) is remarkable for a sensuous richness of a kind that leads one to talk loosely of the author as a 'poet.' (He did indeed write verse, but not much of it is poetry, though it is very interesting in various ways; he rarely attained the level of the *Ballad of a Second Ophelia*). This richness may be seen at its best in the lovely passage at the opening of *The Rainbow*. It derives from his poignant intuition of the common flame in all things that live and grow; from his sense of the mysterious intercourse of man with the world around him.

Sons and Lovers bears obviously a close relation to Lawrence's own history. *The Rainbow* deals with three generations, yet it seems to bear much the same kind of relation to personal experience. In fact, Lawrence seems here to be exploring his own problems, to be living them through in the book. *Sons and Lovers*, for all its beauty and poignancy, everyone I have discussed it with agrees with me in finding difficult to get through. *The Rainbow* is a great deal more difficult. We do not doubt the urgency for the author of these shifting tensions of the inner life, this drama of the inexplicit in personal intercourse, but for us the effect is one of monotony. Lawrence's fanatical concern for the 'essential' often results in a strange intensity, but how limited is the range! And the intensity too often fails to come through to us. Behind these words we know that there are agonies of frustration, deadlock and apprehension, but we only see words.

In a sense Lawrence is exploring his problems, living them through, in all his novels, but from *The Rainbow* onwards we are aware of certain conclusions. Indeed, he insists on our being aware of them, for, not content to leave them implicit, he enforces them by illustration, comment and symbolism. He becomes, in fact, a prophet, and imposes on the critic the same kind of task as Blake does. His conclusions involve a great deal of declaiming against 'ideas,' 'ideals' and 'mind-knowledge.' For Lawrence arrived at a passionate conviction that man is destroying himself with consciousness, with self-consciousness. Health —life—depends upon complete emotional spontaneity, he believed, and this has been made impossible for us by self-consciousness, by 'mind-knowledge.' ('Blake too,' he says, 'was one of these ghastly, obscene "Knowers." ') The aim, then, is to throw off all ideas of how we ought to feel, all will to feel one way rather than another, 'so that that which is perfectly ourselves can take place in us.' Now these conclusions, so stated, are not very new, and it is in any case not the literary critic's business to discuss them in the abstract. The manner of the critic's concern with them Lawrence himself has indicated:

Art speech is the only speech,

he says in *Studies in Classic American Literature*. And in *Lady Chatterley's Lover*:

It is the way our sympathy flows and recoils that really determines our lives. And here lies the importance of the novel, properly handled. It can inform and lead into new places the flow of our sympathetic consciousness, and it can lead our sympathy away in recoil from things gone dead. Therefore the novel, properly handled, can reveal the most secret places of life—for

·· it is in the *passional* secret places of life, above all, that the tide of
sensitive awareness needs to ebb and flow, cleansing and refreshing.

When, so authorised, we consider as a work of art a novel, say
Women in Love, in which the 'conclusions' are embodied, our judgment cannot be altogether favourable to them. For *Women in Love*
hardly 'informs and leads into new places the flow of our sympathetic
consciousness.' To get through it calls for great determination and a
keen diagnostic interest. One of the reasons for the difficulty is indicated by this passage:

> He (*i.e.*, Birkin-Lawrence), was not very much interested any
> more in personalities and in people—people were all different,
> but they were all enclosed nowadays in a definite limitation, he
> said; there were only about two great ideas, two great streams of
> activity remaining, with various forms of reaction therefrom. The
> reactions were all varied in various people, but they followed a
> few great laws, and intrinsically there was no difference. They
> acted and reacted involuntarily according to a few great laws, and
> once the laws, the great principles, were known, people were no
> more mystically interesting. They were all essentially alike, the
> differences were only variations on a theme. None of them
> transcended the given terms.

Lawrence's main interest lay much lower than personality, and the
characters in *Women in Love* tend to disintegrate into swirls of conflicting impulses and emotions. It is difficult to keep them apart. A
more radical criticism is suggested by this passage from *Studies in
Classic American Literature*:

> I always remember meeting the eyes of a gypsy woman, for one
> moment, in a crowd, in England. She knew, and I knew. What
> did we know? I was not able to make out. But we knew.

It is this kind of 'knowledge' that Lawrence is pervasively concerned with in *Women in Love*: if it can be conveyed at all it is only
by poetic means. But Lawrence uses for the purpose a specialized
vocabulary of terms that he tries to invest with a new potency by
endless re-iteration: 'dark,' 'pure,' 'utter,' 'inchoate,' 'disintegrate,'
'uncreated,' 'violated,' 'abstract,' 'mindless,' 'lapse out,' 'loins of dark-

ness,' and so on. This method is, to use one of Lawrence's own terms of reprobation, mechanical:

'Gerald,' he said, 'I rather hate you.'
'I know you do,' said Gerald. 'Why do you?'
Birkin mused inscrutably for some minutes. 'I should like to know if you are conscious of hating me,' he said at last.
'Do you ever consciously detest me—hate me with mystic hate? There are odd moments when I hate you starrily.'

The great part of the book gets no nearer to concrete particularity than that. Failure of this kind, in a man of Lawrence's genius, would seem to throw doubt on the project of recovering pure spontaneity by getting rid of mind-knowledge. Lawrence himself clearly had misgivings: he tried to settle them by putting them into the mouths of characters:

'What is it but the worst and last form of intellectualism, this love of yours for passion and the animal instincts.'

and

'You *don't* trust yourself. You don't fully believe yourself what you are saying. You don't really want this conjunction, otherwise you wouldn't talk so much about it, you'd get it.'

But even in *Women in Love* the genius of Lawrence is apparent in passages of description, and passages evoking subtle shades of consciousness, strange stirrings of emotion, intuitions of 'unknown modes of being.' In the short stories of such volumes as *The Ladybird, England my England*, and *The Woman who Rode Away*, where he has no room for prophecy and is not tempted to dwell upon his 'conclusions,' his genius triumphs again and again. In critical equity these should receive close attention, but there is not space enough. His novels, as he wanders from country to country—Italy, Australia, Mexico—looking for a new mode of consciousness, exhibit in varying measure the kind of defect indicated above. They are fascinating, exasperating, and very difficult to read through—at least, at the risk of being included under Mr Forster's 'highbrows whom he bored,' I must confess to having found them so. *The Plumed Serpent* describes an attempt to restore the ancient religion of Mexico. The descriptions of the country and the evocations of 'the dark power in the soil' are marvellous, but Lawrence's efforts to persuade himself that he takes the Mexican religion seriously invite the application to himself of certain comments that, in *Studies in Classic American Literature*, he makes on Melville:

> At first you are put off by the style... It seems spurious. You feel Melville is trying to put something over you. It won't do.
> And Melville really is a bit sententious: aware of himself, self-conscious, putting something over even himself...
> ...He preaches and holds forth because he's not sure of himself. And he holds forth, often, so amateurishly.

His last novel, however, is not open to this kind of criticism. *Lady Chatterley's Lover* shows that where sex is concerned he knew what he meant. So far as artistic success can validate his teaching about the relations between man and woman, the book does so: it is beautifully poised and sure. It magnificently enforces the argument of *Pornography and Obscenity*—and so cannot expect free circulation. It is a masterpiece of a rare order. Criticism of it must take the form of the question: How comprehensive or generally valid is this solution?

There is no room to argue the question here, even if I thought myself competent. I will only say that it seems to me too easily assumed that *Lady Chatterley's Lover* represents greater health and vitality than *A Passage to India* (this is not the same as the question of the authors' relative genius): we ought to ask ourselves. If we accepted the first without reserves, how much of what is represented by the second should we have to abandon?

The question is a tribute to both authors.

June 13th, 1930

An Early Romantic

WILLIAM EMPSON

Vaughan is a continual and close imitator of Herbert, both as to images (bees, shooting stars, and so forth, which are not particularly suited to his own mind), actual conceits, subjects and forms of poems as a whole. An example at random is

'Arise, arise, they come.' Look how they run.
Alas, what haste they make to be undone.
How with their lanterns do they seek the sun.

(said by the Christ in Gethsemane—Herbert; and Vaughan, of the
angels running between Heaven and earth on Ascension Day)

They pass as at the last great day, and run
In their white robes to seek the Risen Sun.

A typical borrowing, where the point of the pun is left out. It is
interesting to see how far Herbert's individual style could be used by
so different a mind.

Different, in that his most effective passages are not metaphysical
at all; it is often an apprehension of Nature, not an intellectual activity,
which is at the focus of his consciousness. Wordsworth possessed an
edition of his poems; the accident is historically an important one.
From the poem on Joy:

He weighs not your forced accents, who can have
A lesson played him by a wind or wave.

The point is not that this shows interest in Nature; Herbert often had
such lessons played him, but he was interested in working out the
particular lesson, not in the experience that extracted it from Nature;
at any rate he would not have thought a generalisation about it had
enough point or colour to be poetical. Nor does Vaughan seem anxious
to remember what the lessons were, he is thinking merely of a state
of melancholy peace experienced when he was out walking, and implying that it did him good, without conscious effort of his own.

I have owed to them ('these forms of beauty')
—feelings too
Of unremembered pleasure; such perhaps
As may have had no trivial influence
On that blest portion of a good man's life;
His little, nameless, unremembered acts
Of kindness and of love.

(*Wordsworth*)

Once you are interested mainly in such influences the whole Seventeenth-century emphasis on conscious will and the discursive intellect
becomes unnecessary and unwise. Vaughan's poem goes on

> Thou hast
> Another mirth, a mirth, though overcast
> With clouds and rain, yet full as calm and free
> As those clear heights which above tempests shine.

(I remember some critic producing 'It is a beauteous evening, calm and *free*' as a noble adjective, typical of its author, which was invented to suit the rhyme).

I suppose it was in Wales that he sniffed the wide air of the mountains, and watched the thunder-clouds advancing into the valleys. It is perfectly good Wordsworth. Amusing, incidentally, to compare

> So in sighs and unseen tears
> Pass thy solitary years,
> And, going hence, leave written on some tree
> 'Sighs make joy sure, and shaking fosters thee.'

with Wordsworth's 'Lines left upon a seat in a yew tree which stands near the lake of Esthwaite,' etc., they seem, while adopting this suggestion, to reprove the extravagance of its tone.

> This is the heart he craves; and whose will
> But give it him and grudge not, he shall feel
> That God is true, as herbs unseen
> Put on their youth and green.

> Dear stream, dear bank, where often I
> Have sate, and pleased my pensive eye

(He recited flatly a flat emotion, and expects the reader's indulgence because it is about Nature)

> What sublime truths and wholesome themes
> Lodge in thy mystical, deep streams.

Sublimity mentioned but not expressed, 'wholesome,' the streams of a stream (or of a bank) introduced for the sake of rhyme, and this entirely debased use of 'mystical'—it is surprising to find it all outside the nineteenth century.

As a bridge between this and Herbert, Vaughan's dramatic use of Nature—

> So hills and valleys into singing break;
> And though poor stones have neither speech nor tongue

> While active winds and streams both run and speak
> Yet stones are deep in admiration.

In part it is a conceit about stones in general, as one of the four elements; in part, from the setting, it seems to be the boulders on the hill side, struck dumb in the presence of the precipices, and in a giant silence waiting for their fall. For Palm Sunday

> Put on, put on your best array,
> Let the joyed road make holiday,
> And flowers, that into fields do stray,
> Or secret groves, keep the highway.

Parts of Nature outcast and retiring, like Jesus, are to be brought, on this day of his showing forth, into the agora; there is both a conceit on the connection of Nature and the tribe through the cult-hero and an implied description of the solitary wanderings, the communing with Nature, of the Christ.

> Such was the bright world, on the first seventh day,
> Before man brought forth sin, or sin decay.
> When, like a virgin, clad in flowers and green,
> The pure earth sat; and the fair woods had seen
> No frost, but flourished in their youthful vest
> With which the great Creator had them dressed.
> When Heaven above them shined like molten glass
> While all the planets did unclouded pass,
> And springs, like dissolved pearls, their streams did pour,
> Ne'r marred with floods, nor angered with a shower.

The last four lines do something very impressive with the manner of Dryden; his gong-like note, coming into this exalted and sensuous view of Nature, suggests that before the Fall the whole mechanism of the spheres, an enormous orrery, a circumterrestrial clockwork, could be seen going in the sky. It is these evanescent but powerful suggestions (like Milton's two-handed engine) that Vaughan gains by blurring the outline and losing the energy of the true Herbert conceit.

> God's saints are shining lights; who stays
>   Here long must pass
> O'er dark hills, swift streams, and steep ways
>   As smooth as glass.

One does not separate them in one's mind; it is the romantic movement's effect; dark hair, tidal water, landscape at dusk, are dissolved in your mind, as often in dreams, into an apparently direct sensory image which cannot be attached to any one of the senses. This dream-like or hypnotic intensity is never far out of sight in Vaughan's work (hence, like the Romantics, and unlike Herbert, the ruck of his work is merely bad); when it can be combined with the self-respect of conceits he is very impressive.

(*Of Cain*)

> If single thou
> —Though single voices are but low—
> Couldst such a shrill and long cry rear,
> As speaks still in thy Maker's ear,
> What thunders shall those men arraign
> Who cannot count those they have slain;

(*Sir Walter Scott*)

> Who bathe not in a shallow flood,
> But in a wide, deep sea of blood?
> A sea, whose loud waves cannot sleep
> But deep still calleth unto deep;
> Whose urgent sound, like unto that
> Of many waters, beateth at
> The everlasting doors above
> Where souls behind the altar move
> And with one strong incessant cry
> Enquire How Long of the Most High.

May 31st, 1929

Empson's Criticism*

F. R. LEAVIS

This book is highly disturbing. Here is a man using his intelligence on poetry as seriously as if it were mathematics or one of the sciences. And Mr Empson's is clearly a mind qualified for distinction in fields of thought where serious standards hold. He seems to think

* *Seven Types of Ambiguity*. By William Empson.

that such standards will be tolerated in the field of criticism. How, then, shall the amateur of belles-lettres defend the Muses and himself? There is the well-tried argument against analysis. Mr Empson glances at this—in a kindly way, it is true, but it becomes very difficult to use. There is an amusing passage on page 12 that I should like to quote, but, as Mr Empson says (producing an ambiguity of his own), 'the position of a literary critic is far more a social than a scientific one,' and I prefer to take no risks. It ends (this much is quite proper): 'the reasons that make a line of verse likely to give pleasure, I believe, are like the reasons for anything else; one can reason about them; and while it may be true that the roots of beauty ought not to be violated, it seems to me very arrogant of the appreciative critic to think that he could do this, if he chose, by a little scratching.' Elsewhere he says: 'however wise the view may be that poetry cannot be safely analysed, it seems to me to remain ignoble; and in so far as people are sure that their pleasures will not bear thinking about, I am surprised that they have the patience not to submit them to so easy a destruction.'

But at any rate the analysis of poetry demands something more than intelligence. Mr Empson's is not in question; but what about his sensibility? Well, as we read through Mr Empson's book we become less confident about separating sensibility from intelligence. Is it merely because we have not had a scientific or a mathematical training that we have so often failed to see what was before our eyes? For as Mr Empson again and again convicts us of not having really read familiar passages of poetry we cannot often contend that what we have missed doesn't matter. He has, in short, a very fine sensibility, and is, in every way, an uncommonly adequate reader of poetry. The objector to analysis may take what comfort he can from the sympathy Mr Empson shows him in the last chapter: 'The object of life, after all, is not to understand things, but to maintain one's defences and equilibrium, and live as well as one can; it is not only maiden aunts who are placed like this.' But the objector will hardly have got so far. *Seven Types of Ambiguity* is only for those who believe that they can afford to understand.

We are so unaccustomed to meeting with a first-class mind in criticism that we are apt to lose touch with serious standards. *Seven Types of Ambiguity* is that rare thing, a critical work of the first order; literary criticism that makes a difference to the reader, that increases his efficiency, that improves the apparatus for the future critic. Its

R

range is wider than the title might suggest. Under the head of 'ambiguity' Mr Empson examines many of the most important things about the use of language in poetry. If one feels sometimes that he is apt to be a little too ingenious in detecting ambiguities, one ends by agreeing that it is difficult to exaggerate the subtlety and complexity of English as used by its masters. And if one finds it hard to hold on to his classifications, one is more than satisfied by this modest reply: 'Thus I think my seven types form an immediately useful set of distinctions, but to a more serious analysis they would probably appear trivial and hardly to be distinguished from one another. I call them useful, not merely as a means of stringing examples, but because, in complicated matters, any distinction between cases, however irrelevant, may serve to heighten one's consciousness of the cases themselves.'

In the course of his inquiries he deals with samples of verse of most periods from Chaucer to the present day, and throws out by the way general suggestions about differences between period and period and type and type that are of the highest value. Indeed, there is more of the history of English poetry in this book than in any other that I know.

I will make no pretence of discussing the main topics that Mr Empson raises. I will merely try and fortify my self-esteem by differing with him upon a minor point or two. '... Browning and Meredith, who did write from the world they lived in, affect me as novel-writers of merit with no lyrical inspiration at all,'—I should have thought that Browning's power was lyrical or nothing. 'Wordsworth frankly had no inspiration other than his use, when a boy, of the mountains as a totem or father-substitute.'—Mr Empson does not take this kind of approach (it is not characteristic of the book) too seriously, and in a like spirit I would point questioningly to *The Prelude*, Book II, lines 233–284. This passage, I think, makes it plain that, if we substitute 'mother' for 'father,' Mr Empson's suggestion thus emended finds support in Wordsworth's own avowal.

Then it is possible to comfort oneself by pointing out that Mr Empson's memory, which he appears to have trusted a good deal in quoting, is not perfect. Particularly, he has introduced an ambiguity of his own into Milton. The Mulciber passages as he quotes it runs:

> 'flung by angry Jove
> Sheer o'er the crystal battlements; from dawn

> To noon he fell, from noon to dewy eve,
> A summer's day; and with the setting sun
> Dropped into Lemnos the Aegean isle—'

'Milton is extremely cool about the matter,' comments Mr Empson. But—'dropped into,' as if to supper—no, not so cool as that. There's clearly something more than that 'dawn' for 'morn' wrong with the quotation. And then, on pages 217–218, he puzzles us by quoting from Marvell

> 'And all the jewels that we prize'

and telling us that 'which' (which should have been printed) suggests more than 'that' would have done.

And then there is the further resource of taking up and developing some of Mr Empson's suggestions. When, for instance, he remarks that 'an insensitivity in a poet to the contemporary style of speaking, into which he has been trained to concentrate his powers of apprehension, is so disastrous' I should like to make the application to Milton. But there would be no end to such a commentary, for the book contains like provocations on every page.

Mr Empson's equipment is remarkable, and still more remarkable is the mastery with which he uses it. We have met with critics who could refer lightly to the sciences, to mathematics, to anthropology, to psychology, and this capacity has not appeared a strength. It is impossible to question Mr Empson's command of his resources. His erudition is always relevant, his instruments are always appropriate. His work is so mature that it is difficult to refrain from impertinent references to the year in which his name appeared in the class-lists of the English Tripos. Perhaps it will not be impertinent to remark that he draws many of his examples from books set for that tripos, and to claim for it that it gave him suitable opportunities and did not get in his way. Now had it been any other university school of English—. Yes, Cambridge may pardonably take some credit for him.

His book is the work of a mind that is fully alive in this age, and such a book has a very unusual importance. This is brought home particularly in the last chapter. It is an event to have the response of a younger generation to the problems envisaged by Mr Eliot and Mr Richards, for Mr Empson is as alive as they to the exciting strangeness of the present phase of human history. He implies more than he says, so that we are left expecting.

And, immediately, there is that book of poems which he has given us a right to demand.

January 16th, 1931

The Poetry of William Empson

I. A. RICHARDS

It may not be amiss to draw attention to the suitability of these *Poems* as a present.* Most books of verse put the recipient in a fix. He ought to be able to say something, but nothing comes into his head. At the worst, Mr Empson will allow him to say that modern poetry is in an even more desperate state than he feared. But with a little luck, after a few bouts of puzzling in a carefree and jovial mood, he ought to be able to say much more about this superlative book of riddles. He will have been engaged in some of the most guileful machinations that can be put on foot in poetry, and animated by a wit that mounts, one upon another, more deliberately complex puns than perhaps have yet been seen, but the wit wrings from them, in the best places, lines that resound with an extraordinary and inexplicable passion. The Notes, meanwhile, will have taken him a tour in contemporary physical and anthropological speculation, as he will have been made to laugh repeatedly in a healthy, intellectual, obscure, and satisfying fashion. Little modern poetry—only the best—makes us laugh so.

It is well to begin with *Rolling the Lawn*, *Flighting for Duck*, and *Description of a View*. These introduce us gently to the very peculiar technique, which is more adventurously exploited in *Legal Fiction* and *Earth has Shrunk in the Wash*. It breaks down (for me) in *High Dive* and *Sea Voyage*. Though these are, as Baedeker says, 'repaying,' in other than poster values. The compression is so high and wilful that the mixture ceases to be explosive, and the last line of *Sea Voyage* reads like Meredith in an unhappy moment. But there are plenty of others.

A philosophic interest in Hell marks some of the best:—

---

* *Poems*. By William Empson.

> Your rights reach down when all owners meet, in Hell's
> Pointed exclusive conclave.

but, though what is between is not neglected, visions of the heavens (relativity heavens) are more insistent. Man is the juggler tossing apples (universes of knowledge) which still have 'the central smuggler' at their core, and whether these are worlds of mathematics or of emotion, is here no problem. In none of the more serious poems will a reader, who possesses the 'wise tact' Mr Empson repeatedly approves, be in haste to decide that the meaning certainly is, or certainly is not, within his grasp—for the poems are built upon the very ambiguities of 'meaning.' Only one of them, as he points out, disregards meaning in the verses in which we are accustomed to look for it. But if with the others we strain too hard to see 'just what they mean' we disable our own vision

> And cannot tell. He who all answers brings
> May (ever in the great taskmaster's eye)
> Dowser be of his candle as of springs
> And pump the valley with the tunnel dry.

There is little risk of this with Mr Empson's verses. It is, though, a recurrent theme:

> The god approached dissolves into the air.

But approaches are various:

> Imagine then, by miracle, with me,
> (Ambiguous gifts, as what gods give must be)
> What could not possibly be there,
> And learn a style from a despair.

Mr Empson, I would say, has done this, and what he now writes with it is a matter of extreme interest. I hope he will reduce the compression, be content to score much less than a possible of puns, even when the feat is most tempting, and try a subject with more resistance to manipulation.

It must be harder for a poet to explain his lines in Notes than those who complain of their absence and necessity suppose. Mr Empson has performed this delicate task with an engaging good humour, well aware of the danger that the Notes may turn into an apologetic, and

will, in any case, attempt to replace the poem. The general effect is
to make the reader know better what structures to look for. 'The
thought supposed to be common to the examples is ... ' warns us off
trying for more direct correspondences and interactions between the
examples; and the prose explanations familiarise us with a deliberate
laxity of syntax (not greater than that of conversation) which is, at
first, disconcerting. All through, familiarization is extremely important.
The poems are printed in the order in which they were written, and
to find that my favourites were not Mr Empson's earliest was reassuring; but they are the poems I have known longest. The hardest of the
others, perhaps

> Will ripen only in a forest fire;
> Wait, to be fathered as was Bacchus once,
> Through men's long lives, that image of time's end.

At least they wait for something in the reader's mind that does not
come at will. If they do not grow to full life, that will show, I think,
that excessive demands are being made upon words—not that Mr
Empson's poetic powers are too slight, but that he has been there
experimenting with impracticable modes. Time only will show this.
Meanwhile he seems much the most considerable of the younger
poets.

February 14th, 1936

Seurat

ANTHONY BLUNT

French painting at the end of the last century is so dominated in
the eyes of students to-day by the colossus of Cézanne and the romantic
figures of Gauguin and van Gogh that certain artists of the first importance are passed over with comparatively little tribute. An example
of a painter who has suffered such an eclipse is Seurat, unquestionably
a greater artist than either van Gogh or Gauguin, whose reputations
depend more on their lives and personalities—the former a fascinating
and tragic madman, the latter a Romantic in the Rousseau tradition—
than on the merits of their work. Seurat, who had no life outside his

painting, has none of this superficial interest; and, in addition to this, his paintings have little immediate appeal and often seem dull or even slightly ridiculous at first sight. As with all highly calculating artists, his works only produce their effect after long and careful examination. And so this intellectual, almost scientific, artist, living a perfectly un-romantic life entirely occupied with painting, has to yield in popular estimation to romantic daubers such as van Gogh. But Seurat was really an artist of the highest quality. His contribution to painting was a combination of a study of light effects which surpassed even that of the impressionists with a sense of form and of static design in the purest classical tradition.

In his early works he was near to impressionist methods in his treat-ment of light. Taking Delacroix as his model, he aimed at a greater brilliance of light by using chiefly the pure colours; and in *La Baignade* (in the Tate), the masterpiece of this period, he gains his end by tradi-tional and direct methods. But within the next two years he developed and put into practice his full theory of colour division. In obedience to this theory every colour was analysed into its component primaries which were put on the canvas in small dabs side by side, and by this process the loss of brilliance involved in mixing colours was avoided. Moreover local colour and colour due to particular lighting or re-flexion were carefully distinguished, and the latter was apparently only painted in when the former was fully established. This technique was most suitable for landscape painting, but Seurat used it for interiors and figure-painting also with brilliant success, witness *Les Poseuses*.

In the matter of colour-division Seurat only systematized and carried to their logical conclusion the discoveries of such impressionists as Monet and Pissarro, though he always denied that they had influenced him directly. But in his treatment of form he stands quite apart from them, and his method of designing is different from that of any of his contemporaries.

To the impressionists in question a house or a figure was simply something which gave rise to varieties of light and colour which they were interested in rendering. In their filmy paintings earth, air and water are all equally imponderable. Seurat on the other hand was con-cerned as much with substance as with light and colour. Even in his figure drawings, done in conté almost without the use of line, and more purely studies of light effects than his paintings, he gives by a careful adjustment of values a definite solidity to the forms. In his paintings, notably in *La Baignade*, the figures have a Giottesque weight and solidity; and hills, buildings, and ships have as complete an existence in the round as those of Cézanne. In his landscapes in fact Seurat goes straight back to the early works of Corot, who excelled in the painting of solid objects bathed in light. There is also about his work the quality which Berenson defines as the characteristic of the Umbrian painters of the Renascence, and names *space-composition*. His figures not only exist in a three dimensional space, but the recession takes place in an almost tangible atmosphere.

The real superiority, however, of Seurat over Monet and his group lies in his power of composition. These painters, since they were interested only in effects, made little attempt to give coherence of design to their paintings. In fact they seem almost deliberately to have avoided doing so, tied down by a misplaced realism. In Seurat's paintings on the other hand the composition is calculated with almost geometrical accuracy. Nothing is left to chance and each part fits exactly into its place. His designs are usually perfectly static, without any suggestion of movement, and are built up of heavy vertical figures, preferably either in profile or seen full face, or, in seascapes, of sailing ships seen broadside on. In his early paintings, *La Baignade* and *La Grande Jatte*, which by reason of their monumental simplifications remind one irresistibly of Piero della Francesca, in addition to the emphatic horizontals and verticals, Seurat makes a considerable use of diagonals, established in the former painting by the figure in the foreground and the line of the river bank. But in many of his landscapes and in *La Parade*, his most purely geometrical design, the diagonals are almost done away with, leaving the design absolutely rigid and simplified, sometimes to the point of monotony. These paintings shew a restraint to which Seurat, Puritan though he was, could not keep, and the last two of the half-dozen big paintings which he left are experimental in a new direction.

These are *Le Chahut* and *Le Cirque* (in the Luxembourg), both of them containing, almost alone in Seurat's work, a certain literary interest, in that they are vivid and witty representations, one of the Music Hall, the other of the Circus. But the real novelty about them is that Seurat is here attempting for the first time the representation of movement. The result is certainly curious. Although it is perfectly clear that the acrobats or dancers are moving, we do not realize this directly but only by a process of deduction. Unlike Delacroix, who contrives to give to his figures, often in less violent motion than these, an effect of continuous movement which is immediately grasped, Seurat has seized on a particular instant and crystallized it. His figures, like Poussin's, restricted in a perfectly rigid contour, seem to have been turned to stone in a moment of extreme energy. They give no idea of the movement either preceding or following that particular instant. They have in fact something of the absurdity of photographs of moving figures which, in spite of their accuracy, often give no idea of motion whatsoever.

In attempting the solution of the problems involved in the painting of movement Seurat gives up his earlier ideas of designing primarily in horizontal and vertical lines and masses. The result is a type of composition new in his work, more elaborate and exciting, but less coherent, at any rate in *Le Cirque*, which lacks any centre of interest. This painting is in any case unsatisfactory in its unfinished state; the colour is too thin to support so big and elaborate a composition or even to give solidity to the forms.

In his best paintings Seurat combines the advantages of impressionism with a classical sense of form and design; and yet in spite of his tremendous achievement he had very few followers and none of importance. A good many contemporary painters have experimented in his methods, but they have almost all given them up and come back to the tradition of Cézanne. The reason is that it is almost impossible to develop along the lines which Seurat laid down. The only possible advance on the impressionist study of light was its application to form, and Seurat carried this out so thoroughly that there was nothing more to be done. Signac, seizing on the obvious scientific side of his methods, only went back a step; he is merely an impressionist with the addition of a certain science.

This then accounts for the low estimation in which Seurat is held to-day compared with Cézanne, who, by indicating a really new attitude to the understanding of form, namely by its analysis, founded a method capable of development. The consequences of his art have given him an importance and popularity above Seurat, but that should not blind us to the fact that as an artist pure and simple Seurat was at least his equal.

June 5th, 1929

The Progress of Poetry:
A Letter to a Contemporary

JULIAN BELL

My dear L.

Now that our poetic contemporaries have gathered themselves into a narrowly-defined group, divided only by personal enmities, we have an admirable opportunity to consider the direction in which poetry is moving in Cambridge. As outsiders we are in a position to take a more impartial, if less favourable, view than that of their own critics. My contention is that our contemporaries, believing themselves to be in reaction against the Romantics, are themselves inverted Romantics.

To do this, I must cross the now putrefying battlefield of Romanticism and Classicism, and try my hand at definitions. By classical poetry I mean nearly everything written in France between Malherbe and Chénier, in England between Dryden and Johnson, and I should also call classical the poetry of Crabbe, of Denham, Waller, and Milton. Romantic I should call nearly everything in England after 1798, in France after 1820, except the work of the Parnassiens.

I should say then that the distinguishing characteristics of the Romantics have been most obviously their metrical licentiousness, next their constant appeal to the emotions, and their most valuable quality, their poeticality, their ability to make use of vague suggestions, and to produce aesthetic effects by relying on the overtones of language. On the other hand, one recognises classical poetry by its extreme metrical strictness. Though it is not devoid of overtones, it relies for its effects above all on accuracy and appropriateness of language, on carefully controlled formal design and movement, and on its appeal to the intellect.

To take the question of metre, our contemporaries, following Keats and Coleridge, have disintegrated the staple English metres, and now appear to write as the spirit moves them, hoping that their halting ragged verses may be taken for new and subtle rhythms.

The second Romantic characteristic which is now universal is the habit of appealing to the emotions. True, our contemporaries have ceased to talk of pure love and mountainous nature. But the illusions they have—not destroyed, but inverted—are precisely the stock romantic illusions.

Even more important, you will notice that their idea of what poetry can do is still that of the Romantics. To find an instance of success among our contemporaries would be both difficult and invidious, but let me take two examples from their master, Mr Eliot:

> The circles of the stormy moon
> Slide westward toward the River Plate,
> Death and the Raven drift above
> And Sweeney guards the horned gate.

And the famous passage from 'The Waste Land', too long to quote, describing the copulations of the typist and the clerk. The first of these is surely typical, and very good, romantic poetry, the words and images used largely for the sake of their overtones and associations, and producing a state of mind that is undoubtedly one of aesthetic emotion, but that is coloured and haunted by endless vague suggestions of other remembered emotions. It is poetry of the same kind as, say, 'Keith of Ravelstone,' not at all of the same kind as

> Thick set with Agat, and the azurn sheen
> Of Turkis blew, and Emrauld green.

Milton gets his effect by statement, Mr Eliot, and all Romantics, by suggestion.

You may think this an unfair comparison. But do not think I fail to recognise Mr Eliot's merits. I admire good romantic poetry as much as anyone, whether Mr Eliot's or Dobell's. But do not let us pretend that it is a new discovery. Nor do I believe that it is a good model for us, for I cannot help thinking that even inverted Romanticism has exhausted itself.

It is worth noticing how much the second passage is in the romantic tradition, both the practice of Baudelaire and Rimbaud—either of whom might well have written it—and the Wordsworthian precepts of simple thoughts in simple language. It also seems to me a very good example of the Romantic standing on his head. It is, surely, the subject matter of Romeo and Juliet or of Saint Agnes' Eve made deliberately anti-poetical. It seems to me that it owes its success to much the same qualities as did the previous quotation. Words are used more for the effects of their overtones and suggestions than their agreed meanings.

Finally, I think these passages show the two important virtues of the moderns. They have at least succeeded in destroying the cant of Georgian emotionalism. The stock poetical attitudes of thirty years ago are not common in their verse. In this we should be well advised to imitate them. But, since we are neither of us disillusioned Romantics, let us avoid the faults, not so much of Mr Eliot as of his imitators, our contemporaries. For they, destroying an old cant, have invented a new one even sillier. The attitudes of disillusion into which they throw themselves, the commonplaces in which they express those attitudes, are of an emptiness and dreariness far surpassing the worst products of their old enemies, the now defunct 'Squirearchy.'

The second of the modern virtues, you may also have noticed in these passages, a marked preference for concrete and exact descriptive words and images. In this direction only does there seem to be hope in the present movement of poetry.

You will see that I have turned from our contemporaries to a criticism of Mr Eliot, since it is easier to criticise one good poet than a pack of imitators.

This question of imitation leads me on, by way of Mr Empson, their other model, to that of obscurity. This quality is common enough in romantic poetry, for it is a natural product of emotionalism and confused thinking.

Much contemporary obscurity appears to me to be of this romantic kind. But it has a second source, the metaphysical poetry of the Seventeenth Century. After Pope's parodies of Cowley, to say nothing of the works of the later metaphysicals themselves, one would have thought that anyone wishing to write in this manner would have exercised a certain discretion. Mr Empson, on the contrary, is more extravagant than one would have believed possible. The cleverness that is capable of 'a vile conceit in pompous language dressed' is not uncommon among our contemporaries. Obscurity, however, suits them very well, since under its cover the silliest charlatan may find those who, wishing to be abreast of the times, will admire him as a new and original poet.

The fashionable defence for obscurity is that the poet is attempting to compress so much into so few words that these are unable to contain his meaning. (Observe the extreme Romanticism of this). As an explanation of some obscurity this may be true. But it is no defence, for if the poet had wished to convey his meaning, but was unable to make himself understood, it is a clear sign that he has failed in the purpose with which he set out. Compression may be a virtue, but it is not the only virtue, and compression at the expense of clarity is the worst possible vice of style. When a writer is obscure, it is a proof either that he has failed to convey his meaning, or that he has no meaning to convey, but wishes either to create an atmosphere or to conceal his lack of meaning, which last is the case with most of our contemporaries. Even in the creation of an atmosphere, the one plausible excuse for obscurity, it cannot be conducive to the poet's purpose that the reader should be racking his brains in a state of perplexity and wondering what it is all about. Another use for obscurity, Mr Empson's, is setting ingenious puzzles for old maids to solve in the *Spectator*.

If we pursue the course I shall suggest, we must be prepared to find ourselves in a minority in print, though I think that there is enough good sense left in Cambridge for us to find a favourable hearing. We must refuse to accept critical dogmas, even when they have the authority of Mr Eliot or Mr Richards behind them, without an exceedingly careful and thorough intellectual examination. We must on no account let ourselves be carried away by the constant flow of verse, all of it moving, like the Gadarene swine, in one same direction. This will be the harder, since two modern qualities, freedom from old sentimentalities and the use of concrete and unpoetic words, are essential at the moment to any kind of good writing. And we must discover for ourselves more hopeful directions of advance. Therefore I propose a deliberate return to classical models, and an attempt to recover the virtues of a classical style. I am convinced that the first step in this direction must be a change in our choice and treatment of subjects. These should be more often than at present intellectual, the expression of ideas in verse. Emotional subjects we should as far as possible intellectualize, and always see that in the expression of our feelings we do not make use of strained and false language, fantastic metaphors, or anything offending the canons of good sense.

In description, the virtues we should seek are vividness, and the clearness of mind which makes it possible to describe a mass of crowded details in such a way that a whole scene is apparent.

In the matter of prosody, I suggest a more frequent use of the decasyllabic and octasyllabic couplets, and of the forms employing regular combinations of iambic feet. For whilst overuse has made all those having strongly marked rhythms echo with memories of past users, these plain and simple metres, admitting only the lightest and subtlest changes, remain as fresh and ready to our hands to-day as ever.

Above all, let us seek to be clear, simple and forcible in expression, plain, precise and appropriate in our language, accurate and polished in our metres, and in our working take great care
That all is round, and full and fair.

March 7th, 1930

Julian Bell: An Obituary

F. L. LUCAS

This summer Julian Bell was killed by the Nationalists in Spain.

My memory of him goes back nearly to another war; in that summer of 1919 he was an independent little boy of nine or so with a strange likeness, I remember thinking, to portraits of Rupert Brooke. He would have laughed loudly at the idea in after years, when he had come to look so different; and yet when one recollects the ends of both, one is less drawn to laugh. Some ten years later I should not have known the pale, already rather burly youth who came up to King's; took History and English; then retired to a farm at Elsworth to write a dissertation on Pope and grow a beard that, while it lasted, made him look formidably like a Robber Baron.

And yet, typical Kingsman as he soon became, he always kept traces of the place where I saw him first. Even when he argued past midnight in the most Cambridge style about the nature of good, or the reality of cows when no one is looking at them, there remained something un-academic about him, some touch of the countryside; as if, had he thrown up the window, one of his Sussex owls might have taken up the debate across the lawn of King's and, instead of the Backs in the moonlight, there might have glimmered behind him the white chalk roads of Charleston and the dark rampart of the Sussex Downs, that will henceforth watch in vain for him from Alfriston to Firle.

I have said that he became in some ways a typical Kingsman; but one of the most typical things about Kingsmen, I believe and hope, is that they are not really typical—too individual, rather, to fit into any mould after the docile fashions of to-day. One of my most vivid memories is an essay he wrote me on *Piers Plowman*. It was a cry of concentrated horror and loathing for Langland in particular and the Middle Ages in general. Now it is possible (and, I think, preferable) to love much that is mediaeval and even to have a certain compassionate fondness for that fourteenth-century Carlyle, so waspish and prudish, nagging and uncouth, yet honest and moving in his way. But here at least was a young man with passion and independence and the power to express them. That was the rare and the essential gift. To-day, when the grovelling servility of modern Europe seems at moments to leave even Cambridge not quite untouched and a bleat is heard from certain sheep reading English because their shepherds do not all pipe the identical tune (as if any body of persons who think at all could think, let alone feel, alike), I remember with the more regret one who, right or wrong, could think for himself and, as time showed, act on it.

Perhaps that was the central thing about him. That the son of Clive and Vanessa Bell should have critical and artistic gifts was only to be expected, impish as heredity can be; but Julian Bell's gift of robust vitality is not too common among intellectual youth. He was never sicklied over. Brief as his life was, he was so full of it that he got more out of it than many who live twice as long.

He was not, I think, made for learning. He was impatient of detail. His originality extended its charming vagaries even to his orthography. That careful accumulation of a thousand facts needed for scientific results was too irksome. He was too wild a bird for the cage.

Nor do I think his future lay in abstract thought; though with characteristic courage he suddenly abandoned Pope for a dissertation on ethics, which won the praise of Mr J. M. Keynes. But his temper was nearer Johnson than Berkeley.

He was happier writing poetry. His *Winter Movement* has two voices. He inherited from Clive Bell (he was too original to react for the sake of reacting, as the new generation often does against the old) a passion for Pope; but he curiously combined it with an equal passion for that Richard Jefferies who inspired so many of his happiest hours, as well as one of his happiest poems. Pope is a dangerous master, as his own century found. He sits on the very summit of his own lower peak of Parnassus; and on it you can only sit in his shadow. The prose of Jefferies was a safer guide. Following him away from Twickenham and out into the countryside, Julian Bell could quickly find himself alone with that wilder nature he knew so well how to observe. The danger here was rather that his eye was too good and tempted him to try to paint in words, while his ear was, I think, a little uncertain when released from the strict pattern of Pope. But after all he was young; and far wiser in serving an apprenticeship with masters of his own choosing than those who think that, like the infant Hermes, they can outwit Apollo the day they are born. Already he had shown himself a true poet, as well as a prophet but too true.

> 'But the grey skeleton may stand more close
> Than sixty years a-cupboard: flying chance
> May jolt her shuttles to a swifter dance,
> And death be nearer than we could suppose.
>   The other day I saw his face,
>   True, but for half a moment's space,
> But now a shadow's at my back, and grows
> As if a guttering candle burned apace.'

When that candle was snuffed out, he had at least made the most of its brief light. Books were, rightly, only the lesser half of his world. Even so, he had produced two volumes of verse and two dissertations; a nearly finished selection of Pope for the Nonesuch Press; a collection of essays by Conscientious Objectors called 'We Did Not Fight' (life is clever at irony); and, with Charles Mauron, an edition of Roger Fry's *Mallarmé*. He had been two years Professor at Hankow; and if he froze the blood with his picture of what English literature can become as studied in an Oriental University, he contrived to study the Orient himself by methods more direct. For he was admirably free from insularity. In a blue blouse in France he could look the robust image of a French workman; and I shall always be able to picture him at the table of a Provençal *mas*, arguing in a flood of fluent and picturesque, though not impeccable French about metaphysics or psychology, poetry or politics. For politics were another passion, at times a ruling one. He never let himself be rammed into a Marxist pigeon-hole. He was too vital and too intelligent. But he was an 'homme de bonne volonté,' a good European, a citizen of the future, in a world of blind newts that cannot look beyond the next frontier, the next dividend, or the next dog-race.

That cost his life. Returned from China, he went out at once in

June, despite all dissuasion, to drive an ambulance on the Madrid front. A few weeks later, after impressing all who knew him by his quiet courage and efficiency, he was bombed with his ambulance, according to the usual chivalry of the modern representatives of the Cid, the gentlemen of Catholic Spain.

It always seemed regrettable that he should go. To employ one with his gifts as a motor-driver was cutting blocks with a razor. I had liked to picture him in years to come as a village Hampden, combining poetry with politics, the countryside he loved with that modern world he could not forget. Now he is dead, murdered by some stupid wretch in a machine supplied by criminals in Rome or Berlin; and who is the better?

But perhaps the historian of the future, if there is one, may see it differently. He and his readers may be thankful to find that the England of 1937 was not perfectly represented, as at the Paris Exhibition, by specimens of a Prime Minister fishing and fools equipped for killing foxes. They may be comforted to feel that not everything was sordid in this period when Foreign Secretaries brought to their office the minds of pettifogging attorneys or wept publicly for their career before a sympathetic House of Commons, which shed no tears for the unhappy nation they had encouraged, then betrayed, and only laughed at the capture of British ships, on an errand of mercy, under the guns of British men-of-war; when learned professors explained in *The Times* that General Franco's cruelties were as justified as the 'punishment' meted out to the Paris Commune in the massacres of 1871, and noble peers could see nothing but 'sentimentality' in saving Basque children from the bombers of Guernica. We are only beginning as yet to count the cost of that mixture of snobbery and panic which refused the Spanish Government at the outset the customary right to buy arms in its own defence. Part of the cost is lives like these. But such things matter no longer to Julian Bell in his grave north of Madrid. Our ministers may fish and fumble on. For him the epitaph of Stendhal—

Visse, scrisse, amò.

October 15th, 1937

S

W. B. Yeats

J. BRONOWSKI

W. B. Yeats made his reputation with a poetry which was vivid, distraught and intangible. He has sustained it with a poetry which has grown from year to year sharper and more purposeful: a poetry as heavy and turbulent with imagery, but with a harsh colloquial pleasure, an acrid idiom, a poetry active with doctrine, which are wholly new. Yeats's later poems may well be understood as didactic poetry, of the highest order. In the change, Yeats has matured from a fine poet of his generation into, I would hold, the greatest poet of a hundred years. He has remained within his century, but he has brought it to that tart perfection to which Goethe brought the previous century. The analogy to Goethe might be pressed, for example in the impulse which each gains from the idiom of knotty but common speech. It suggests another reflection, that no modern poetry is likely to build beyond the poetry of Yeats which is not founded in a doctrine as single and self-sufficient as the doctrine which Wordsworth pitched against the century of Goethe. No modern poet who has hitherto achieved wide reputation holds such a doctrine.

Yeats's early poetry was filled with one belief, which, having inspired such poems as *The Wanderings of Usheen*, reached its fulfilment in *The Countess Cathleen*. It is the belief in the supreme grace of purpose. The Countess Cathleen sells her soul to the devil in order to buy bread for her famine-stricken people. She dies: but her action does not damn her, and raises her instead to the high altar of heaven. This was the theme again and again of the early poems. It was overlaid by poetic sensuousness, the delight in the mere material of verse, and with this it never made a truce. How steadfast was the conflict between them may be instanced by a later poem, *The Grey Rock*, where it is fought visibly both in the manner and content. *The Grey Rock* is a story, but it is broken up by long passages of reflection which explain, as it were, how difficult it is to tell the story while its sheer forces of beauty and drama are so overwhelming:—

> We should be dazed and terror struck,
> If we but saw in dreams that room,

Those wine-drenched eyes, and curse our luck
That emptied all our days to come.
I knew a woman none could please,
Because she dreamed when but a child
Of men and women made like these.

But the story is told. It is the story of the goddess Aoife who, to preserve her lover in a battle in which he insisted upon fighting, gave him
a pin which made him invisible. He, in pride, throws away the pin
and is killed; and she bitterly asks the gods to harass him for his
faithlessness. But her purpose and its conflict with her lover's mannish
pride are too easily defeated by the gods, who each

Stretching forth his arm and cup
To where she moaned upon the ground,
Suddenly drenched her to the skin;
And she with Goban's wine adrip,
No more remembering what had been,
Stared at the gods with laughing lip.

It is a solution which Yeats himself then too often accepted. And this
is one of his finest poems because it is in this vividly personal, a
moment of self-recognition more profound than the many pathetic
moments which fill his later poems.

How important was this deep faith in, this constant struggle to
realise a purpose, may be seen in the hammered strength which it gave
to such poems as this. It forces into these poems a vast compression of
sensuous beauty in the sharp and just word at the just moment, and it
continually urges the verse forward, continually binds and harnesses it.
When, those few years later which closed the century, another poet,
James Joyce, was moved by the same material beauties (indeed by
Yeats's beauties—a quotation from Yeats shapes the end of Joyce's
Portrait of the Artist as a Young Man) the faith in purpose had been lost.
Joyce therefore fell rapidly into the mere elaboration of verbal graces
and echoes, with no other directing power than the belief that the
human mind is cluttered with these.

Yeats was born at the very turn of the tide. Before him had been the
smug purposefulness of Browning, certain not only of the reality of a
purpose but of its nature; believing that he understood, not only what
effect followed what cause, but by what agency the cause grew into

its effect. After Yeats, the belief in purpose and in ordered and intelligent sequence died. Yeats lived, therefore, in that poetically fruitful state in which there is felt the compulsion of a purpose, but in which the purpose itself remains always undiscovered. This appears strikingly in the very form of Yeats's verse. The verse appears to be continuous, yet when it is carefully read it is found to move spasmodically from phrase to phrase. Almost any early passage will illustrate this:

> What matter if your head's below your arms
> Or you've a horse's tail to whip your flank,
> Feathers instead of hair, that's but a straw,
> Come share what bread and meat is in the house.

Each line begins explosively afresh, has been written with separate energy and contributes a discrete energy to the passage. The verse thus accurately reflects the state of mind in which, beginning and end being seen, a connection is felt to be present but remains elusive. It is verse which has sequence but no consequence.

It may be that it is this quality, and Yeats's steady search for the connection of cause with effect which he felt but could not trace, which make his contemporary appeal. But him it led much further. He came to despair of finding such a connection rationally, and he looked for it in mysticism. In that mysticism his faith in purpose survived, and his poetry was re-energised and became stronger and more precise than his youthful, comparatively rational poetry. For with mysticism he gained suddenly a new command of his imagery. Yeats had been happy from the first in taking his imagery from an ancient mythology, so that it always possessed, potentially, a richness of meaning which no one mind can invent. He had therefore never to exhaust himself in that enormous demand of energy which is asked of a poet whose imagic world does not flower of itself, and which returns no truth to him but that upon which he has himself founded it. Yeats's poems had always that unexpectedness, that quality which shows that a poem has suddenly dictated its own end beyond the meditated peroration of the poet, which comes to the poet whose world is a living imagination and not a tortured and personally energised fancy. Now Yeats's symbols hardened into their place and made their own poems. His poems of this period—*The Phases of the Moon* is an example—are not his best poems, but they begin that self-dependent close which marks his later poems.

For now Yeats came also to doubt, not indeed purpose, but his own purpose. The doubt appears in the introductory poem to *Responsibilities*. It may be seen even in the title of that book, a title which does not accord with his old, fervent view of his own purpose, and which suggests instead that his purpose may be mistaken but is inexorable— *In dreams begins responsibility*, he quotes at the beginning of his book. This new and growing doubt so overshadows Yeats's later poems that it masks his earlier struggle for purpose. Yeats now becomes concerned to justify his life. He sees a conflict between living, in the most human sense, and poetry. He wishes to own allegiance to both, and he therefore regards their conflict as a matter for regret. In one of his latest poems (of a series characteristically called *Vacillation*) he says, dividedly and bitterly.

> Get all the gold and silver that you can,
> Satisfy ambition, animate
> The trivial days and ram them with the sun
> And yet upon these maxims meditate:
> All women dote upon an idle man
> Although their children need a rich estate;
> No man has ever lived that had enough
> Of children's gratitude or woman's love.

Yeats has never believed the world of poetry to be absolute and beyond the human world. Now he regrets that he should have written poems while his contemporaries have lived, hunted, loved. What is strangest in this view is that a poet should find the division pathetic—so intensely pathetic as to say,

> The intellect of man is forced to choose
> Perfection of the life, or of the work,
> And if it take the second must refuse
> A heavenly mansion, raging in the dark,
> And when the story's finished, what's the news?
> In luck or out the toil has left its mark:
> That old perplexity an empty purse,
> Or the day's vanity, the night's remorse.

This final regret of Yeats rests upon a view of poetry, not as an absolute, but as only one of the greatest of human activities—an activity whose greatness may be equalled by the greatness of fine living.

To him, *Byzantium*, the world of poetry, is therefore only the real world stripped of its *mere complexities, the fury and the mire of human veins*. The journey to it is difficult only because it must be taken across *that dolphin-torn, that gong-tormented sea* of life—the sea, that is, in which the dolphins of human desire conflict with the gong of final beauty. This is the faith which now stamps Yeats's poems, and gives them a lavish and almost brittle richness which is the perfection of his poetry. It is a faith which implies also that human beauty is as permanent as poetry, though it be the lost beauty of a woman as soured as the woman he describes in *Quarrel in Old Age*. Everything created survives, unchangeably somewhere, merely by virtue of having lived: the faith has its epitome in that secondary mysticism,

> Things out of perfection sail,
> And all their swelling canvas wear,
> Nor shall the self-begotten fail
> Though fantastic men suppose
> Building yard and stormy shore,
> Winding sheet and swaddling clothes.

In a sense, this is the perfect anti-poetic faith; and the outstanding achievement of Yeats is thus to have built the monument of his poetry as it were against poetry. It is a strange opposition of poet and poetry, and only a poet of gigantic stature could have used it for the foundation of a great poetry. Yeats has proved himself a poet of such stature.

June 8th, 1933

T. S. Eliot's 'Failures' in Criticism*

JOAN BENNETT

Mr Eliot's criticism illuminates by flashes, his strength does not lie in sustained argument. It would be rash to expect from him, perhaps indeed from anyone, an answer to the large questions he raises in his introduction: 'Let me start with the supposition that we do not know what poetry is, or what it does or ought to do, or of what use it is, and try to find out, in examining the relation of poetry and criticism,

---

* *The Use of Poetry and the Use of Criticism*. By T. S. Eliot.

what the use of both of them is.' If that is indeed what Mr Eliot tried to do in these lectures, he did not succeed. Nor does the book supply an answer to that other question which concerns some of us even more nearly, and with which the introduction closes, the question 'whether the attempt to teach students to appreciate English literature should be made at all; and with what restrictions the teaching of English literature can rightly be included in any academic curriculum, if at all.' The solution of these problems will not be found in the ensuing pages. High hopes are raised and they are not fulfilled. But Mr Eliot's failures are more illuminating than the successes of cruder minds. He feels his way, recalls with scrupulous fidelity his own adventures among poets and critics, confesses his own hopes and ambitions as a poet, even allows us a glimpse into his workshop. Anyone who has hitherto assumed that Mr Eliot writes poetry for an intellectual minority will be much shaken by this book. On the contrary, he questions whether any poet ever deliberately restricts his public: 'From one point of view, the poet aspires to the condition of the music-hall comedian. Being incapable of altering his wares to suit a prevailing taste, if there be any, he naturally desires a state of society in which they may become popular, and in which his own talents will be put to the best use.' Later on he tells us that 'the worst fault a poet can commit is to be dull,' and he notices of what great value it was to the Elizabethan dramatist that he had to earn his living by amusing 'an alert, curious, semi-barbarous public, fond of beer and bawdrie, including much the same sort of people whom one encounters in local outlying theatres to-day.' His own preferred audience would be one 'which could neither read nor write.' It is difficult to see how such an audience could deal with Mr Eliot's intricate allusiveness, but at least we can now be sure that he is not deliberately writing for a cultivated minority.

Anyone who has felt the fascination of Mr Eliot's poetry will inevitably turn greedily to such passages as these and others which throw light on its inception. But Mr Eliot is modest: he has not written a book about himself, though it is above all a personal book, refreshing in its candour and in its fidelity to his own experience. For instance, 'It is perhaps as well to warn you that Addison is a writer for whom I feel something very like antipathy... the smugness and priggishness of the man,' or of Shelley 'I find his ideas repellent.' This is as refreshing as meeting a friend at a dinner party. On these terms real opinions can be exchanged. Mr Eliot takes his own taste as a basis and in its light considers his problem,—the function of criticism in Queen Anne's day, or the effect upon poetry of a doctrine which the reader 'rejects as childish and feeble.' But if his critical opinions are personal, they are never perverse. He may sanction our distaste for Addison's complacency or for Shelley's lack of judgment; but he will not encourage the exclusion of Milton from the company of great poets, nor the elimination of whole centuries of poetic endeavour. 'When a poet has done as big a job as Milton has, is it helpful to suggest that he has been up a blind alley?', he asks, with reference to Mr Herbert Read's assertion (*Form in Modern Poetry*) that Milton is outside the main English tradition; and, again in connection with Mr Read, 'it is rather strong to suggest that the English mind has been deranged ever since the time of Shakespeare, and that only recently have a few fitful rays of reason penetrated its darkness. If the malady is as chronic as that, it is pretty well beyond cure.'

In a modest preface to these lectures, Mr Eliot writes that 'such success as they had was largely dramatic, and they will be still more disappointing to those who heard them than to those who did not.' But it is hard to believe that they were in fact better heard than read. They lack the compelling form of good lectures; no conclusion is reached, no plan is fulfilled. Their value lies in those incidentals and asides which are likely to escape a listener; but to which a reader can return and over whose implications he will wish to linger.

November 24th, 1933

H. G. Wells and Ourselves

C. P. SNOW

I

This is a magnificent book.* It was bound to be, of course. The raw materials of Wells' life are enough in themselves, without the aid of a great writer, to make a story that catches at the heart; however it was told, one could not read of this fight through poverty, illness,

---

* *An Experiment in Autobiography.* By H. G. Wells.

maladjusted love, without being enriched at second-hand by the courage of an experimental life. It is a life that not many men could have lived; and, as it happened to a writer of genius, it makes an autobiography of a kind that has not been written before. It must be, in fact, one of the great autobiographies of the world, far more the honest record of a man's full life than either Augustine's or Rousseau's.

If I were writing in anything but a Cambridge magazine, I think I should finish there. But it is probably fair to say that various bodies of 'Cambridge' opinion have shown more unanimity in disapproving of Wells' work than in anything else whatever. Of all reputations grudgingly conceded, his has been the most grudging. If Chairs in Progress or Contemporary English were established, his chances of either would be negligible beside Major Walter Elliot and T. S. Eliot, and the opposition would prefer Leonard and Virginia Woolf. Undergraduates can be led to say that Gerard Manley Hopkins was the only justification for the nineteenth century, or that Joyce is the only hope of the twentieth, or that all art should be collective: they can be led to say pretty nearly anything—and yet I wonder when anyone said a good word for Wells.

It is all very silly. It is also a pity. For when we have the luck to possess the most richly endowed artist of his time, and when he has deliberately spent much of his intelligence in making plans for the years ahead, it is rather stupid of us to deny that he is an artist because he has plans for the future and to deny that the plans are any use because he is an artist. That is what we have done, in our Cambridge provinciality. And the Cambridge attitudes have been an exaggeration, a sort of academic caricature, of the world's. A great deal has been lost by this frigidity; in the very fine introduction to the autobiography, Wells himself is suggesting that most of his work has been wasted; the least one can do now is to try to find the reasons.

For the resentment directed at his schemes for the future of mankind, it is not difficult to see the explanations; but since the Open Conspiracies do not enter much into the first volume (which stops when he is thirty, just beginning to make a success of writing) I shall leave them until the review of the second volume. The resentment of the novels is not quite so straightforward; it seems possible to disentangle two defensible reasons for it, as well as a large assortment of unworthy ones. The last can be disposed of without any serious consideration. In so many ways he is a reproach to sterility; and he has aroused more than the usual jealousies, more than the usual barriers of culture (with his science and his zest and his gibes at the older universities and the pretensions about Art). These things have not put off serious people, though they have a disastrous effect on people who take themselves seriously—upon that class of academic figure in particular, who in Wells' own phrase 'are not distinguished people: they confer distinctions upon one another.'

Apart from these trivialities, though, there are the two reasons which deserve to be looked at more closely. The first of them is a little difficult to convey without the use of a jargon that is widely mistrusted; unfortunately I cannot try to make it more acceptable by saying at some length what all these things mean, and why these words are no more offensive than any other words, if one is in the way of using them. And so I should like this taken as a sketch of an argument, rather than an argument itself. However, in the autobiography Wells spends considerable time in explaining how important the conception of the 'persona' seems to him, the persona defined by Jung as the private conception a man has of himself, his idea of what he wants to be and how he wants other people to take him. Beneath it there lie all the unconscious urgencies, the medley of desires and fears, that are at the root of a man's thoughts and actions; his 'persona' is the control by which these urgencies are presented to himself. There are people with complex and fluctuating personas, some with scarcely any at all, and some with them very definitely and rigidly developed. Wells himself seems always to have had a self-picture as the thinker and worker for the benefit of mankind; it shines through so many of his books, more clearly in his autobiography perhaps than anywhere. He admits it, discusses impartially and acutely the relation between it and the deeper unconscious desires. But yet, it seems to me, he has not the profoundest intuitive grasp of these deeper urgencies; too intelligent and honest not to recognise them, he still does not *feel* their importance as a man of less rigid persona might do; he has not the sense of the inner life that Dostoievski had, or in some ways Proust. Perhaps there is a law of compensation; a rigid idea of oneself is a useful possession in driving a way through life; the looser persona will often involve much disillusion and misery; but maybe just because the rigid persona can be so useful in effect, it cuts a man off from some parts of himself. And possibly in creative literature too, the rigid persona will be a help and also a hindrance. Seeing himself so clearly, a writer will deal with difficulties and incongruities in other people; he will tend to give them personas as definite as his own, make them stand out clear, in more conscious outline, than they do in fact; he will be preoccupied with conscious problems and conscious conflicts. His characters will gain in vividness (roughly, a 'character which comes to life' in a novel is one with a well-marked persona) and comedy; but on the other hand he may sometimes fail to show the deeper understanding.

To some extent, that seems to me true of Wells. I am not sure how important it is; my own bias leads me to suggest that the complete understanding of people is the most important part of a novelist's work, but very likely I am overstressing it. In any case, no novelist in English has shown anything like this understanding yet; and though in Wells it seems to me deficient by the side of his other qualities, there is nevertheless a great deal of it. But I fancy it is that lack which has made itself felt to readers unsympathetic to his temperament; and they have gone to writers without a tenth of his qualities, such as Bennett, and decided that because occasionally they could find in him a glimmer of a deeper understanding than Wells' that therefore he was far the better novelist.

The other reason which may have led to a depreciation of Wells is much simpler and shorter. He is the least nostalgic of great writers. He is a human being in action towards the future, planning, contriving, fighting. Most writers, perhaps because they are often less than adult, have been more than preoccupied with dreams of the past than plans for the future. Wells' note is new and strange, so active and intelligent and full of hope that it strikes hostilely against those brought up on the nostalgic memories. And perhaps the only statement one can make is that if art must be all gestures of futility, despair and home-sick escape, then Wells is less of an artist than anyone who ever wrote.

II

In this volume Wells concludes his autobiography. It begins when he is writing his first scientific romances and making a comfortable living from incidental journalism; it shows him preoccupied with his personal life and starting to shape his thoughts in the world state of the future. As his struggle for fame and money became successful, these two desires (one remembers the New Machiavelli—'the scarlet thread of passion and the white thread of service') came more and more to dominate his life; with the more impersonal one, the real creative longing to put order into the world, taking a larger place as the years rush on, creeping into his novels, coming to some sort of final expression in *The World of William Clissold*, and now in this autobiography.

And the autobiography ends in fact with his account of the present situation in the world, his impatience with its muddles and his own solutions for them; through the impatience, though, there sounds the serenity of an ultimate faith in the future of mankind.

It is an unfamiliar note to end an autobiography on; so unfamiliar that it will probably be always a little resented during the many years in which this book will be read. It is the same note, of course, which made people dubious of *The New Machiavelli* and bitter about *The World of William Clissold*. But they could always be dismissed with the stock phrase—'they are not novels at all.' It will be rather more difficult to dismiss this last book — 'it is not an autobiography at all.' Somehow that seems to be going a little too far—or am I being too naïve, too unsuspicious of what criticism is capable, when it really sets its mind to the job? It will either have to be dismissed, however, or else the hard fact faced that for this man at any rate the future of the world, the Idea of a Planned World, was a reality right from his youth, that much of his thought and emotions have been about it, that it has taken up a large part of his life. That is simply the truth; and being so, had to be put down in the autobiography, for otherwise it would have been less than complete, a good deal less than honest. And yet, to most people perhaps the book would have seemed truer, just as the later novels would have seemed truer, if this side of a man's life had been diminished or left out altogether.

It is interesting that we make these conventions of the kinds of experience we choose to have described for us. It is interesting, and a little difficult, to see why they are made—why, in particular, should Wells' social passion seem repugnant (or uninteresting or unreal) to a very large number of readers? Universality obviously is not the criterion; at least as many people want to get some order into the world as have Proust's curious reactions to Time; both attitudes are a little unusual, but without the Proust experience most readers are willing to admit this was true for the writer if not for them, while Wells' experience seems unacceptable unless one has already had a touch of it oneself. There does not seem an explanation ready made for this colour-blindness of the emotions—except maybe that most of us are so made that we do not want the world to change, and that we not only do not share the social passion but find it actively breaking into our securities.

However, if any book can make the urge for a planned world seem an integral part of a life, this can. And there is much more which is the common stuff of human experience, the record of a packed life. All through, the book is lively and humorous and stimulating as the best of Wells—and that is enough to say. It is written with singular tranquillity and generosity. To compare it with other autobiographies seems, on reflection, impertinent to Wells. It is perhaps better to think of it as one of the most vivid and glowing and complete of books. It is a book that warms one with the echo of its own vitality, the masterpiece of a great writer, the life of a remarkable man.

October 19th and November 30th, 1934

The Energy of Dylan Thomas*

THOM GUNN

One of the reviewers has remarked that Dylan Thomas has reached the collected-works status early in life; for he is not yet forty. He has been writing for almost 20 years, yet we still feel at something of a loss when faced with one of his poems, and especially when someone demands a judgment of it. There is so often a deliberate attempt to intoxicate us with words. Is not such intoxication, we enquire cautiously, a little dishonest? It should reassure us that hangovers after Thomas' poems are exceptional, and that with the best among them the intoxication is renewed, and is just as great, at each re-reading. We cannot get nearer to his meaning by closer inspection, as we can with, say, Eliot or Yeats at their obscurest, nor will a knowledge of what pernes and gyres may be or of what Dame Juliana of Norwich said help us one bit. With Thomas, the first impression is essentially the lasting one, and the closer we examine his logic and even his syntax the more blurred they become—we have to take each poem whole and not phrase by phrase. True, many of his poems are not satisfying

* *Collected Poems.* By Dylan Thomas.

as a whole but only in parts; yet both the scheme of the sense and the repetition of the metrical patterns require that the parts should not be appreciated in isolation, as would be so easy.

It is not presumptuous to compare him with Yeats: for he too dares things on a big scale—and if he fails where Yeats does not it is through trying to include fantastically too much. In 1937 he said, rather surprisingly, in praise of Auden: 'He makes Mr Yeats's isolation guilty as a trance.' It is worth trying to see why Thomas himself is not 'isolated' in this way. He writes his verse,

> 'Not for the proud man apart
> ... But for the lovers, their arms
> Round the griefs of the ages
> Who pay no praise nor wages
> Nor heed my craft or art.'

Though he can be impossible, pretentious, or downright phoney, he does take as his subject the palpable things which are the common experience—and usually at not many removes from the direct experience of the reader himself. And he is besides *hopeful*. If we compare, as we well may, 'Do not go gentle into that good night' with any of Yeats' later poems that it so resembles ('Why should not old men be mad?'), we see that the difference is not so much between the subject, as between the hope the writers have in persuading themselves of their success. Yeats knows that he is working against terrific odds and will finally fail, and Thomas knows that life and instinct are on his side.

> 'Old age should burn and rave at close of day;
> Rage, rage against the dying of the light.'

The plea for opposing resignation and for fighting without forgiveness is there in Yeats too, but whereas he fights in circles, and realises so with a giant frustration, Thomas fights forward, and knows when he gains ground. There is in Thomas a lack of timidity that is more genuine than cocksureness and a lack of pessimism (as in *A Winter's Tale*) that makes him one of our few imperfect poets from whom we can still expect signs of life. When we put one of the new poems included in these collected works, *Lament*, beside the weak despairs of our latter-day Georgians, there is perceptible an energy in his very mourning of the past which makes us realise that there is still strength, and what is more a greater strength and one allied with humour, in the present. His poems are reprinted almost without omission in this volume, and in them we see this strength mount up again and again, unembarrassed and hopeful.

The lack of timidity extends to his way of writing: he is always willing to risk being outrageous. Sometimes a huge confusion reigns —but much more often than not the confusion becomes coherent. His method is to accumulate suggestions so that they finally pile up to a meaning. Every important word (and the important words are crammed in) suggests about six ideas. This leads at the best to an enrichment of language, it is a sort of portmanteau-ing of syntax which does not prevent there emerging a *single* meaning. And in his most successful poems he does qualify the meaning of just the words one would expect to be most imprecise. Take, for example, the line quoted above, 'Do not go gentle into that good night'—'good' has more than one sense in the poem, but each sense is made clear to us by its context. Nor do his images have to be *worked out*—they strike us at once, or not at all:

> 'And then to awake, and the farm, like a wanderer white
> With the dew, come back, the cock on his shoulder.'

This method of suggestions can lead at the worst to an unresolvable chaos or, as in even *Fern Hill*, to the mere gasping inadequacy of 'it was lovely.' No doubt it was lovely; there should be no need for him to say so. But the very gasping is evidence of vitality; and the very fact that he has such vitality as to be incoherent is refreshing, to say the least, in a time when almost every other poet is contented with being dull, with writing in safe, acknowledged, dead traditions, and with lacking the strength of mind to be original. Originality is despised rather too level-headedly nowadays. It is as well to remember that its context in history or society can make it a virtue. One of Thomas' favourite Biblical figures is Samson—and he himself is still a sort of Samson in the modern poetic world, shocking us by laying about him with a verbal jaw-bone, and perhaps in the end pulling the pillars of the prison of logic, in which we have chained him and ourselves, down about our very ears.

November 22nd, 1952

The Death of a Stranger

THOM GUNN

A stranger boy was seen. His ready hand
　　Was there to raise the sunken wheel
　　　From mires of deep remembrance.
　　Free in its midst, what could he feel
But what it made him feel, this sunny land?

Mountain to mountain went his ready foot.
　　His charity the handled crust
　　　He ate from cottage hoarded.
　　Unbreakable his pitch of trust
But swelling welcome each place it was put.

The streams were ready for his ready lip.
　　Some called him Christ Child, and to all
　　　His was not comfort merely.
　　He wrested one from dizzy fall
Who could remember neither slide nor trip.

And when the time came for his ready breath
　　To link a wind, no person saw
　　　The movement of transference.
　　So easy this—no dropping jaw
Or white eyes—you could hardly call it death.

They buried him upon the road in sight
　　Of houses: he would have no ghost.
　　　Already from his gravestone
　　Sprung flowers ignorant of frost.
He had no ghost. Now no one fears the night.

　　　　　　　　　　　　　　October 17th, 1953

Le Modulor*

NIKOLAUS PEVSNER

To commemorate the tercentenary of Inigo Jones's death, Professor Wittkower gave a lecture at the Royal Institute of British Architects two years ago in which he proved that Inigo had designed according to an ingenious and complicated system of proportions worked out from a module which was divided into parts which were divided into sixty minutes each. Can any eye be sensitive enough to recognise the aesthetic advantages of an order expressed in such small fractions? Can the results be more satisfying to the eye than those an architect of genius would choose instinctively? Inigo certainly could not recognise visually what he stipulated; for Professor Wittkower quoted a note in his copy of Palladio's treatise: 'The sweet rustick aboufe is near half ye diameter of the Pillar.' Near half—that is what he saw, the modules and minutes were applied later. And in Inigo's own works the results were sometimes as perfect as in the Queen's House, sometimes as awkward as in the first design for the front of St Paul's.

Le Corbusier is the Inigo Jones of to-day, and nothing is changed except two letters. It is Modulor now,* not module, but the mystic background is the same: the sacredness of mathematics and the sacredness of the human body normalised artfully to six feet height (women are abnormal) and a fixed position of the solar plexus and the length of arms and legs. That would not matter much, if Le Corbusier were satisfied with simple divisions into parts only, but he, too, has his minutes. In studying the book they grow quickly to hours, but the time spent is not without its rewards. It convinces the reader of the arbitrariness of the system, but reveals much of the psychology of the most brilliant architect of our time. Le Corbusier was born at La Chaux de Fonds in Switzerland. It is a Calvinist country and a watchmaker's district. Both are reflected in Le Corbusier's hankering after purity and exactitude. His genius, however, which allows him to break his own rules happily, comes straight from Heaven, and where his superb showmanship comes from, Heaven only knows. The book on the Modulor, in spite of its mathematics, is dramatic reading, the fight

* *The Modulor.* By Le Corbusier.

T

of Le Corbusier for acceptance of his invention, friends and foes, the German occupation, the *Unité* at Marseilles—they all come in.

Le Corbusier pleads for an international acceptance of Modulor for the manufacturing of standard parts, windows as well as crates. We have now in this country a Modulor Society fighting for the same. The necessity of such standardisation is undeniable. Modulor would do as well as any other system, provided it were accepted universally. That is a matter of diplomacy. Meanwhile, the disadvantage of Modulor is that Le Corbusier in the zest of his discovery and under the spell of mathematics, divides so far that in the end everything, with the smallest adjustments, would have the blessings of Modulor.

This is not an exaggeration. We have a friend in Johannesburg, an excellent architect. He designed a house for himself and demonstrated it to us as an example of Modulor applied throughout. The result was convincing, but when we asked him how he had done it, we found that he had designed it first, and then found that with minute alterations all his measurements could be made to fit Modulor.

As is always the case with Le Corbusier, there are two mainsprings to Modulor, the thrill of aesthetic theory and the thrill of industrial production. The way in which, in the book, they play into each other's hands is admirable, and as long as one does not expect either a recipe how to design well or an explanation of the beauties of Le Corbusier's buildings, one can enjoy it wholeheartedly. The format of the book incidentally is 29·2 by 29·2 cm. bound. Is that a Modulor unit? I cannot find it in any prominent place. Perhaps measuring was for the untrimmed page or the trimmed page minus binding—which all goes to show.

May 15th, 1954

In Defense of Yvor Winters*

TONY TANNER

Keats and other romantics thought that poetry should come as naturally as leaves on a tree—or not at all. Since trees are not noted for their capacity for thought this image implies an anti-rationalist bias. Eliot and other symbolists seemed to react against romantic poetry by talking of pure poetry and autotelic art. This implied a poetry which could refine away the impure admixture of reality contained in previous writing. It was non-referential—it had no use for the cognitive powers of the mind. Another connected theory—also supported by Eliot—maintained that as the modern world is disordered and atomistic, poetry should attempt to imitate that disorder. Thus *The Waste Land* is a great poem because it is as chaotic as the 1920's. Poetry according to these ideas either works as unconsciously as nature, or ignores nature, or capitulates to nature. But there is another, older, view of the job of poetry. It can be suggested by the following lines from Milton if we substitute the poet's word for God's Word.

> I saw when at his Word the formless Mass,
> This worlds material mould, came to a heap:
> Confusion heard his voice, and wilde uproar
> Stood rul'd, stood vast infinitude confin'd;
> Till at his second bidding darkness fled,
> Light shon, and order from disorder sprung:

By this view the poet stands against nature and from it tries to elicit meaning (which Arthur Miller has called 'the ultimate reward for having lived'): his work will not beguile us with sensation but nourish us with sense—it will make the firmest grasp at the consolations of

---

* This piece was written while I was a graduate student just after I had returned from America. At that time nobody seemed to be much aware of Winters' work—I recall a couple of footnotes by Donald Davie as exceptions to this generalisation—so the tone of my article was somewhat polemical and I allowed myself some strategic over-emphases. I would not now write such a piece, either in the same tone or with the same amount of agreement with some of Winters' specific value judgments. However, I still have great respect for the best of Winters' criticism, and I am happy to let the piece stand as an example of the stimulation he then provided for someone fresh from the Cambridge English school.

T.T., 1969

truth. An American critic named Yvor Winters has long stood out for this view of the poet. His work is only now available in this country and many may ignore it because of the mischief of such men as Stanley Hyman who have been content to extrapolate a few of his more un-conventional judgements and hold them up for cheap scorn, instead of trying to do justice to the great bulk of vigorous thought and pondered wisdom which his work contains. I want to try and redress the balance.

First of all Winters insists that the critic should not only make value judgements but also that he should be honest about them. Like most critics he makes certain philosophic assumptions: unlike most critics he also makes the intellectual effort involved in clarifying these assump-tions instead of hiding them in prevarication and wary circumlocutions. (Significantly he was calling attention to the triple-tiered confusion in Eliot's criticism at a time when most other critics were content to bow the knee and parrot the famous oracular hints.) He has little time for critics who are unwilling to commit themselves to principles. His own he makes clear from the start. His position is that of a reactionary and a classicist: he speaks out firmly for order, thought, intelligence, control, and generally applicable wisdom, in an age which he considers to have overvalued confusion, reverie, emotionalism, impulse, and the un-related details of private sensory experience. He is a moralist—and admits it; and since he maintains that any value judgement implies an absolutist position (remember Bertrand Russell's trouble with Father Copplestone) he defends that position bravely. He realizes that his absolutism implies a theistic position—and he doesn't shirk the im-plication. Though he phrases it less dogmatically than many have supposed.

> The absolutist believes in the existence of absolute truths and values. Unless he is very foolish, he does not believe that he person-ally has free access to these absolutes and that his own judgements are final; but he does believe that such absolutes exist, that it is the duty of every man and of every society to endeavor as far as may be to approximate to them.

The welcome notes in Winters' criticism are the consistency of a man with the courage of his convictions, the lucidity of a rare common-sense, the invigorating toughness of a mind determined to master its materials and confident it can do so without recourse to esoteric jargon.

If there is also at times a stern note then that is because he thinks life and literature are serious matters. He is convinced that such an attitude is indispensable to civilization and I think he is right.

What does he ask of poetry? The answer is readily available in the clearest language.

The poem is a statement in words about a human experience. Words are primarily conceptual, but through use and because human experience is not purely conceptual, they have acquired connotations of feeling. The poet makes his statement in such a way as to employ both concept and connotation as efficiently as possible. The poem is good in so far as it makes a defensible rational statement about a given human experience (the experience need not be real but must be in some sense possible) and at the same time communicates the emotion which ought to be motivated by that rational understanding of the experience.

Some question begging perhaps—but because of his announced absolutist position he has a right to words like 'defensible' and 'ought.' Because of his demand for evaluation, comprehension, and judgement he attacks what he calls the fallacy of expressive form ('the procedure by which the poet surrenders the form of his statement to the formlessness of his subject'), he deprecates the use of poetry for irresponsible self-expression, and he flatly refuses to believe that such a thing as 'pure poetry' exists. (Words being what they are, he is right—the nearest you can get to it is nonsense verse.) Because of his stated ideals he prefers historiography ('the complete thought of the great mind') to the novels of Joyce and late James which offer us the confused processes of thinking of fictional characters. For the same reason he considers the lyric or short poem superior to all other forms of poetry. It is in this latter preference that he makes his position particularly clear. He prefers the logical lyric of Wyatt and Nashe to the associationist lyric of Collins, and in the best poems of men like Greville, Herbert and Jonson, he finds 'a concentration of meaning, a kind of sombre power.' Instead of just *presenting* us with experience they offer us, by an effort of intense contemplation, a profound *understanding* of it—wisdom in its most compressed form. So far from disliking abstractions and generalizations (words of opprobium to some) he demands them. 'A race that has lost the power to handle abstractions with discretion and dignity may do well to confine itself to sensory impression, but our ancestors were more fortunate, and we ought to labor to regain what we have lost.' Not details, but the conclusions to be drawn from the details; not the spectacle but the theory; not the imitation of an event but the meditation upon it, not fragmentary romantic particularizing but 'the classical gift of generalizing'—this is the emphasis in Winters' work. On this count he differs with many conventional estimates. Pound is 'a barbarian on the loose in a museum,' 'a sensibility without a mind' (this seventeen years ago—Pound's subsequent work has only endorsed the justice of these remarks). Hopkins is 'a poet of fragments for the most part' and a large portion of his verse contains 'an element of emotional violence which is neither understood nor controlled' (is that so wrong?). Hart Crane, who at his best fulfills Winters' high demands often slips into 'brilliant, but disconnected, epithets and ejaculations.' Eliot offers us 'a discreetly modulated diffuseness.' Too much poetry of the last hundred and fifty years has exploited the connotations of words (the emotional aura) at the expense of their denotative function (the hard core of thought). Not that this is as exclusive as it sounds. At one point, for instance, he writes: 'Frost's instinctualism, his nostalgia for dream and chaos, are merely symptoms of sentimental obscurantism' yet elsewhere he concedes that Frost frequently celebrates 'the minor incident and fleeting perception with extraordinary beauty, and I trust he will long remain an ornament to our literature.' Similarly he dislikes what he calls Stevens' hedonism, but considers *Sunday Morning* one of the great poems of the century because it so beautifully enunciates and portrays that particular attitude to life. Writers like Masters, Lindsay and Sandburg writing in the Whitmanesque tradition he judges 'sentimental poets with no gift for thought.' On the other hand, dry exposition does not always earn his uncritical approval and he faults Edwin Arlington Robinson for 'a distrust of the suggestive power of language.' Always the central concern is—what leads towards greater intelligence and invigorating comprehension, because 'poetry should increase the intelligence and strengthen the moral temper.' To this end he asks, not that we reject most modern and romantic poetry, but that we recognize it as a partial poetry and do not confuse it with the best, the most complete. Without falling into the error of identifying the poem with its paraphrasable content he yet insists that poetry contains ideas, or should, and that these ideas are eligible for intelligent discussion and final evaluation.

Of course all this insistence on ideas and intelligence would be arid indeed if it was not working in conjunction with a sensitivity to good poetry, an ear for the mesh of nuances which makes poetry the richest form of human utterance, and a capacity to respond to the mingled rhythms of verse which can emphasize or qualify the words they carry in the subtlest way. Winters has that sensitivity, that ear, that capacity. He is a critic—not a philosopher. But he is also a critic who is honest about his philosophy. There are—as in all critics—limitations. He does leave too much out and I think he underestimates the ways in which poems can construct and convey meanings. Perhaps he is sometimes too quick to dismiss a poet if he finds his ideas unsympathetic (he seems to me too harsh on Yeats—but that piece of his criticism is not available over here) and he too severely circumscribes the valid functions of literature and drama. But the compensations are a rare consistency, a challenging view of poetry, and the example of a vigorous mind at work. Unlike many critics he is profitable to disagree with—because you cannot argue with him without being intelligent. You have to join him on his own ground. He clears the air: he makes for sense by demanding it. And by his continual insistence upon excellence he dignifies poetry, he renews our sense of how much 'the best words in the best order' can contribute to civilized living. He rescues the mind from the limbo to which it has been effectively relegated by too much misguided romantic anti-rationalism—mind, which Thomas Mann called 'life's self-criticism'—and invites it to full participation in poetry and criticism. He calls poetry back to its most serious function —the attempt to understand life and give it meaning. Not that poetry cannot do other things, but this, he would maintain, is the best thing it can do. Such a critic deserves more sympathetic, more serious attention.

November 26th, 1960

Poems from the
'Cambridge Manuscript'

SYLVIA PLATH

STREET SONG

By a mad miracle I go intact
Among the common rout
Thronging sidewalk, street,
And bickering shops;
Nobody blinks a lid, gapes,
Or cries that this raw flesh
Reeks of the butcher's cleaver,
Its heart and guts hung hooked
And bloodied as a cow's split frame
Parceled out by white-jacketed assassins.

Oh no, for I strut it clever
As a greenly escaped idiot,
Buying wine, bread,
Yellow-casqued chrysanthemums
Arming myself with the most reasonable items
To ward off, at all cost, suspicions
Roused by thorned hands, feet, head,
And that great wound
Squandering red
From the flayed side.

Even as my each mangled nerve-end
Trills its hurt out
Above pitch of pedestrian ear,
So, perhaps I, knelled dumb by your absence,
Alone can hear
Sun's parched scream,
Every downfall and crash
Of gutted star,
And, more daft than any goose,
This cracked world's incessant gabble and hiss.

resolve

day of mist: day of tarnish

with hands
unserviceable, I wait
for the milk van.

the one-eared cat
laps its grey paw

and the coal fire burns.

outside, the little hedge leaves are
become quite yellow.
a milk-film blurs
the empty bottles on the windowsill.

no glory descends.

two water drops poise
on the arched green
stem of my neighbour's rose bush.

o bent bow of thorns.

the cat unsheathes its claws.
the world turns.

today
today I will not
disenchant my twelve black-gowned examiners
or bunch my fist
in the wind's sneer.

AERIALIST

Each night, this adroit young lady
Lies among sheets
Shredded fine as snowflakes
Until dream takes her body
From bed to strict tryouts
In tightrope acrobatics.

Nightly she balances
Cat-clever on perilous wire
In a gigantic hall,
Footing her delicate dances
To whipcrack and roar
Which speak her maestro's will.

Gilded, coming correct
Across that sultry air,
She steps, halts, hung
In dead center of her act
As great weights drop all about her
And commence to swing.

Lessoned thus, the girl
Parries the lunge and menace
Of every pendulum;
By deft duck and twirl
She draws applause; bright harnass
Bites keen into each brave limb.

Then, this tough stint done, she curtsies
And serenely plummets down
To traverse glass floor
And get safe home; but, turning with trained eyes,
Tiger-tamer and grinning clown
Squat, bowling black balls at her.

Tall trucks roll in
With a thunder like lions; all aims

And lumbering moves
To trap this outrageous nimble queen
And shatter to atoms
Her nine so slippery lives.

Sighting the stratagem
Of black weight, black ball, black truck,
With a last artful dodge she leaps
Through hoop of that hazardous dream
To sit up stark awake
As the loud alarmclock stops.

Now as penalty for her skill,
By day she must walk in dread
Steel gauntlets of traffic, terror-struck
Lest, out of spite, the whole
Elaborate scaffold of sky overhead
Fall racketing finale on her luck.

                                    February 7th, 1969

Sylvia Plath: The Cambridge Collection

A. ALVAREZ

It would seem that Sylvia Plath came to think none too highly
of this Cambridge collection of her poems. Only five of them survive
in *The Colossus*, despite the fact that a number she later rejected had
already been published in respectable, eminently professional magazines: the *Atlantic Monthly*, *Harper's*, *London Magazine*, *Mademoiselle*,
The Nation, *Poetry* (Chicago), among others. For an undergraduate,
her list of acknowledgements is prodigious. Yet when she came to
select poems for her first published collection she turned her back on
these early, accepted successes, just as she later rejected the poems in
The Colossus. In the British Council interview made shortly before
her death, she remarked,

May I say this: that the ones I've read are very recent, and I have found myself having to read them aloud to myself. Now this is something I didn't do. For example, my first book, The Colossus—I can't read any of the poems aloud now. I didn't write them to be read aloud. In fact, they quite privately bore me.

Presumably, these Cambridge poems had come to bore her earlier still. Which is as it should be, since every serious artist is more aware of the inadequacy of what he has done than of his achievements. Sylvia, particularly, never lost a certain critical edge of dissatisfaction; in the last months of her life, when she was writing with a fertility, newness and power which surprised even her, she always seemed sharply aware of how little her poems measured up to the inner vision she was trying to reveal. Her tone, when she read them, was apologetic, faintly self-knocking.

But just as *The Colossus* is a necessary stepping-stone to the last poetry, so the Cambridge poems obviously precede *The Colossus*. Both collections exhibit everywhere the technical skill and fizzling verbal energy without which she could never have gone on to do what she did in *Ariel*. At every stage in her career images came easily to her, so her progress as a poet was a matter of stripping the inessentials down and away until she arrived at that final, utterly authentic simplicity—at once highly disciplined, highly charged and colloquial. Evidently, it was a long, slow and, at all levels, a difficult process. In these earliest poems—and a number of them were published before she went up to Cambridge, while she was still an undergraduate at Smith—there is often a tense and excessive thickness of texture: the diction is rich but self-conscious, the movement dandified, the landscape ornate. The action, in short, is nearly all on the surface.

This, of course, was also very much the manner of the day: in American poetry the 'fifties was a period of high style, of cadenced, slightly mandarin verse of which Wallace Stevens was the grand master. In England, less ambitiously, it was the reign of the Movement: nor surprisingly, Sylvia included a clutch of the villanelles in order, perhaps, to show her Cambridge examiners that she could do the obligatory British thing as well, or better, than any of the natives. Her list of acknowledgements shows how successful she was. Yet, inevitably, a good deal of this work has dated; she was right not to republish it. Even by the time *The Colossus* appeared, four years or so later, she was getting closer to her own individual style and had no need to fall back on the poetic manners of the time.

It is the same with her characteristic themes: the dead father, the New England seacoast of her childhood, and a crowd of baleful, destructive, more or less supernatural figures and influences who wish her no good. They are already broodingly present in these poems, but only at a considerable distance. Her dealings with them are oblique, even a bit arty; perhaps her style was still not sufficiently her own to allow her to tackle the obsessional themes head-on. There is a poem, for example, called 'The Shrike' which has much the same theme as a short story she wrote at this time called 'The Wishing Box' (it was published posthumously in the *Atlantic Monthly*). In both a woman finds herself bedded down with a man whose dream-life is so rich that she, in comparison, is made to feel commonplace, emptied out. The story ends with the girl killing herself—partly in revenge, partly to regain a lost childhood world of imagination. In the poem, equally dramatic, she feeds on her lover, vampire-like, as Sylvia's father, in 'Daddy', was later to feed on her. The story is relaxed, rather witty, not particularly intense, yet by its close it has gathered to itself far greater power than the poem ever quite generates, for all its wrought language. It is as though the huge precociousness of her verse technique were still an end in itself and almost an inhibition.

Not, alas, that this will discourage the amateur analysts; no doubt they will ransack these poems, as they have the others, for their own devious, undiscriminating and wholly uncritical ends. So it might be as well to point out that here, as in her later work, when Sylvia takes as her subject a couple of mildly persecuted dreams, she was able to use the material positively, creatively and with very great objectivity in order to make autonomous poems. Which is an activity a good deal less sick and uncontrolled than the interpretations which will, almost certainly, be wished on it.

But perhaps this is altogether by the way, since these poems show that her preoccupations as an undergraduate were largely technical. They are, literally, apprentice work. She was trying out a wide variety of styles, tones and subjects in a continually dissatisfied search for her own particular manner. If nothing else, these poems prove again what we can already infer from *The Colossus*: that her apprenticeship was professional, thorough and dedicated to an extraordinary degree.

Yet every so often, from among these several provisional voices,

U

her own utterly distinct voice speaks. Sometimes it is only for a single
line:

> *Water will run by rule; the actual sun*
> *Will scrupulously rise and set;*
> *No little man lives in the exacting moon*
> *And that is that, is that, is that.*
>
>   (*'Two Lovers & a Beachcomber by the Real Sea'*)

'The actual sun' and 'exacting moon' 'scrupulously' going about their
business belong to the world of Wallace Stevens. But that last line is
wholly her own. It catches the same note of dead-end emphasis as she
sounded often in the last poems; for example, in 'Elm': 'These are the
isolate, slow faults / That kill, that kill, that kill'. Or in a brilliant poem
called 'The Jailor', published posthumously in *Encounter* and not reprinted since:

> *... What would the dark*
> *Do without fevers to eat?*
> *What would the light*
> *Do without eyes to knife, what would he*
> *Do, do, do without me?*

Yet only one poem in the collection is, I think, written in the
manner she later developed so brilliantly and profoundly; it is called
'resolve'. Apparently, she didn't much like it, since she left it out of
The Colossus. Certainly, it has nothing much to do with the taut,
highly textured language she was assiduously using elsewhere. It seems
in comparison more casually written and considerably more subdued.
Perhaps it is also less ambitious, concerned neither to make large statements nor stake out wide territories of the imagination. Instead, its
business is with a mood, with defining accurately and with the mini-
mum of fuss and ornament the kind of slow autumnal melancholy in
which inner depression fuses inextricably with the blurred, silent
weather outside. It is very close, in tone and movement, to one of the
most poignant of the late poems, 'Sheep in Fog', where guilt and inadequacy also dissolve into weariness. Both poems turn on a central,
locking image:

> *... o bent bow of thorns ...*
> *... O slow / Horse the colour of rust ...*

The image of the rose reappeared, and both poems were finally perfected, in that most beautiful of all her poems, 'Edge', a poem about death written a couple of days before she died.

It is strange how, from among the several different styles of this collection, one voice, which she had seemed to discard, could later reemerge to express strengths the others were wholly unequal to. Maybe the key is the depression and apparent casualness. It is as though it were first necessary for her to give up trying to force the technical pace, as though the willed, highly self-conscious styles she was experimenting with at Cambridge diverted too much attention to themselves. Later, when she began to explore those themes which were wholly central to her, she needed a style at once relaxed and inward in which all the necessary skills could be assumed instinctively and without labour.

Perhaps this accounts for the intense and deliberate professionalism of these poems, that determination to do things the hard way, which makes them so unlike most university verse. Everywhere there is evidence of an unwavering artistic seriousness; she seems to be preparing herself carefully to do battle with the heavyweights. And beyond that—even in the many poems which don't come off, which she was right to discard—everything points to a life led at a considerable pitch of awareness, to an unequivocally creative consciousness. Yet I doubt if, from these poems, even the sharpest of those 'twelve black-gowned examiners' could have possibly guessed what was to come.

February 7th, 1969

In Extremis

GEORGE STEINER

In the summer of 1952, a young woman came to interview me in London. She was writing an all-too-predictable article on 'Poets on Campus' for *Mademoiselle*, an American glossy with literary spurts. I recall little of the occasion, except that the young lady was poised and conventionally inquisitive as were all the young 'guest editors' such magazines picked up. It was the weedy photographer who made an impression. Now this failure of distinct recollection haunts me. I never met Sylvia Plath again.

The shock of her last poems, the *Ten Poems* as they stood side by side in *Encounter* in October 1963, is, I imagine, reverberating still. Here was an act of extremity, personal and formal, obliging one to try and re-think the whole question of the poet's condition and of the condition of language after modernism and war. It is doubtful whether Sylvia Plath had ever come across T. W. Adorno's dictum 'no poetry after Auschwitz' or whether she was aware of the European poets who felt that language itself had been damaged, possibly beyond creative repair, by the politics of terror and mass-murder. But it is to that possibility, and to the consequent self-mutilation of the poet, that 'Daddy', 'Getting There', 'Lady Lazarus', 'Childless Woman' (which was not included in *Ariel*) address themselves.

The memorable terror of the reader's experience lay not only in the matter of the poems, in the gold teeth 'melting to a shriek'. It lay in the authorizing fiction:

> *An engine, an engine*
> *Chuffing me off like a Jew.*
> *A Jew to Dachau, Auschwitz, Belsen.*
> *I began to talk like a Jew.*
> *I think I may well be a Jew.*

Sylvia Plath was not a Jew. So far as I know, she had no personal connections with the holocaust. But Daddy became a 'panzer-man', the swastika replaced the sky, and the poet rode the death-cars to the ovens. I am not concerned with the private, domestic agonies which may have triggered this black piece of mimicry. But without this assumption of a doomed persona, the final poems, the work through which Sylvia Plath now matters, could not have been done.

Her success was drastic. Some of the poetry of the Polish writer Zbigniew Herbert, and Paul Celan's *Fugue of Death* is probably all one can set beside the *Ten Poems*. In most other verse, fiction and drama about the world of Belsen, the enormity of the facts, their location outside the common bounds of speech and the imagination, stomps the life out of language. Sylvia Plath communicated her apprehension of horror, the racking passage of humiliation and death through her own consciousness, by extreme concentration. She made the jagged fragment somehow comprehensive of the whole. Emily Dickinson

can do that with a darting abstraction, with a camera-quick implication of allegory; in Sylvia Plath's last poem the focus is physical: 'A
cake of soap, / A wedding ring, / A gold filling.' These stand out
sharp and clean as glass. And it is this effort at hideous clarity which
seems to me to underlie the bone-spareness of the metrics and such
constant effects as the juxtaposition of *l* and *r* sounds. The last poems
are full of words such as *bell* and *glitter* on which the contrasting *r* cuts
with a scratching desolate note:

> *Herr God, Herr Lucifer*
> *Beware*
> *Beware.*

Both sounds are active in the title *Ariel*, and it tells something of Sylvia
Plath's presence that in that name the Shakespearian ring is, just now,
muffled.

Yet this grim fiction leaves me uneasy. Does any writer, does any
human being other than an actual survivor, have the right to put on
this death-rig? Auschwitz and Belsen lodge at the centre of our current
lives and sensibilities like the energized, malignant void of a Gnostic
vision of damnation. The imagination touches on them at its peril; in
some corrosive way, the material flatters those who, in safety and at a
distance of time, invoke it. Pathos can corrupt when images which
exceed pathos are too deliberately used. Particularly for the benefit
of art.

What extra-territorial right had Sylvia Plath—she was a child,
plump and golden in America, when the trains actually went — to
draw on the reserves of animate horror in the ash and the children's
shoes? This is precisely where the private issues intrude. Even where
the chosen fiction is most impersonal, where the poet's fierce honesty
bears witness against hell, betrayingly private images of surgery,
mental breakdown and attempted suicide crop up. Do any of us have
license to locate our personal disasters, raw as these may be, in
Auschwitz?

I can't get this question of the poet's 'overdraft' clear in my own
mind. It can be argued that Sylvia Plath's death balanced the account
and that there is no more to be said. But there was, even in this death,
a mimesis, an acting out of some of the circumstances of the *Ten
Poems*—or, as Wallace Stevens would put it, 'a supreme fiction'. I

don't know the answer; but the issue will need to be clarified, gradually, if we are to see the poems whole, if we are to see what life of their own they have apart from the life of a human being whom they seem to have 'eaten like air'.

I don't think we know, as yet. Will Sylvia Plath come to occupy a place, say, after Lowell and well ahead of W. D. Snodgrass or Anne Sexton in the recent movement of 'Confessional' poetry? Of poetry motivated by the peculiarly public conventions of contemporary American neurosis and domestic drama? Or will *Ariel*, and notably the *Ten Poems* move into a more durable context as among the few valid responses of language and imagination to the root disaster of this age (some of Berryman's recent poems pose the same difficulty)?

The newly uncovered, early poems raise no such problem. Many are better, more 'necessary' than the usual run of undergraduate verse, and it is worth recalling that Sylvia Plath had already come to Cambridge with something of a poet's reputation. Very few are thoroughly flat—though 'Natural History' comes near. But little in this submission of 'independent work' to the Part II examiners in the English Tripos announces the poet of the *Ten Poems* (but then, not much in *Colossus* did either).

In these early pieces, the influence of Ted Hughes is very marked. Claws grip, beaks flash, the night is hunted by prowling, heraldic fauna. In pure Hughes ornithology, thoughts

> *Now fold their wings like bats and disappear*
> *Into the attic of the skull.*

There are touches of Empson: especially in 'To Eva Descending The Stair' and the 'Mad Girl's Love Song' with its Empsonian ritornel, 'I think I made you up inside my head'. I have always thought that something of Empson's 'clear and queer' register can be heard in the late poems. We find a lot of Yeats, of the ceremonious, violent Yeats who comes down through the 50's and Ted Hughes. The crazed queens, 'foul sluts' and 'common rout' stem from Yeats, as does Sylvia Plath's trust, not invariably justified, in the efficacy of half-rhymes. Without Yeats, a whole number of these early poems are difficult to imagine.

But there is another presence. It has, until now, been little noticed but seems to me very important. I take it that Sylvia Plath was strongly influenced by the poetry of John Crowe Ransom, that it is via Ransom that her own American-ness can best be made out. Echoes of Ransom are subtle but pervasive: in her use of his *blues* and *greens*, in the repeated *bruit*, a favourite Ransom archaicism. 'Tinker Jack And The Tidy Wave' is almost a variation on Ransom. Such turns as 'fallen from lustre', 'bleared', 'beauty from hag', come close to being a pastiche of Ransom's stately, ascetic yet implicitly violent mode. I would guess that 'Captain Carpenter' was among the decisive moments in Sylvia Plath's realization of herself as a poet. There are few tonal finds and stately frenzies in that astonishing ballad which we do not hear echoed or modulated in Sylvia Plath's work. Right down to the 'red vitals of his heart' and the kites who 'whet their beaks clack clack'. It is this rhetoric of violence, none the less honest for being oratorical, that makes Sylvia Plath so American, so much a cousin to Mr Poe and Mr Tate.

'Epitaph For Fire And Flower', in these early poems, is a good test. Would one, seeing it fresh, have guessed at the future? There are poignant, delicately-paced strokes in it; there are also lapses and derivations (a touch of Wallace Stevens in that 'fluent air'). But the stone in the camera-eye and the 'mouth's instant flare', with its confident dual reference to the flash-bulb and the shape illumined, announce the real poet. What did the examiners make of it? Did they do more than glance at this whole sheaf? Did anyone spot the typing-error in stanza four of the 'Aerialist' (already the word *Ariel*) on page 298? To me, that trivial typo is almost intolerably immediate and of a live presence.

Sylvia Plath did not get a First. Which is as it should be. Poets need not be taught by English dons; it is their poems that the dons shall teach.

February 7th, 1969

Biographical Notes

LORD ACTON (John Emerich Edward Dalberg Acton) (1834–1902), historian and political publicist, was educated at Munich. He edited the Catholic journals *The Rambler* and the *Home and Foreign Review* until the infallibility controversy brought him into conflict with Cardinals Wiseman and Newman and the Church. A Member of Parliament from 1859 to 1865 he was elected to succeed Sir John Seeley as Regius Professor of History at Cambridge University in 1895. He founded the *English Historical Review* and planned the *Cambridge Modern History* but died before its volumes appeared. Although his output of historical writing was small, his impact as a teacher, and his commitment to liberalism were profoundly influential.

A. ALVAREZ (b. 1929), literary critic and poet, was educated at Corpus Christi College, Oxford. He became a friend of Sylvia Plath's after she returned to England in 1959, and is the author of an influential essay on her work collected in *Beyond All This Fiddle: Essays 1955–67* (1968).

JULIAN BELL (1908–37), poet, was the son of Clive and Vanessa Bell. He was educated at King's College, Cambridge, and died in Spain, driving an ambulance for the Loyalists. His brother, Quentin Bell, edited *Julian Bell: Essays, Poems and Letters* (1938), with contributions from J. M. Keynes and E. M. Forster.

JOAN BENNETT (b. 1896), literary critic, was educated at Girton College, Cambridge. She lectured in the English Faculty at Cambridge from 1936 to 1964, and is the author of studies on the metaphysical poets, Virginia Woolf, George Eliot and Sir Thomas Browne.

SIR ANTHONY BLUNT, K.C.V.O. (b. 1907), art historian, was educated at Trinity College, Cambridge. He is Professor of the History of Art in the University of London, Director of the Courtauld Institute, and author of numerous studies in European art.

R. B. BRAITHWAITE, F.B.A., (b. 1900), philosopher, is Emeritus Professor of Moral Philosophy at Cambridge. He was educated at King's College, Cambridge, and has been a Fellow since 1924. He lectured on Moral Sciences at Cambridge from 1928 and held the Knightbridge Chair from 1953 to 1967. Among his publications is *The Theory of Games as a Tool for Moral Philosophy*.

SIR DENIS BROGAN, F.S.A. (b. 1900), historian and journalist, is Emeritus Professor of Political Science at Cambridge and a Fellow of Peterhouse, Cambridge. Educated at Glasgow University, Balliol College, Oxford, and Harvard, he was a lecturer successively at University College, London, Corpus Christi College, Oxford, and at Cambridge. Among his many publications on American and French history are *The Development of Modern France 1870-1939* (1940) and *An Introduction to American Politics* (1955).

LOUIS DE BROGLIE (b. 1892), physicist, is the brother of the sixth Duc de Broglie. He has been Professor of Theoretical Physics at the Henri Poincaré Institute at the Sorbonne since 1928. He was awarded the Nobel Prize in 1929 for the discovery of the wave nature of electrons.

JACOB BRONOWSKI (b. 1908), scientist and literary critic, was educated at Jesus College, Cambridge. He is Senior Fellow of the Salk Institute for Biological Study, and is the author of numerous studies in literary criticism.

GERALD BULLETT (1893-1958), novelist, was educated at Jesus College, Cambridge. Among his many novels was *The Quick and the Dead*. He also wrote biographies of George Eliot and Sydney Smith.

SIR HERBERT BUTTERFIELD, F.B.A. (b. 1900), historian, was educated at Peterhouse, Cambridge, where he was a Fellow from 1923 to 1955. He was Professor of Modern History at Cambridge from 1944 to 1963 and Regius Professor from 1963 to 1968. He was President of the Historical Association from 1955 to 1958, editor of the *Cambridge Historical Journal* from 1938 to 1952 and Master of Peterhouse from 1955 to 1968. He is the author of *Man on His Past* (1955) and *George III and the Historians* (1957).

SIR JOHN CLAPHAM (1873-1946), economic historian, was educated at King's College, Cambridge, where he was elected Fellow in 1898. He was a lecturer in economic history from 1898 and Professor of Economic History at Cambridge from 1928 to 1938. Among his many publications *An Economic History of Modern Britain* (1926-38) remains an important quantitative study.

R. G. COLLINGWOOD (1881-1943), philosopher, was educated at University College, Oxford. Beginning a career as an archaeologist, he turned to philosophy and in particular to the philosophy of history. He became a Fellow and Lecturer at Pembroke College, Oxford, in 1912, and later Waynflete Professor of Metaphysical Philosophy from 1935 to 1941.

G. G. COULTON, F.B.A. (1858-1947), historian, was educated at St Catharine's College, Cambridge, and Heidelberg University. He was Birkbeck Lecturer in Ecclesiastical History at Trinity College, Cambridge, and Ford's Lecturer at Oxford in 1930-31. Among his publications are *The Medieval Village* (1925) and *Romanism and Truth* (1930-31).

WILLIAM CUNNINGHAM (1848–1919), economist and churchman, was educated at Edinburgh, Tübingen and Cambridge. He was, successively, Professor of Economics at London University, Vicar of Great St Mary's, the University Church at Cambridge, and Archdeacon of Ely. He was the author of *The Growth of English Industry and Commerce*.

MAURICE DOBB (b. 1900), economist, was educated at Pembroke College, Cambridge. He has been Visiting Lecturer in Russian Economic Studies at the University of London School of Slavonic Studies, and is Emeritus Reader of Economics at Cambridge University and a Fellow of Trinity College. He has published many works on Russian economic history including *The Development of the Soviet Economy Since 1917*.

JOHN DUNN (b. 1940), historian of ideas, was educated at King's College, Cambridge, where he is now a Fellow. He is the author of *The Political Thought of John Locke* (1969).

G. R. ELTON, F.B.A. (b. 1921), historian, was educated at London University and lectured in history at Glasgow University before coming to Cambridge in 1948 where he became Reader in Tudor Studies in 1963, and Professor of English Constitutional History in 1967. He has made many important contributions to sixteenth-century constitutional history including *The Tudor Revolution in Government* (1953). He is the author of *The Practice of History* (1967).

T. S. ELIOT, O.M. (1888–1965), poet and literary critic, was educated at Harvard, the Sorbonne and Oxford. His was the major influence on Cambridge English in the 'twenties and 'thirties. I. A. Richards has written a reminiscence of Eliot in Cambridge in *T. S. Eliot: The Man and his Work*, edited by Allen Tate (1966). Eliot's earlier essay on Pascal appears in his *Selected Essays*.

WILLIAM EMPSON (b. 1906), poet and literary critic, was educated at Magdalene College, Cambridge, where he was I. A. Richards's pupil. He is Professor of English at Sheffield University. *Seven Types of Ambiguity* appeared in 1930.

M. I. FINLEY (b. 1912), Ancient historian, was educated at Columbia University and Jesus College, Cambridge. He was Assistant Professor of History at Rutgers University from 1948 to 1952 and has lectured in the Classics Faculty, where he is Professor of Ancient History, since 1955. He is the author of *The World of Odysseus* (1954) and *A History of Ancient Sicily* (1969).

ROGER FRY (1866–1934), painter and art critic, was educated at King's College, Cambridge. He was Slade Professor of Fine Art in Cambridge from 1933 until his death.

C. W. GUILLEBAUD (b. 1890), economist, was educated at St John's College, Cambridge, where he became a Fellow in 1915. He is the Emeritus Reader in Economics at Cambridge and the author of *The Economic Recovery of Germany 1933–1938*.

THOM GUNN (b. 1929), poet, was educated at Trinity College, Cambridge, and now lives in San Francisco. His most recent volume of verse is *Touch* (1967).

FRED HOYLE, F.R.S., (b. 1915), radio astronomer and novelist, was educated at Emmanuel College, Cambridge. Since 1958 he has been Plumian Professor of Astronomy and Experimental Philosophy at Cambridge. He is the author of many works of science fiction including *The Black Cloud* (1957).

H. M. HYNDMAN (1842–1921), socialist politician, was educated at Trinity College. He founded the *Social Democratic Federation* in 1884, the leading Marxist organization outside the Trade Union Movement. In 1889, the year he appeared at the Union, Hyndman and the S.D.F. received a great deal of the publicity and the credit for instigating the London Dock Strike.

J. M. KEYNES (1883–1948), economist, was born and educated at Cambridge where he became a Fellow of King's College in 1908 as well as a lecturer in economics. His has been a revolutionary influence in modern economics, both in public and academic life. *The Economic Consequences of the Peace* (1919), written when he left the Treasury, provided a popular and major critique of reparations policy. *The General Theory of Employment Interest and Money* (1936) has had incalculable effect in the formulation of public economic policy. In 1930, when the *Treatise on Money* appeared, Keynes was appointed by MacDonald to advise the government on unemployment.

G. KITSON CLARK, Litt. D., (b. 1900), historian, was educated at Trinity College, Cambridge. He is Emeritus Reader in Constitutional History and was Ford's Lecturer at Oxford in 1959–60. His many works on Victorian history include *The Making of Victorian England* (1962). In 1929 he published *Peel and the Conservative Party*.

PETER LASLETT (b. 1915), social historian, is Reader in Politics and the History of Social Structure at Cambridge University and a Fellow of Trinity College, Cambridge. He is Director of the Cambridge Group for the History of Population and Social Structure and the author of *The World We Have Lost* (1965).

E. R. LEACH (b. 1910), anthropologist, is the Provost of King's College and University Reader in Social Anthropology. From 1947 to 1953 he was Lecturer, then Reader, in Social Anthropology at the London School of Economics. Among his numerous publications are the Reith Lectures for 1967, *A Runaway World?*

F. R. LEAVIS (b. 1895), literary critic, was educated at Emmanuel College, Cambridge. He was Fellow of Downing College from 1936 to 1962 and was a founder of *Scrutiny*.

F. L. LUCAS (1894–1967), literary critic and novelist, was educated at Trinity College, Cambridge, and became Fellow of King's. He edited the standard edition of Webster and wrote several books of criticism.

J. ELLIS MCTAGGART (1866–1925), philosopher, was educated at Trinity College, Cambridge, where he became a Fellow in 1891 and a lecturer in philosophy. Among his many works on Hegel are *Studies in Hegelian Dialectics* (1896).

DENIS MACK SMITH (b. 1920), historian, was educated at Peterhouse, Cambridge. He was a Fellow of Peterhouse, Cambridge, and is now a Research Fellow of All Souls' College, Oxford. Among his many works on Italian history are *Cavour and Garibaldi 1860* and *A History of Modern Sicily* (1969).

F. W. MAITLAND (1850–1906), jurist and legal historian, was educated at Trinity College, Cambridge. After being called to the bar and training in equity and conveyancing he took up legal history of which he became a practitioner of the utmost distinction. His prolific output included *Canon Law in England* (1898) and his Rede lecture *English Law and the Renaissance* (1901). He was elected as Downing Professor of the Laws of England at Cambridge in 1888 but declined to succeed Acton in the Regius Chair in 1902.

G. E. MOORE, O.M. (1873–1958), philosopher, was educated at Trinity College, Cambridge, where he was awarded a Prize Fellowship in 1898. He published the *Principia Ethica* in 1903 which gave great impetus to the attack on Kantian and Hegelian metaphysics. He was Professor of Philosophy at Cambridge from 1925 to 1939, and editor of *Mind* from 1921 to 1947.

WILLIAM MORRIS (1834–96), poet, designer and socialist. His talk on 'Art Under the Plutocracy', in an expanded version, appears in *William Morris on Art and Socialism* edited by Holbrook Jackson (1947).

JOSEPH NEEDHAM (b. 1900), biochemist and Sinologist, is Master of Gonville and Caius College, Cambridge. He was Fellow of Caius College from 1924 to 1966, Sir William Dunn Reader in Biochemistry from 1933 to 1966 and Director of the Department of Natural Sciences at UNESCO from 1946 to 1948. He is the author of the seven-volume *Science and Civilisation in China* (1954–65).

MICHAEL OAKESHOTT (b. 1901) is University Professor of Political Science at the London School of Economics since 1951. He was educated at Gonville and Caius College, Cambridge, where he has been a Fellow since 1925. His many publications on philosophy and politics include his first, reviewed by R. G. Collingwood in this collection, *Experience and Its Modes* which appeared in 1933.

MAX PERUTZ, C.B.E., F.R.S., (b. 1914), biologist, was awarded the Nobel Prize for Chemistry, jointly in 1962, for work on Nucleic Acids. He is the Chairman of the Medical Research Council Laboratory of Molecular Biology at Cambridge.

NIKOLAUS PEVSNER (b. 1902), historian of art and architecture, was educated at the Universities of Leipzig, Munich, Berlin and Frankfurt. He has been Slade Fellow of Fine Art at Cambridge and a Fellow of St John's.

SYLVIA PLATH (1932–63), poet, was educated at Smith College, Massachusetts, Newnham College, Cambridge, where she met and married the English poet Ted Hughes. Wendy Campbell has written a memoir of Sylvia Plath in Cambridge, originally in the *Cambridge Review* (1969), which has been collected in *The Art of Sylvia Plath*, edited by Charles Newman (1970).

J. B. PRIESTLEY (b. 1894), novelist, was educated at Trinity Hall, Cambridge.

SIR ARTHUR QUILLER-COUCH ('Q') (1863–1944), literary writer and anthologist, was educated at Trinity College, Oxford, where he lectured in classics. He was the anthologist of the *Oxford Book of English Verse* (1900) and was the King Edward VII Professor of English Literature at Cambridge.

I. A. RICHARDS (b. 1893), literary critic and poet, was educated at Magdalene College, Cambridge. He lectured at Cambridge until 1929, during which time his *Principles of Literary Criticism* (1924) and *Practical Criticism* (1929) appeared. He is University Professor Emeritus at Harvard.

E. A. G. ROBINSON, C.M.G., O.B.E., F.B.A., (b. 1897), economist, is Emeritus Professor of Economics at Cambridge and a Fellow of Sidney Sussex College. He was educated at Christ's College and Corpus Christi College, Cambridge, and was the editor of the *Economic Journal*.

JOAN ROBINSON (b. 1903), economist, is Professor of Economics at Cambridge, a Fellow of Newnham College, and is married to E. A. G. Robinson. Educated at Girton College, Cambridge, she has lectured in economics at Cambridge since 1931, is the author of *Essays in the theory of employment* (1937) as well as of works on contemporary China, including *The Cultural Revolution* (1967).

JACQUES RUEFF (b. 1896), economist, was made Inspecteur-général des finances under the Third Republic in 1923. One of France's most influential economists, he was financial counsellor to the French Embassy in London from 1930 to 1936, and a close adviser to General de Gaulle from 1944 to 1946 and again from 1958 to 1968. An opponent of Keynesian economics he is the author of the *Théorie des Phénomènes Monétaires* (1927).

W. G. RUNCIMAN (b. 1934), sociologist, was educated at Trinity College, Cambridge, where he became a Fellow. He is now Reader in Sociology at the University of Sussex and is the author of *Social Science and Political Theory* (1963).

BERTRAND RUSSELL (Earl Russell), O.M. (1872–1970), philosopher, mathematician and political writer, was educated at Trinity College, Cambridge, where he was elected to a Fellowship in 1895. From 1910 to 1913 he published the *Principia Mathematica* together with Alfred North Whitehead and became a lecturer in philosophy at Trinity in 1910. His writings on Bergson include 'The Philosophy of Bergson' *Monist*, xxii (July 1912), and 'Mr. Wildon Carr's Defence of Bergson', *Cambridge Magazine*, April 26th, 1913, and *The Philosophy of Bergson* (1914). Rex v. Bertrand Russell originally appeared in G. H. Hardy, *Bertrand Russell: A College Controversy of the Last War* (1942). As a result of this case, Trinity deprived Russell of his Fellowship in 1918.

SIR ERNEST RUTHERFORD (Baron Rutherford of Nelson and Cambridge), F.R.S. (1871–1937), physicist, was educated in New Zealand and at Trinity College, Cambridge. He worked with J. J. Thomson from 1895 to 1899 at the Cavendish before going to Montreal to continue work on radioactivity with Frederick Soddy. *Radioactive Substances and their Radiations*, a summary of this work appeared in 1913, and he was awarded the Nobel Prize for Physics in 1908. In 1919 he succeeded Thomson as the Cavendish Professor of Physics at Cambridge.

QUENTIN SKINNER (b. 1940), historian of ideas, was educated at Gonville and Caius College, Cambridge. He is Lecturer in History at Cambridge and a Fellow of Christ's College. His publications include 'Meaning and Understanding in the History of Ideas' (*History and Theory*, 1969).

C. P. SNOW (Baron Snow) (b. 1905), scientist and novelist, was educated at Christ's College, Cambridge, where he was Fellow from 1930 to 1950. He delivered *The Two Cultures and the Scientific Revolution* as the Rede Lectures in 1959 which provoked F. R. Leavis's reply, *Two Cultures? The Significance of C. P. Snow* (the Richmond Lecture, 1962).

GEORGE STEINER (b. 1929), literary critic, was educated at Harvard and has been a Rhodes scholar. He is an Extraordinary Fellow of Churchill College, Cambridge, where he was, until 1969, Director of Studies in English. His many Publications include *The Death of Tragedy* (1961). His review of Sylvia Plath's *Ariel* ('Dying in an Art') is collected in *Language and Silence* (1967).

TONY TANNER (b. 1935), literary critic, was educated at Jesus College and King's College, Cambridge, where he is now Fellow and Director of Studies in English, and the University of California, Berkeley. He is the author of *The Reign of Wonder* (1965), and other studies in American fiction.

J. J. THOMSON (1856–1940), F.R.S., physicist, was educated at Trinity College, Cambridge. In 1884, he succeeded Rayleigh as Cavendish Professor of Experimental Physics and held the Chair until 1919. In 1906 he was awarded the Nobel Prize in Physics for his work in the conductivity of gases. It was largely under his influence that the Cavendish Laboratory became the nucleus of research in atomic physics. He was Master of Trinity College from 1918 to his death.

G. M. TREVELYAN, O.M., C.B.E., F.B.A. (1876–1962), historian, was educated at Trinity College, Cambridge, where he succeeded J. J. Thomson as Master in 1940. The third son of the historian George Otto Trevelyan, and a disciple of Acton's liberalism, he was elected to the Regius Chair of History at Cambridge in 1927. His many works of popular history include the Garibaldi trilogy and the *Illustrated English Social History* (1949–52).

W. C. D. WHETHAM (Lord Dampier), F.R.S. (1867–1952), physicist, was educated at Trinity College, Cambridge, where he was elected a Fellow in 1891. He lectured in physics at Cambridge from 1895 to 1922 and was Senior Tutor at Trinity from 1913 to 1917. His work with Thomson at the Cavendish was mostly in the field of experimental electricity.

RAYMOND WILLIAMS (b. 1921), critic and literary historian, is a Fellow of Jesus College and University Reader in Drama. He was educated at Trinity College, Cambridge, and is the author of *Culture and Society* (1958).

JOHN WISDOM (b. 1904), philosopher, was educated at Fitzwilliam House, Cambridge. He lectured in moral sciences at Cambridge and was elected a Fellow of Trinity College. He is now Professor of Philosophy at Oregon University. His publications include *Other Minds* (1952).

LUDWIG WITTGENSTEIN (1889–1951), philosopher, was educated at Vienna, Mainz and Trinity College, Cambridge. His review of Coffey's book appeared in the *Cambridge Review* less than a year after his arrival at the University. After serving in the Austro-Hungarian Army in the First World War, and working as a teacher and then as an architect, he returned to England and lectured in Cambridge from 1930 to 1935 when he was elected to a Chair of Philosophy which he held until 1947. A formative influence in the development of modern epistemology and linguistics, the *Tractatus logico-philosophicus* was published in 1922.

JOHN ZIMAN, F.R.S. (b. 1925), physicist, was educated in New Zealand and at Balliol College, Oxford, where he was junior lecturer in Mathematics from 1951 to 1953. He was lecturer in Physics from 1954 to 1964, Fellow of King's College from 1957 to 1964 and editor of the *Cambridge Review* in 1958–9. He is now Professor of Theoretical Physics at Bristol University. He was the author, with Jasper Rose, of *Camford Observed* (1964).